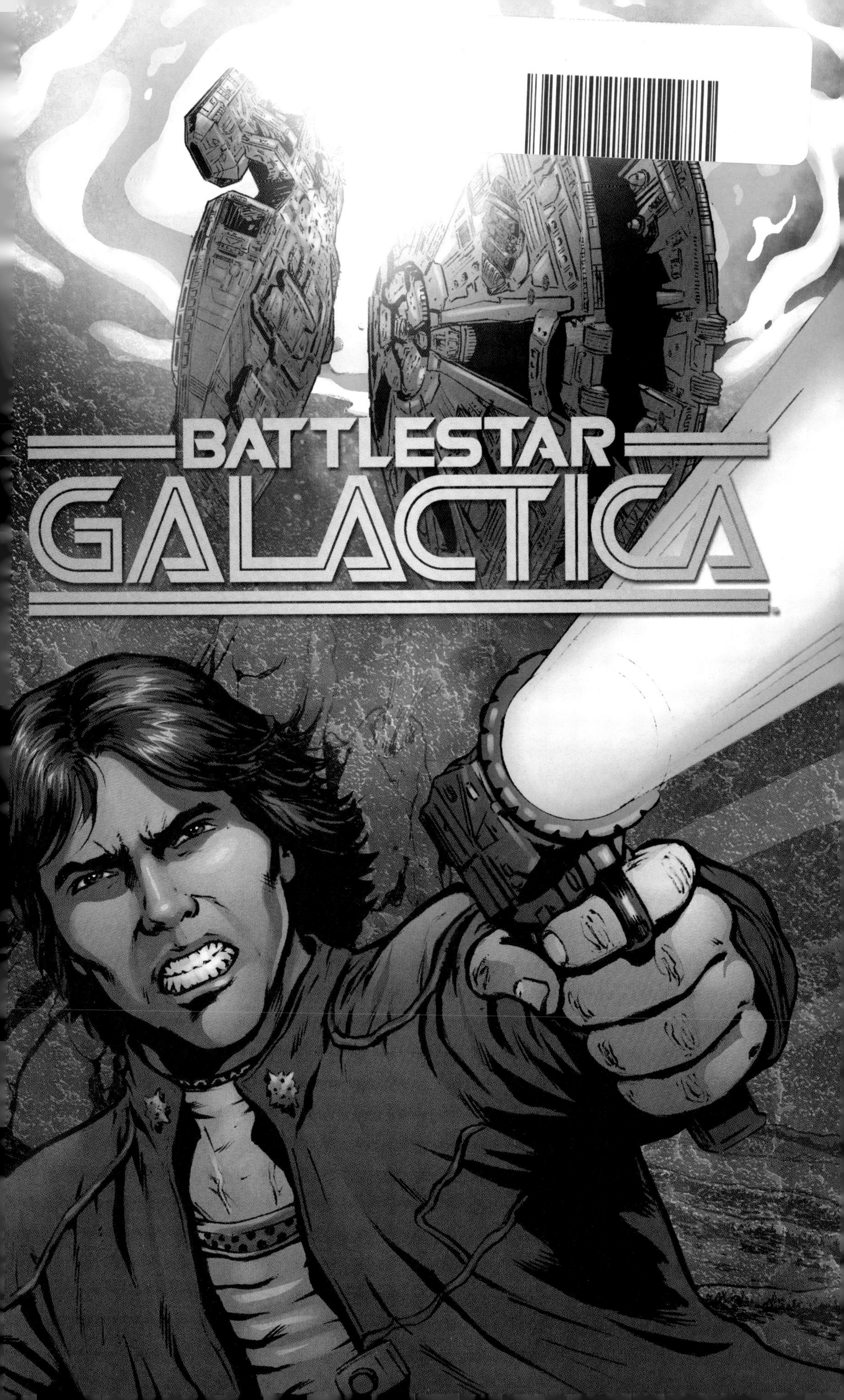
BATTLESTAR
GALACTICA

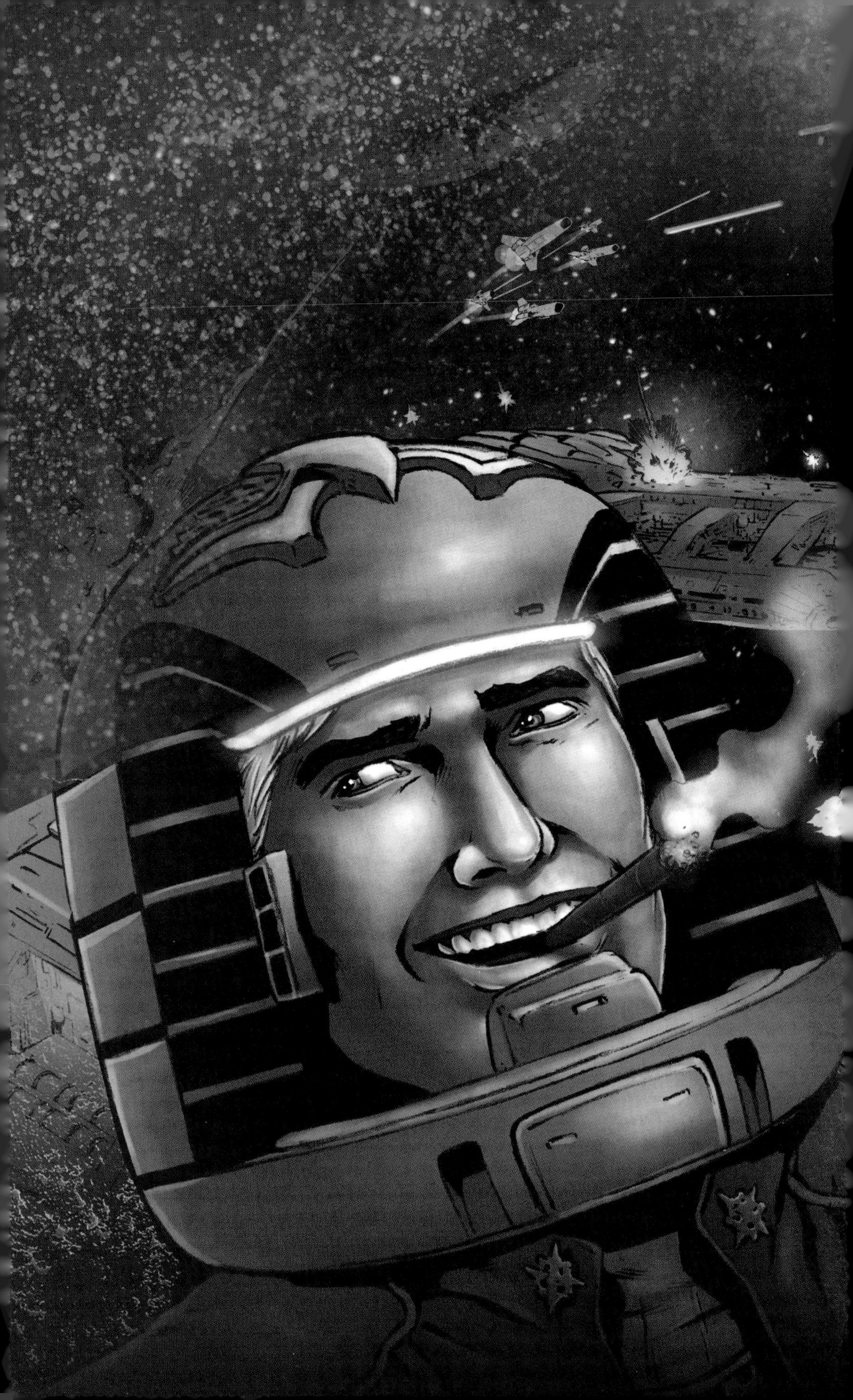

BATTLESTAR GALACTICA™

VOLUME ONE
MEMORIAL

WRITTEN BY
DAN ABNETT
ANDY LANNING

ART BY
CEZAR RAZEK

COLORED BY
VINICIUS TOWNSEND

LETTERED BY
SIMON BOWLAND

COLLECTION COVER BY
ALEX ROSS

COLLECTION DESIGN BY
KATIE HIDALGO

SPECIAL THANKS TO KIM NIEMI, ED PRINCE AND CHRISTOPHER LUCERO

BASED ON THE UNIVERSAL TELEVISION SERIES "BATTLESTAR GALACTICA" CREATED BY GLEN A. LARSON

THIS VOLUME COLLECTS ISSUES 1-5 OF BATTLESTAR GALACTICA BY DYNAMITE ENTERTAINMENT.

DYNAMITE®

lick Barrucci, CEO / Publisher
uan Collado, President / COO
lich Young, Director Business Development
leith Davidsen, Marketing Manager

oe Rybandt, Senior Editor
osh Green, Traffic Coordinator
Aolly Mahan, Assistant Editor

osh Johnson, Art Director
ason Ullmeyer, Senior Graphic Designer
Katie Hidalgo, Graphic Designer
Chris Caniano, Production Assistant

Visit us online at **www.DYNAMITE.com**
Follow us on Twitter **@dynamitecomics**
Like us on Facebook **/Dynamitecomics**
Watch us on YouTube **/Dynamitecomics**

ISBN-10: 1-60690-446-9 ISBN-13: 978-1-60690-446-6 First Printing 10 9 8 7 6 5 4 3 2 1

For information regarding press, media rights, foreign rights, licensing, promotions, and advertising e-mail:
marketing@dynamite.com

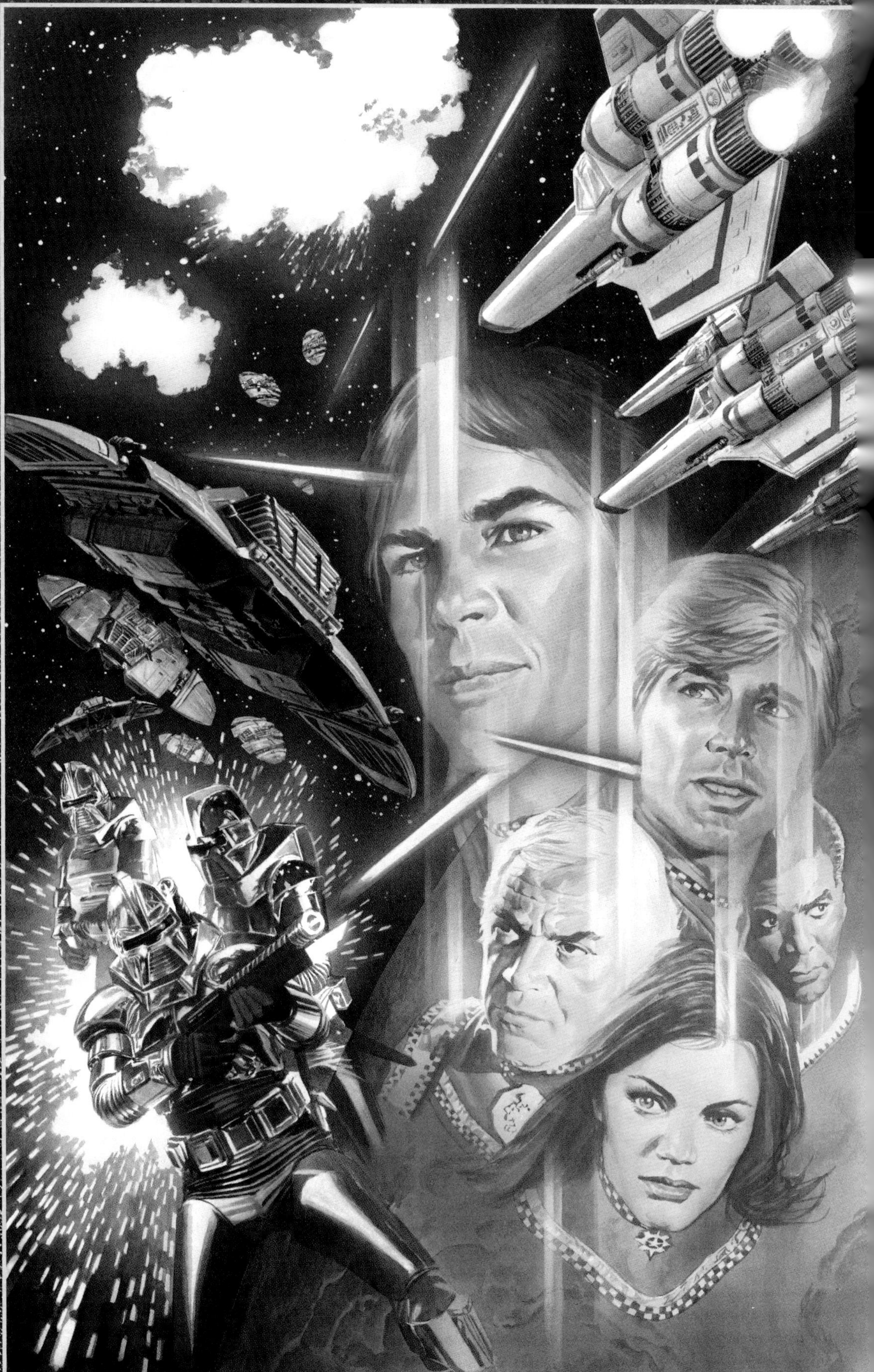

ISSUE 1

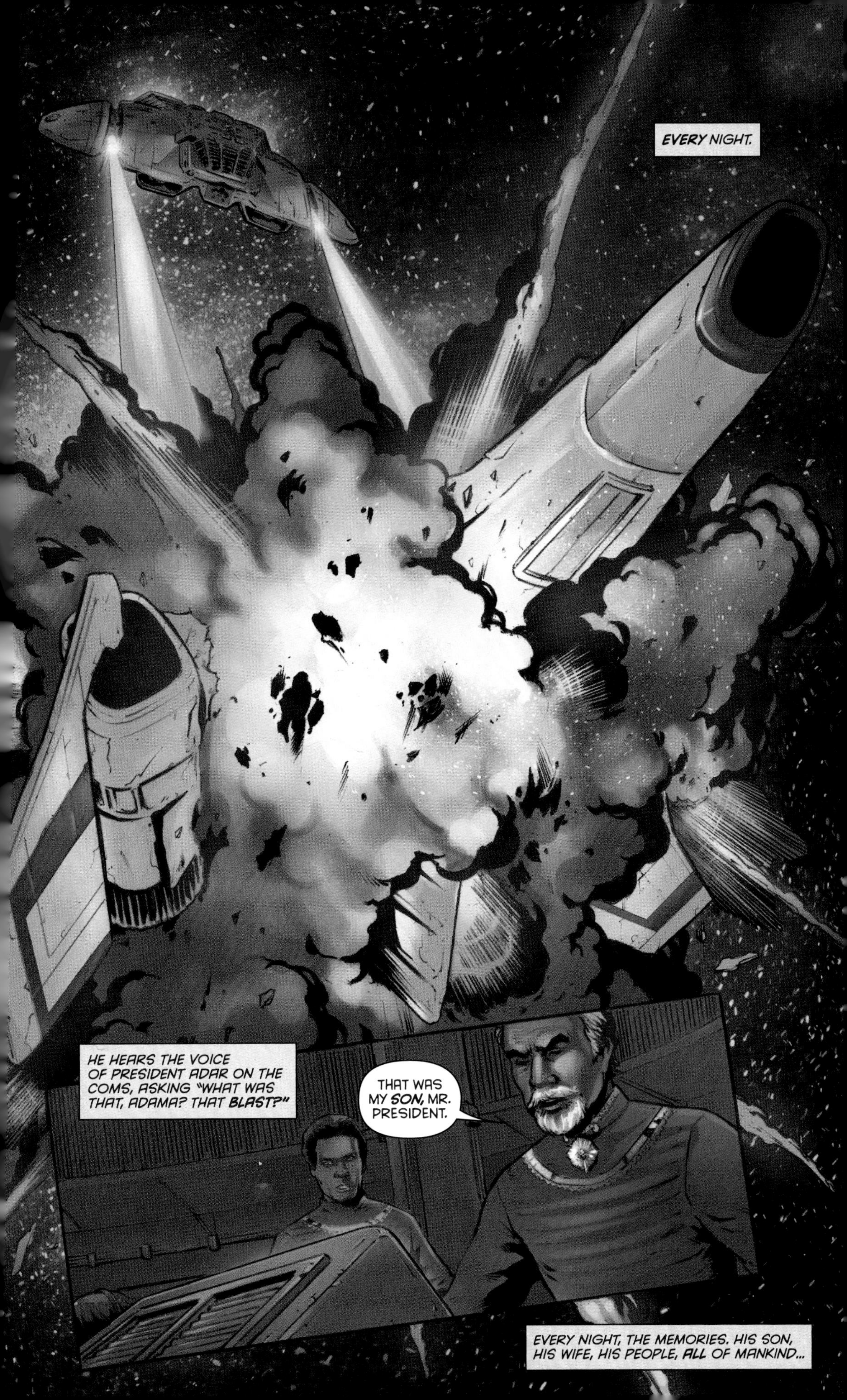
EVERY NIGHT.
HE HEARS THE VOICE OF PRESIDENT ADAR ON THE COMS, ASKING "WHAT WAS THAT, ADAMA? THAT BLAST?"
THAT WAS MY SON, MR. PRESIDENT.
EVERY NIGHT, THE MEMORIES. HIS SON, HIS WIFE, HIS PEOPLE, ALL OF MANKIND...

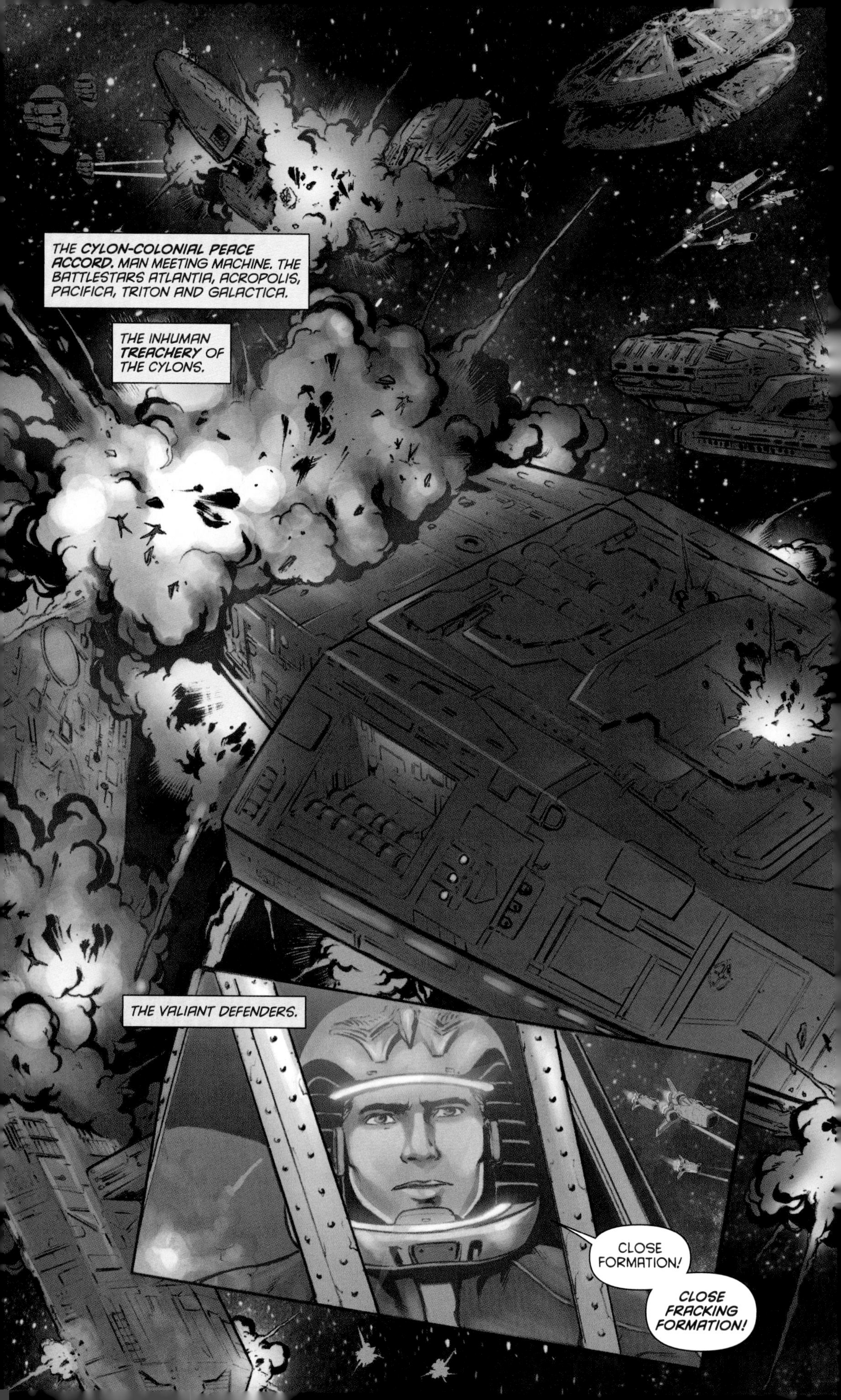
THE CYLON-COLONIAL PEACE ACCORD. MAN MEETING MACHINE. THE BATTLESTARS ATLANTIA, ACROPOLIS, PACIFICA, TRITON AND GALACTICA.
THE INHUMAN TREACHERY OF THE CYLONS.
THE VALIANT DEFENDERS.
CLOSE FORMATION!
CLOSE FRACKING FORMATION!

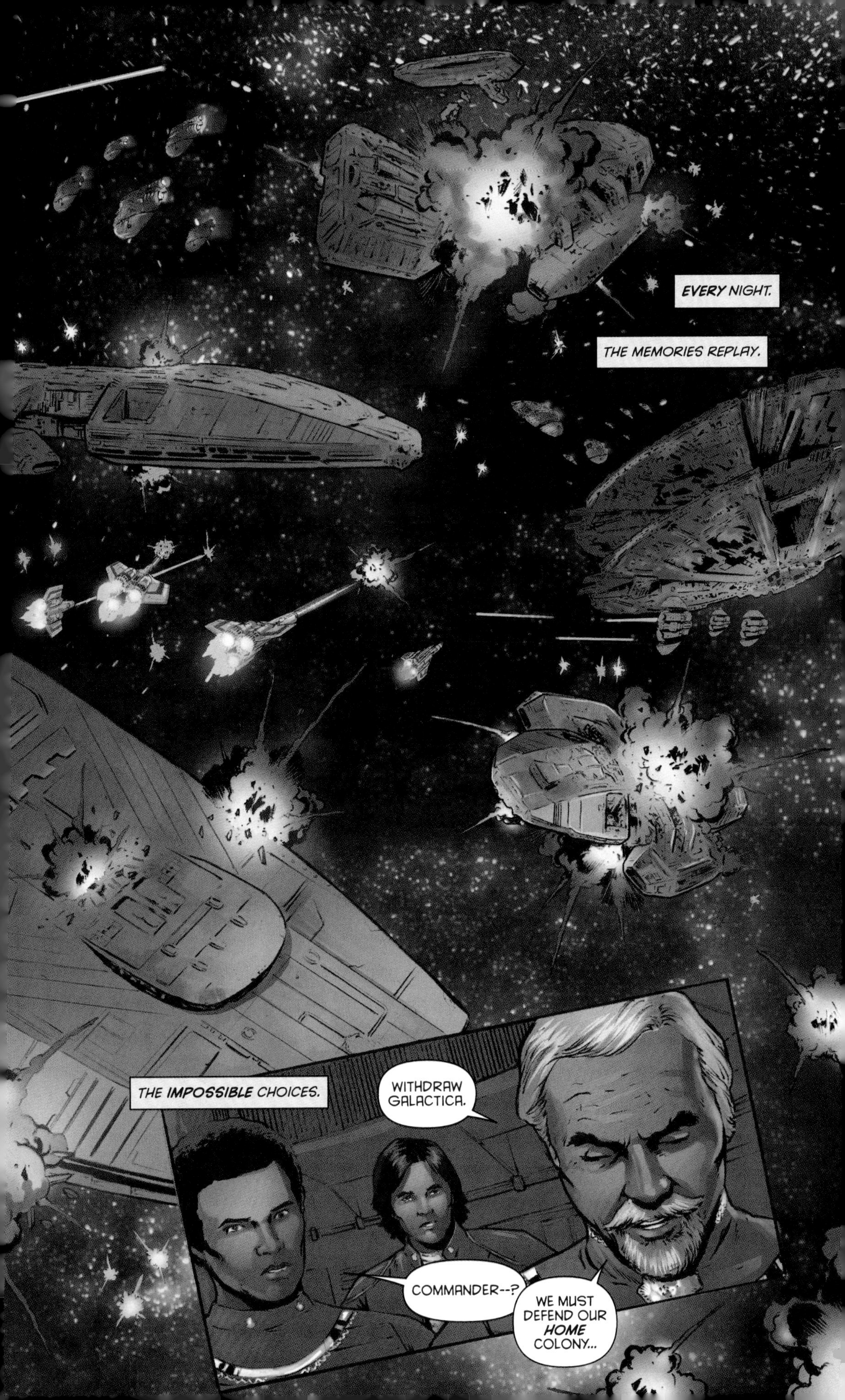
EVERY NIGHT.
THE MEMORIES REPLAY.
THE IMPOSSIBLE CHOICES.
WITHDRAW GALACTICA.
COMMANDER--?
WE MUST DEFEND OUR HOME COLONY...

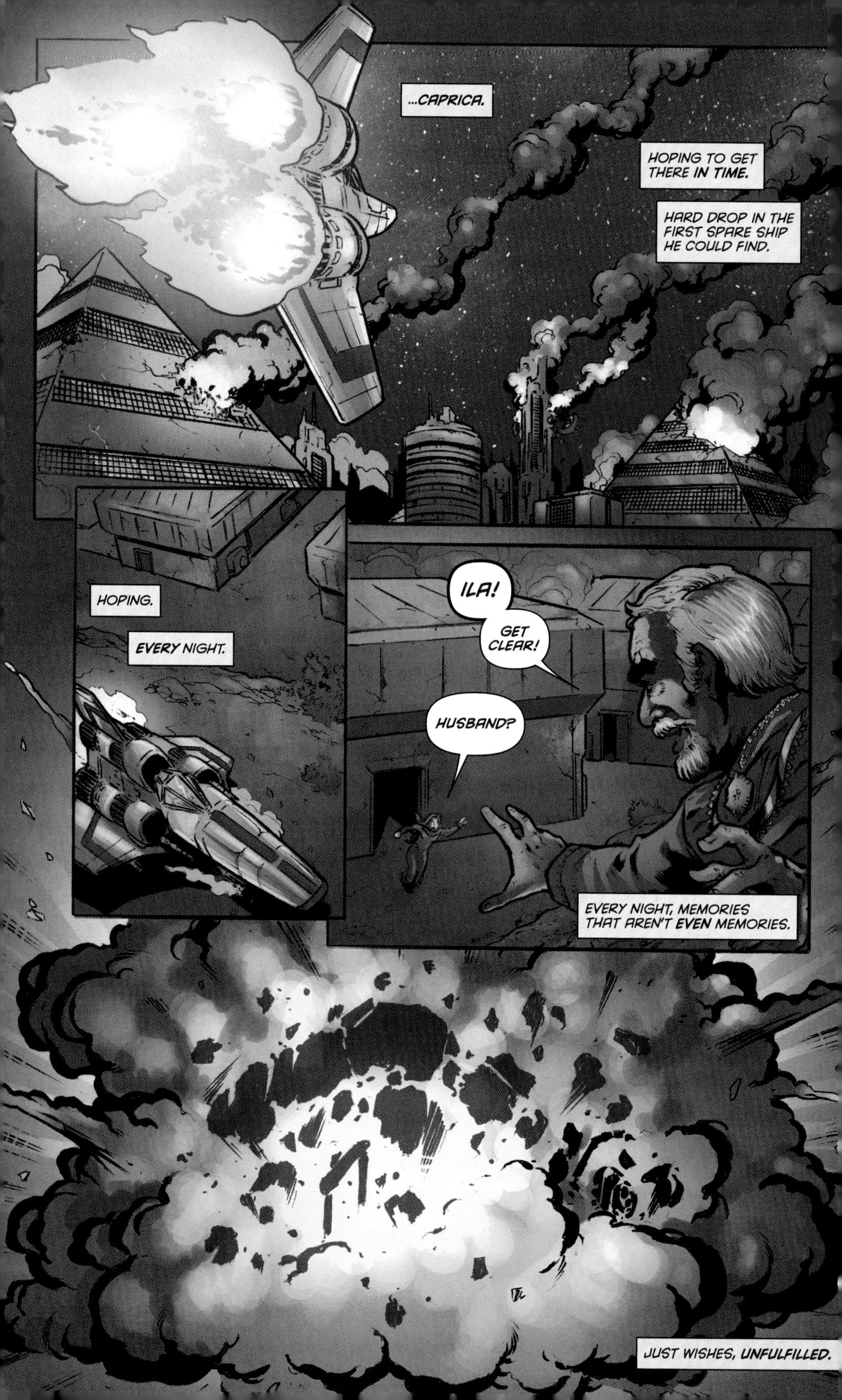
...CAPRICA.
HOPING TO GET THERE IN TIME.
HARD DROP IN THE FIRST SPARE SHIP HE COULD FIND.
HOPING.
EVERY NIGHT.
ILA!
GET CLEAR!
HUSBAND?
EVERY NIGHT, MEMORIES THAT AREN'T EVEN MEMORIES.
JUST WISHES, UNFULFILLED.

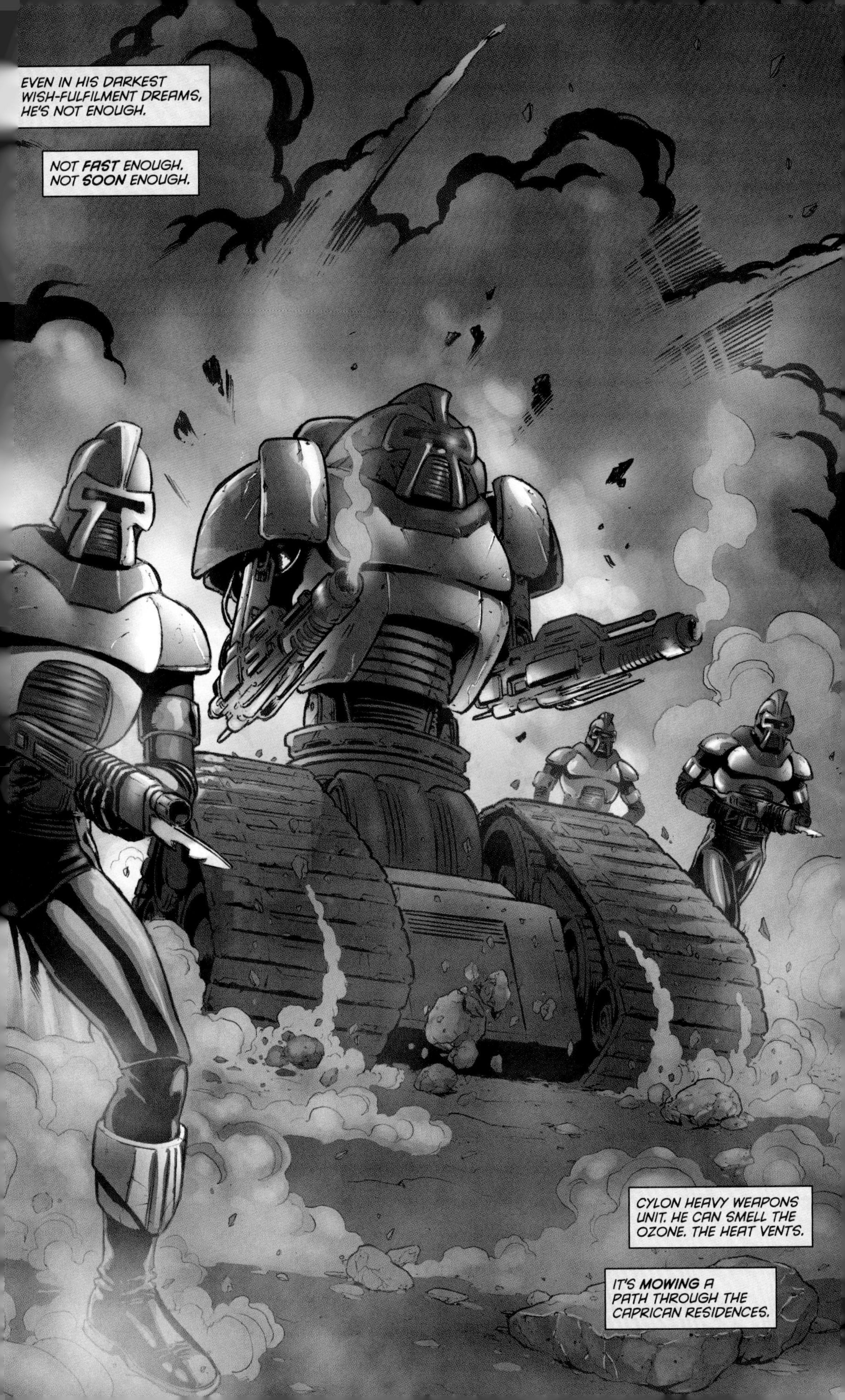
EVEN IN HIS DARKEST WISH-FULFILMENT DREAMS, HE'S NOT ENOUGH.
NOT FAST ENOUGH. NOT SOON ENOUGH.
CYLON HEAVY WEAPONS UNIT. HE CAN SMELL THE OZONE. THE HEAT VENTS.
IT'S MOWING A PATH THROUGH THE CAPRICAN RESIDENCES.

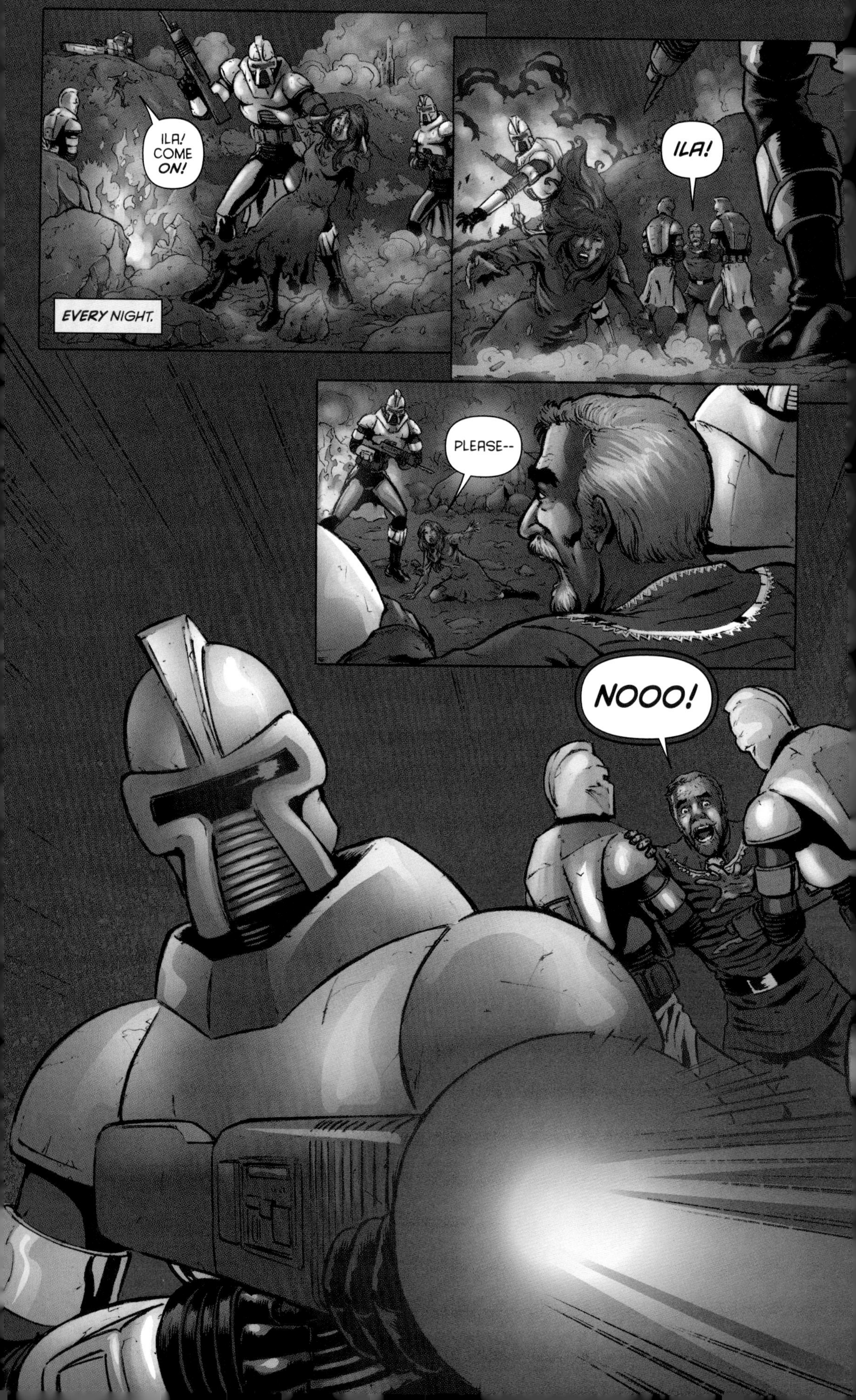
ILA! COME ON!
EVERY NIGHT.
ILA!
PLEASE--
NOOO!

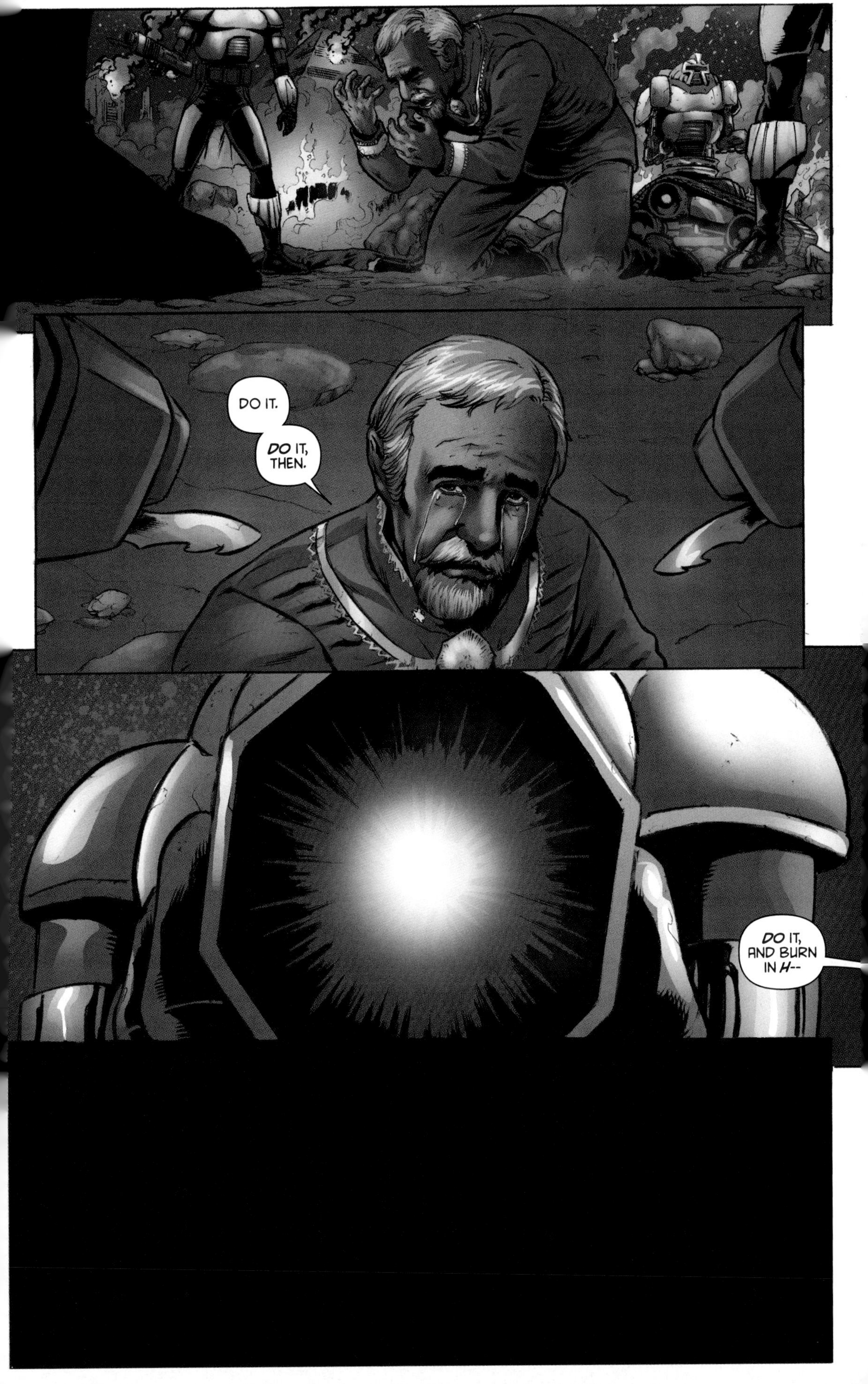
DO IT.
DO IT, THEN.
DO IT, AND BURN IN H--

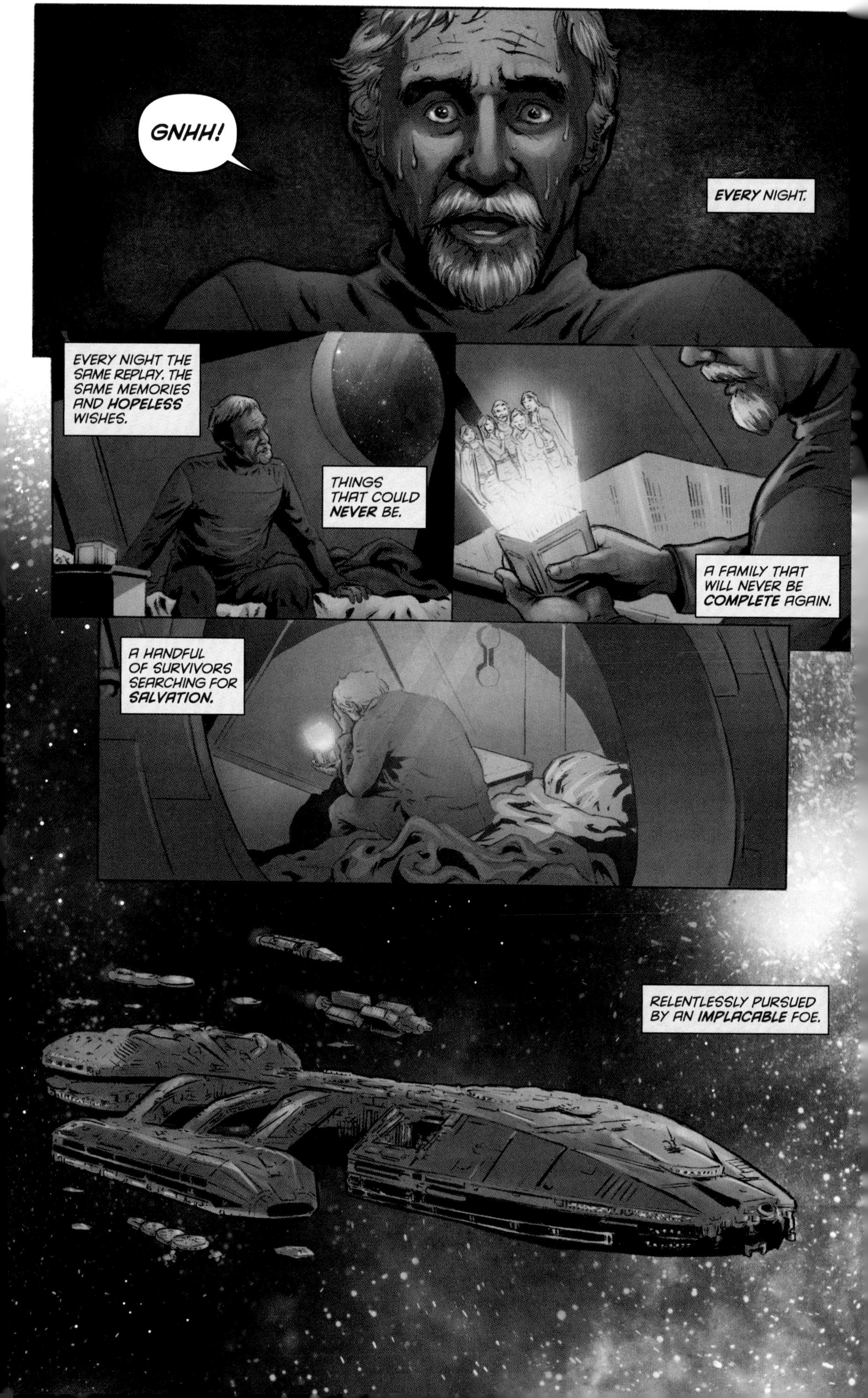
GNHH!
EVERY NIGHT.
EVERY NIGHT THE SAME REPLAY. THE SAME MEMORIES AND HOPELESS WISHES.
THINGS THAT COULD NEVER BE.
A FAMILY THAT WILL NEVER BE COMPLETE AGAIN.
A HANDFUL OF SURVIVORS SEARCHING FOR SALVATION.
RELENTLESSLY PURSUED BY AN IMPLACABLE FOE.

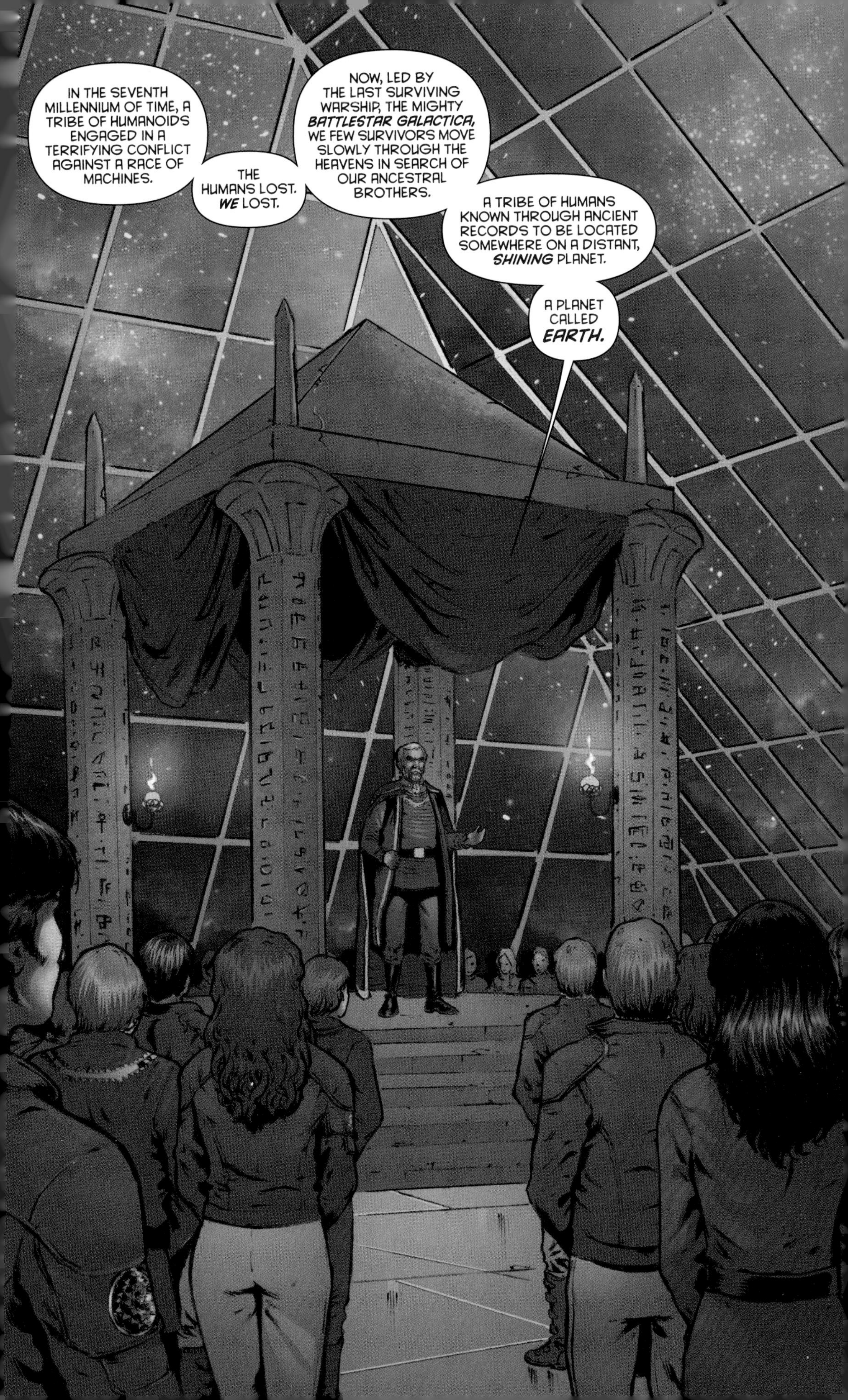
IN THE SEVENTH MILLENNIUM OF TIME, A TRIBE OF HUMANOIDS ENGAGED IN A TERRIFYING CONFLICT AGAINST A RACE OF MACHINES.
THE HUMANS LOST. *WE* LOST.
NOW, LED BY THE LAST SURVIVING WARSHIP, THE MIGHTY ***BATTLESTAR GALACTICA,*** WE FEW SURVIVORS MOVE SLOWLY THROUGH THE HEAVENS IN SEARCH OF OUR ANCESTRAL BROTHERS.
A TRIBE OF HUMANS KNOWN THROUGH ANCIENT RECORDS TO BE LOCATED SOMEWHERE ON A DISTANT, *SHINING* PLANET.
A PLANET CALLED ***EARTH.***

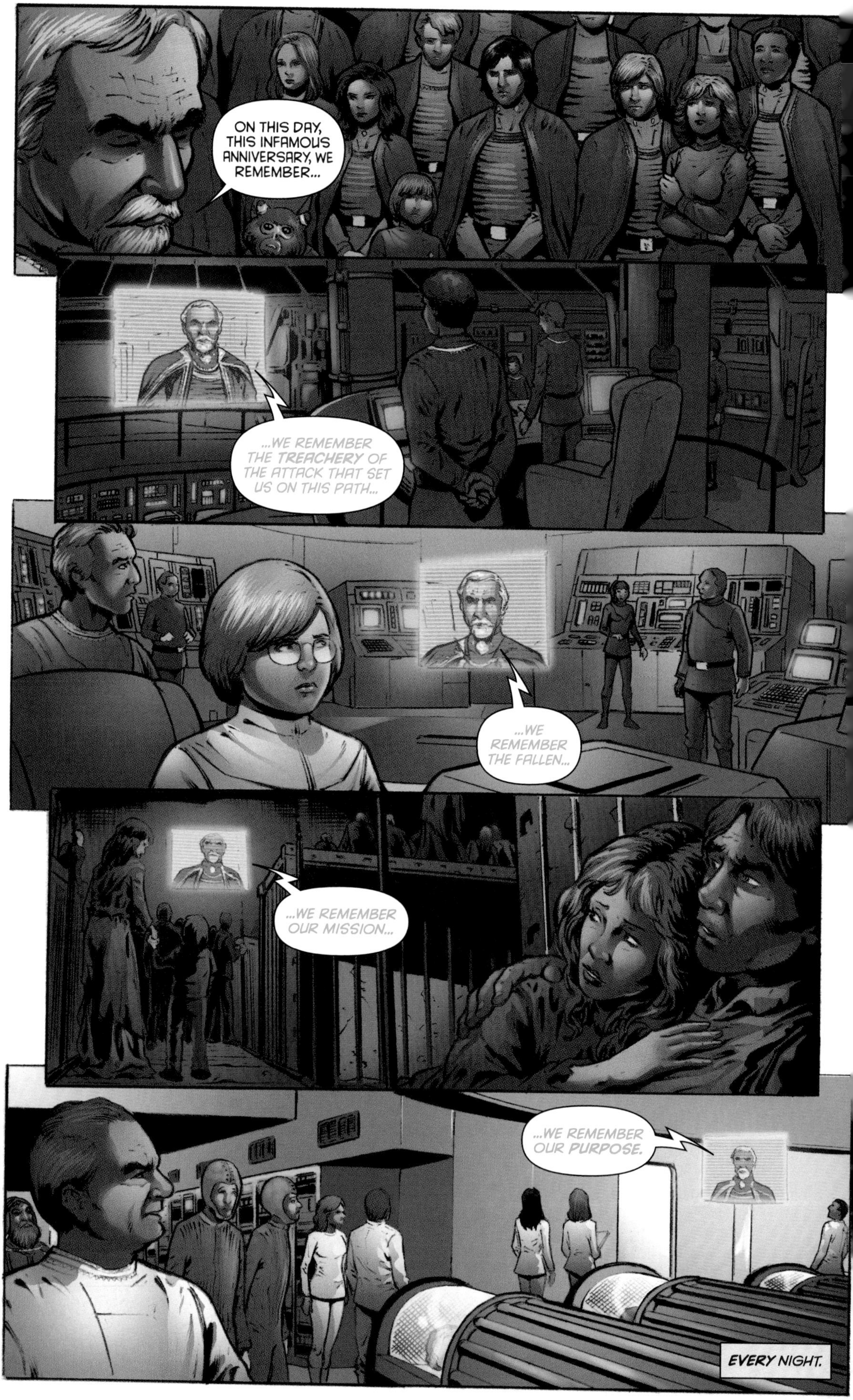
ON THIS DAY, THIS INFAMOUS ANNIVERSARY, WE REMEMBER...
...WE REMEMBER THE TREACHERY OF THE ATTACK THAT SET US ON THIS PATH...
...WE REMEMBER THE FALLEN...
...WE REMEMBER OUR MISSION...
...WE REMEMBER OUR PURPOSE.
EVERY NIGHT.

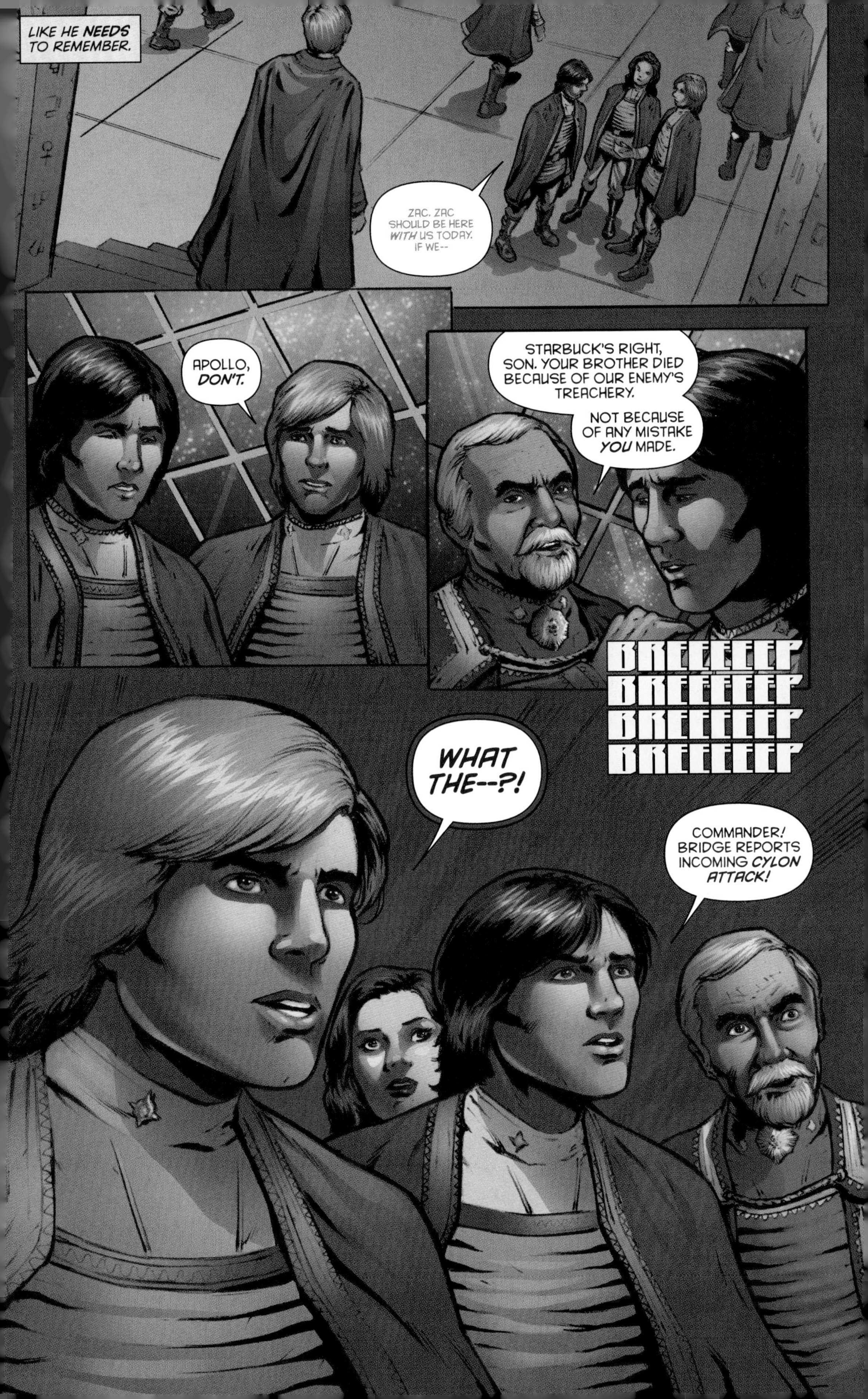
LIKE HE NEEDS TO REMEMBER.
ZAC. ZAC SHOULD BE HERE WITH US TODAY. IF WE--
APOLLO, DON'T.
STARBUCK'S RIGHT, SON. YOUR BROTHER DIED BECAUSE OF OUR ENEMY'S TREACHERY.
NOT BECAUSE OF ANY MISTAKE YOU MADE.
BREEEEEP
BREEEEEP
BREEEEEP
BREEEEEP
WHAT THE--?!
COMMANDER! BRIDGE REPORTS INCOMING CYLON ATTACK!

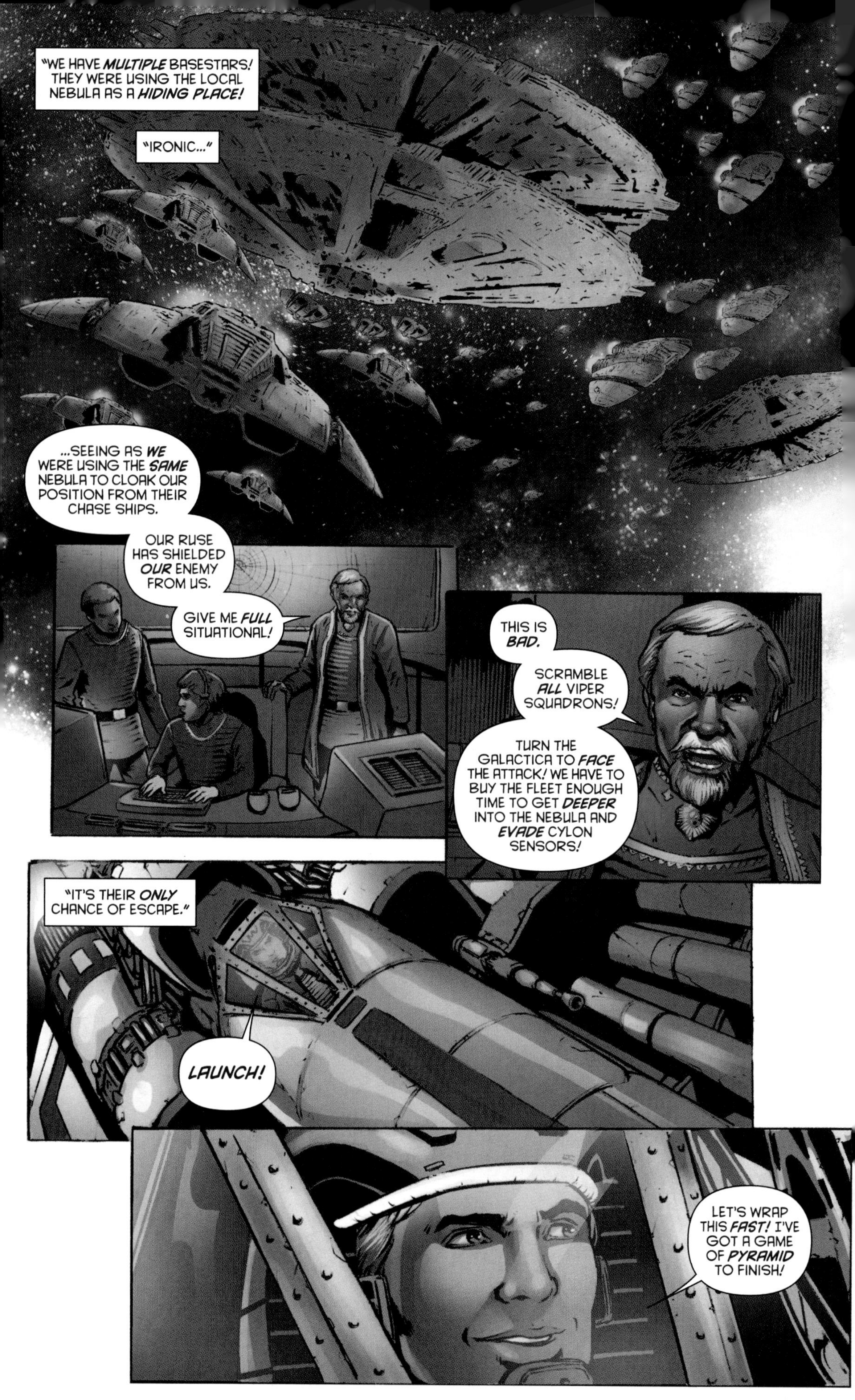
"WE HAVE MULTIPLE BASESTARS! THEY WERE USING THE LOCAL NEBULA AS A HIDING PLACE!
"IRONIC..."
...SEEING AS WE WERE USING THE SAME NEBULA TO CLOAK OUR POSITION FROM THEIR CHASE SHIPS.
OUR RUSE HAS SHIELDED OUR ENEMY FROM US.
GIVE ME FULL SITUATIONAL!
THIS IS BAD.
SCRAMBLE ALL VIPER SQUADRONS!
TURN THE GALACTICA TO FACE THE ATTACK! WE HAVE TO BUY THE FLEET ENOUGH TIME TO GET DEEPER INTO THE NEBULA AND EVADE CYLON SENSORS!
"IT'S THEIR ONLY CHANCE OF ESCAPE."
LAUNCH!
LET'S WRAP THIS FAST! I'VE GOT A GAME OF PYRAMID TO FINISH!

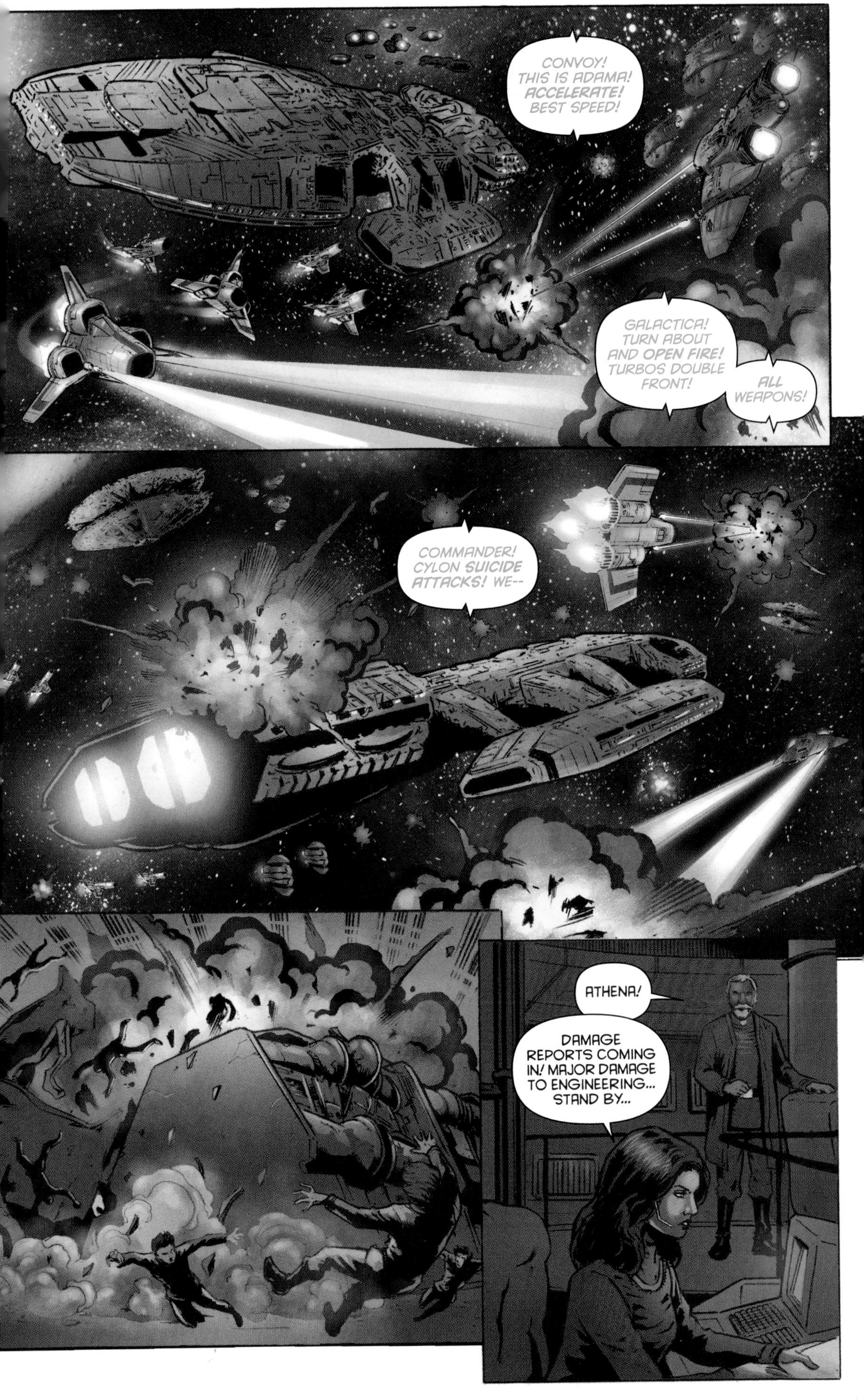
CONVOY! THIS IS ADAMA! ACCELERATE! BEST SPEED!
GALACTICA! TURN ABOUT AND OPEN FIRE! TURBOS DOUBLE FRONT!
ALL WEAPONS!
COMMANDER! CYLON SUICIDE ATTACKS! WE--
ATHENA!
DAMAGE REPORTS COMING IN! MAJOR DAMAGE TO ENGINEERING... STAND BY...

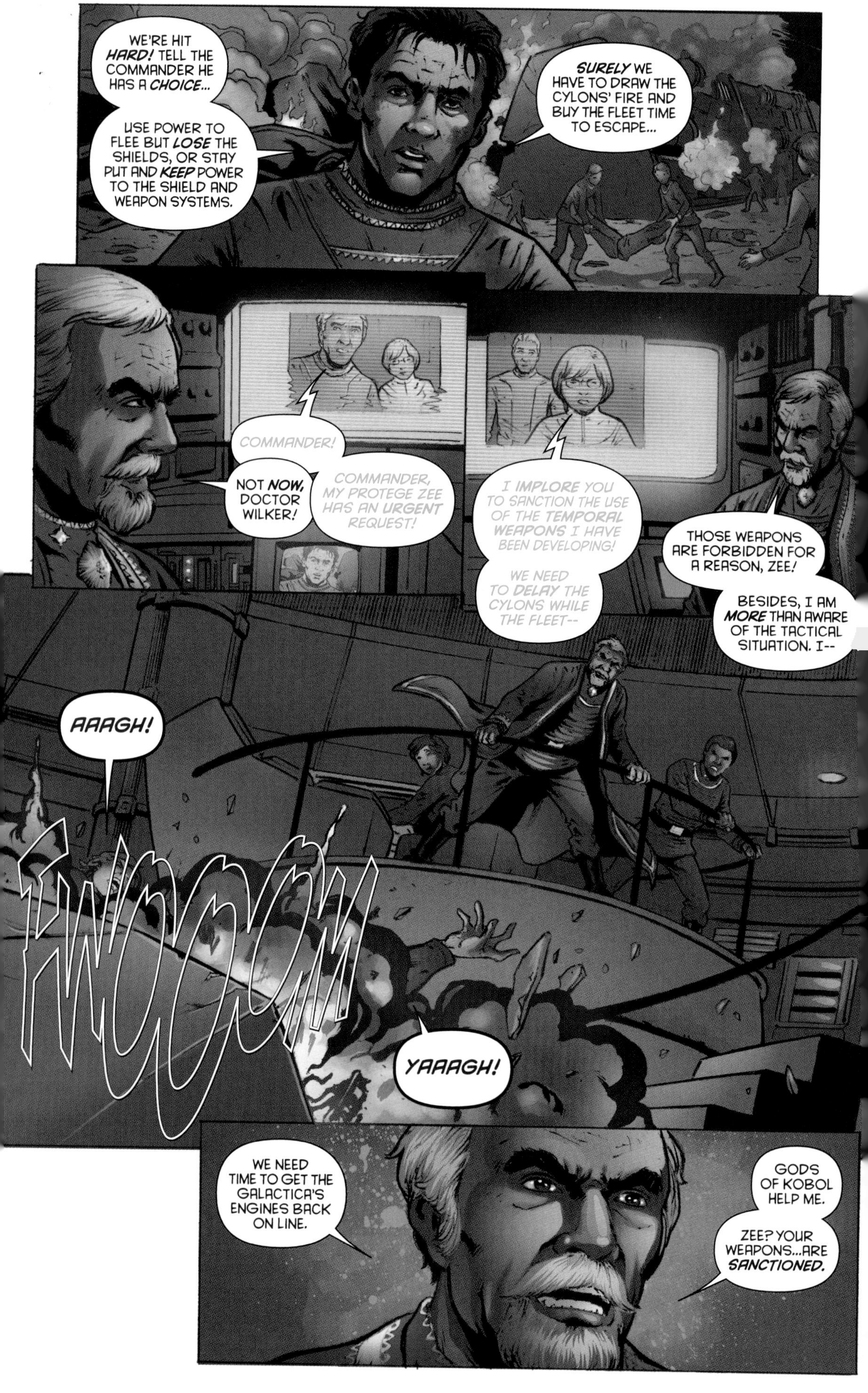
WE'RE HIT HARD! TELL THE COMMANDER HE HAS A CHOICE...
USE POWER TO FLEE BUT LOSE THE SHIELDS, OR STAY PUT AND KEEP POWER TO THE SHIELD AND WEAPON SYSTEMS.
SURELY WE HAVE TO DRAW THE CYLONS' FIRE AND BUY THE FLEET TIME TO ESCAPE...
COMMANDER!
NOT NOW, DOCTOR WILKER!
COMMANDER, MY PROTEGE ZEE HAS AN URGENT REQUEST!
I IMPLORE YOU TO SANCTION THE USE OF THE TEMPORAL WEAPONS I HAVE BEEN DEVELOPING!
WE NEED TO DELAY THE CYLONS WHILE THE FLEET--
THOSE WEAPONS ARE FORBIDDEN FOR A REASON, ZEE!
BESIDES, I AM MORE THAN AWARE OF THE TACTICAL SITUATION. I--
AAAGH!
FWOOOM
YAAAGH!
WE NEED TIME TO GET THE GALACTICA'S ENGINES BACK ON LINE.
GODS OF KOBOL HELP ME.
ZEE? YOUR WEAPONS...ARE SANCTIONED.

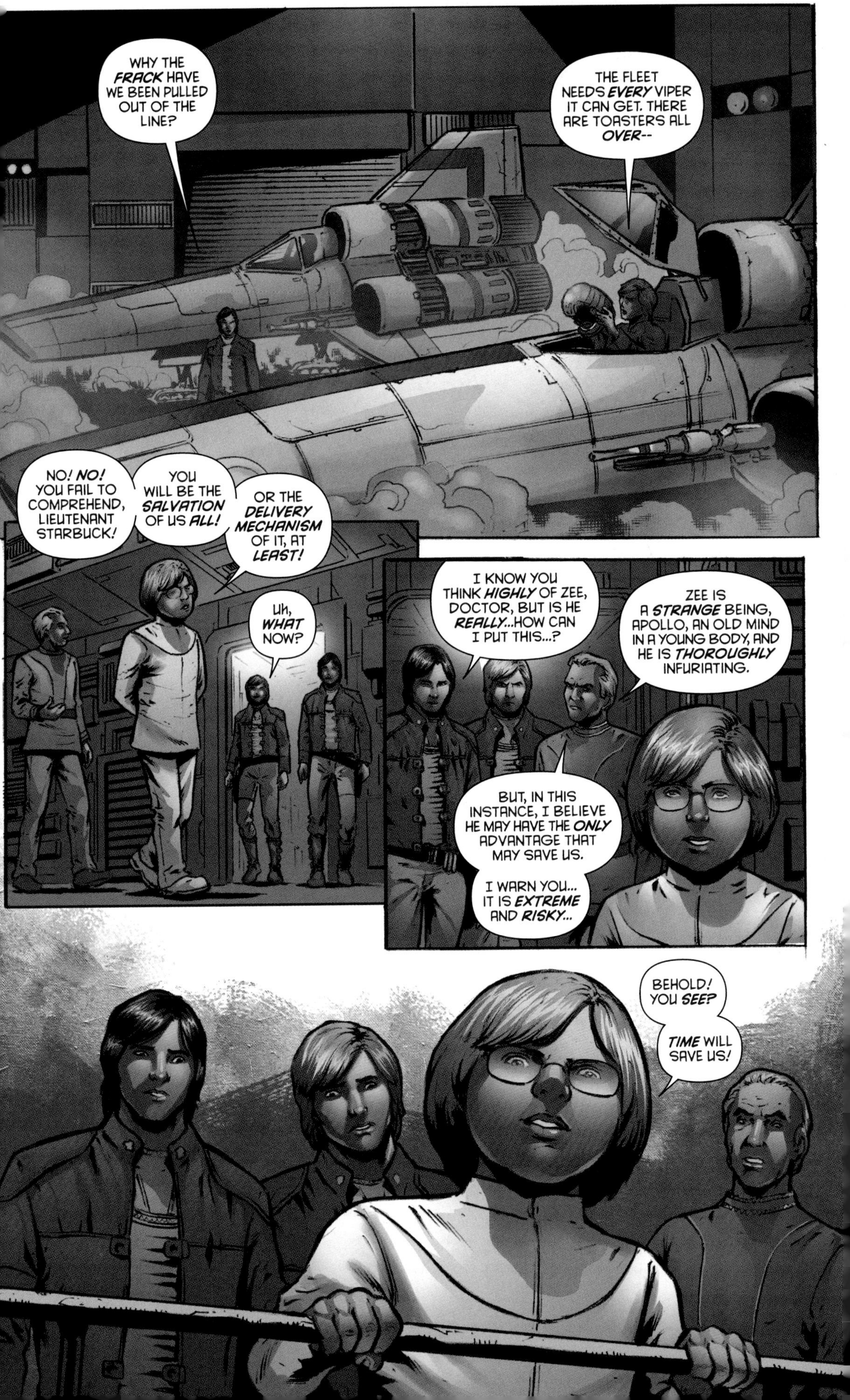
WHY THE FRACK HAVE WE BEEN PULLED OUT OF THE LINE?
THE FLEET NEEDS EVERY VIPER IT CAN GET. THERE ARE TOASTERS ALL OVER--
NO! NO! YOU FAIL TO COMPREHEND, LIEUTENANT STARBUCK!
YOU WILL BE THE SALVATION OF US ALL!
OR THE DELIVERY MECHANISM OF IT, AT LEAST!
UH, WHAT NOW?
I KNOW YOU THINK HIGHLY OF ZEE, DOCTOR, BUT IS HE REALLY...HOW CAN I PUT THIS...?
ZEE IS A STRANGE BEING, APOLLO, AN OLD MIND IN A YOUNG BODY, AND HE IS THOROUGHLY INFURIATING.
BUT, IN THIS INSTANCE, I BELIEVE HE MAY HAVE THE ONLY ADVANTAGE THAT MAY SAVE US.
I WARN YOU... IT IS EXTREME AND RISKY...
BEHOLD! YOU SEE?
TIME WILL SAVE US!

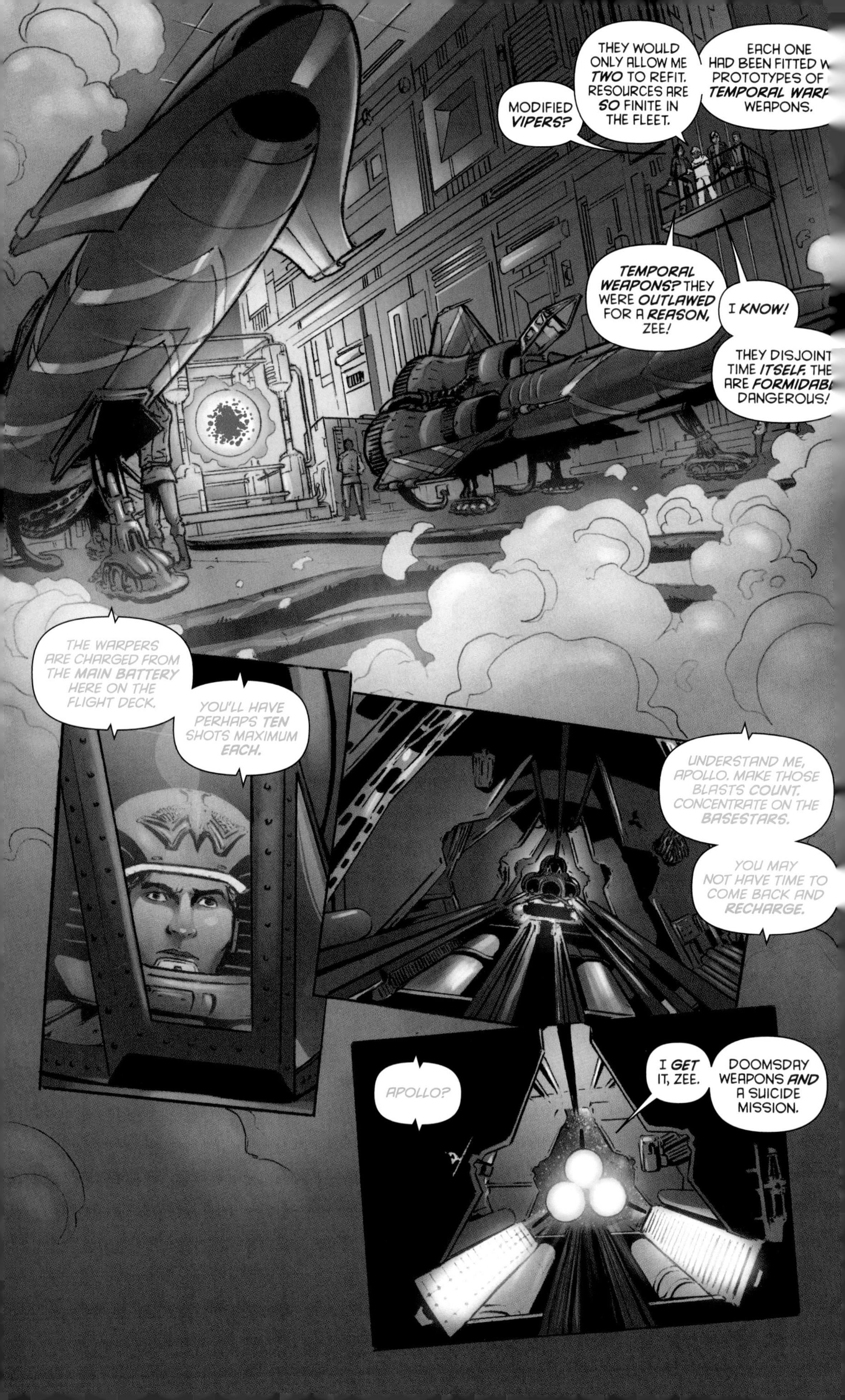
MODIFIED VIPERS?
THEY WOULD ONLY ALLOW ME TWO TO REFIT. RESOURCES ARE SO FINITE IN THE FLEET.
EACH ONE HAD BEEN FITTED W PROTOTYPES OF TEMPORAL WARP WEAPONS.
TEMPORAL WEAPONS? THEY WERE OUTLAWED FOR A REASON, ZEE!
I KNOW!
THEY DISJOINT TIME ITSELF. THE ARE FORMIDABL DANGEROUS!
THE WARPERS ARE CHARGED FROM THE MAIN BATTERY HERE ON THE FLIGHT DECK.
YOU'LL HAVE PERHAPS TEN SHOTS MAXIMUM EACH.
UNDERSTAND ME, APOLLO. MAKE THOSE BLASTS COUNT. CONCENTRATE ON THE BASESTARS.
YOU MAY NOT HAVE TIME TO COME BACK AND RECHARGE.
APOLLO?
I GET IT, ZEE.
DOOMSDAY WEAPONS AND A SUICIDE MISSION.

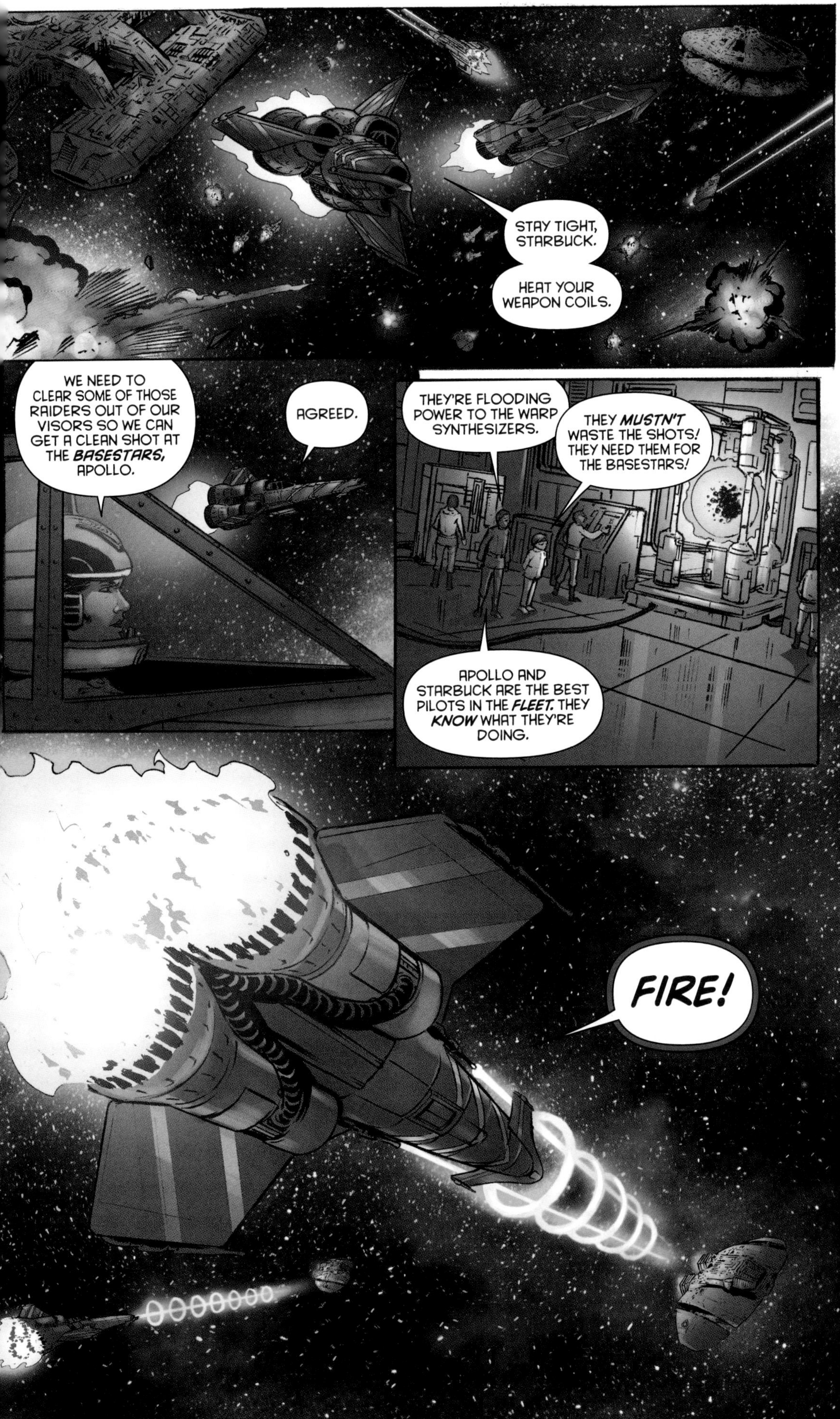
STAY TIGHT, STARBUCK.
HEAT YOUR WEAPON COILS.
WE NEED TO CLEAR SOME OF THOSE RAIDERS OUT OF OUR VISORS SO WE CAN GET A CLEAN SHOT AT THE BASESTARS, APOLLO.
AGREED.
THEY'RE FLOODING POWER TO THE WARP SYNTHESIZERS.
THEY MUSTN'T WASTE THE SHOTS! THEY NEED THEM FOR THE BASESTARS!
APOLLO AND STARBUCK ARE THE BEST PILOTS IN THE FLEET. THEY KNOW WHAT THEY'RE DOING.
FIRE!

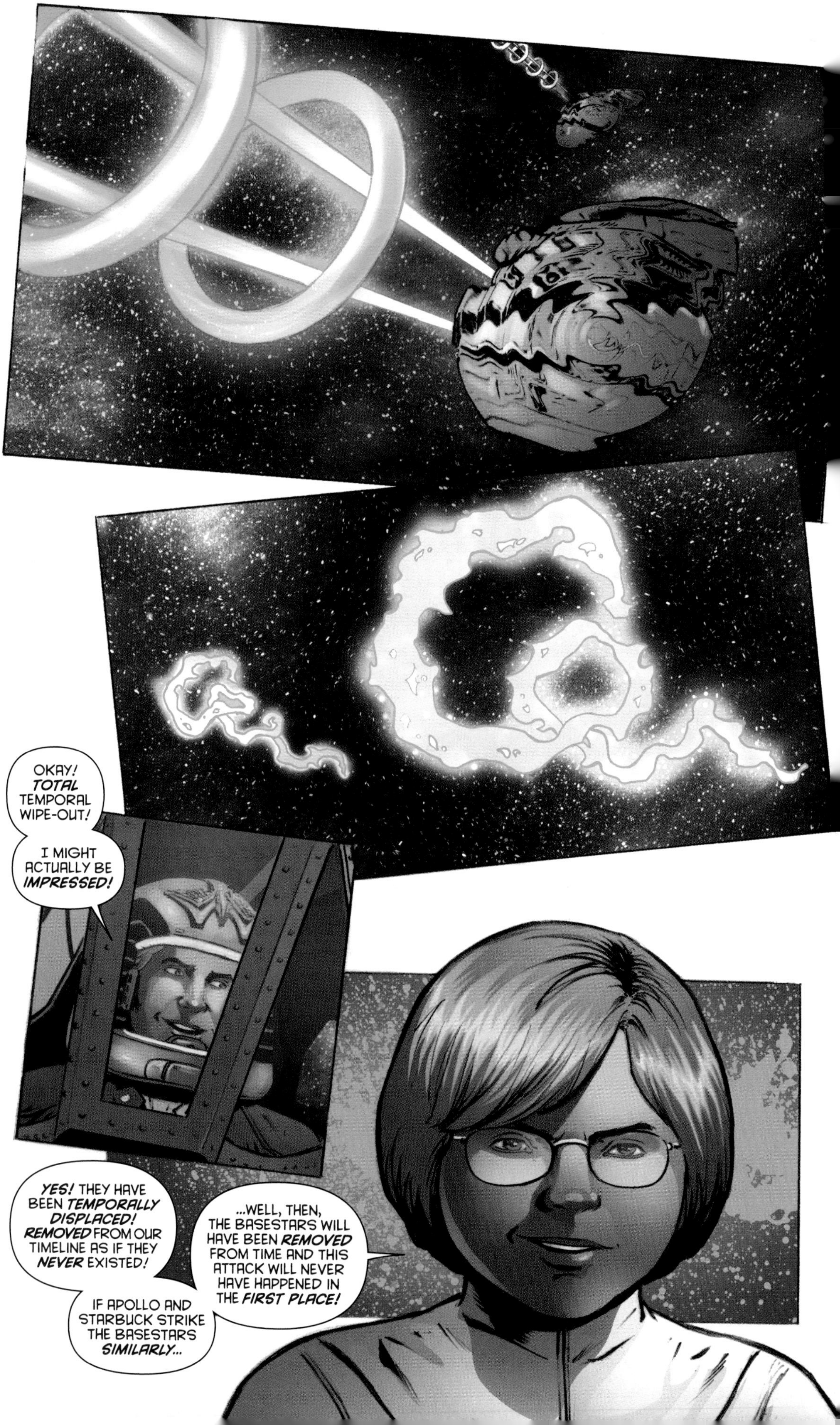
OKAY! TOTAL TEMPORAL WIPE-OUT!
I MIGHT ACTUALLY BE IMPRESSED!
YES! THEY HAVE BEEN TEMPORALLY DISPLACED! REMOVED FROM OUR TIMELINE AS IF THEY NEVER EXISTED!
IF APOLLO AND STARBUCK STRIKE THE BASESTARS SIMILARLY...
...WELL, THEN, THE BASESTARS WILL HAVE BEEN REMOVED FROM TIME AND THIS ATTACK WILL NEVER HAVE HAPPENED IN THE FIRST PLACE!

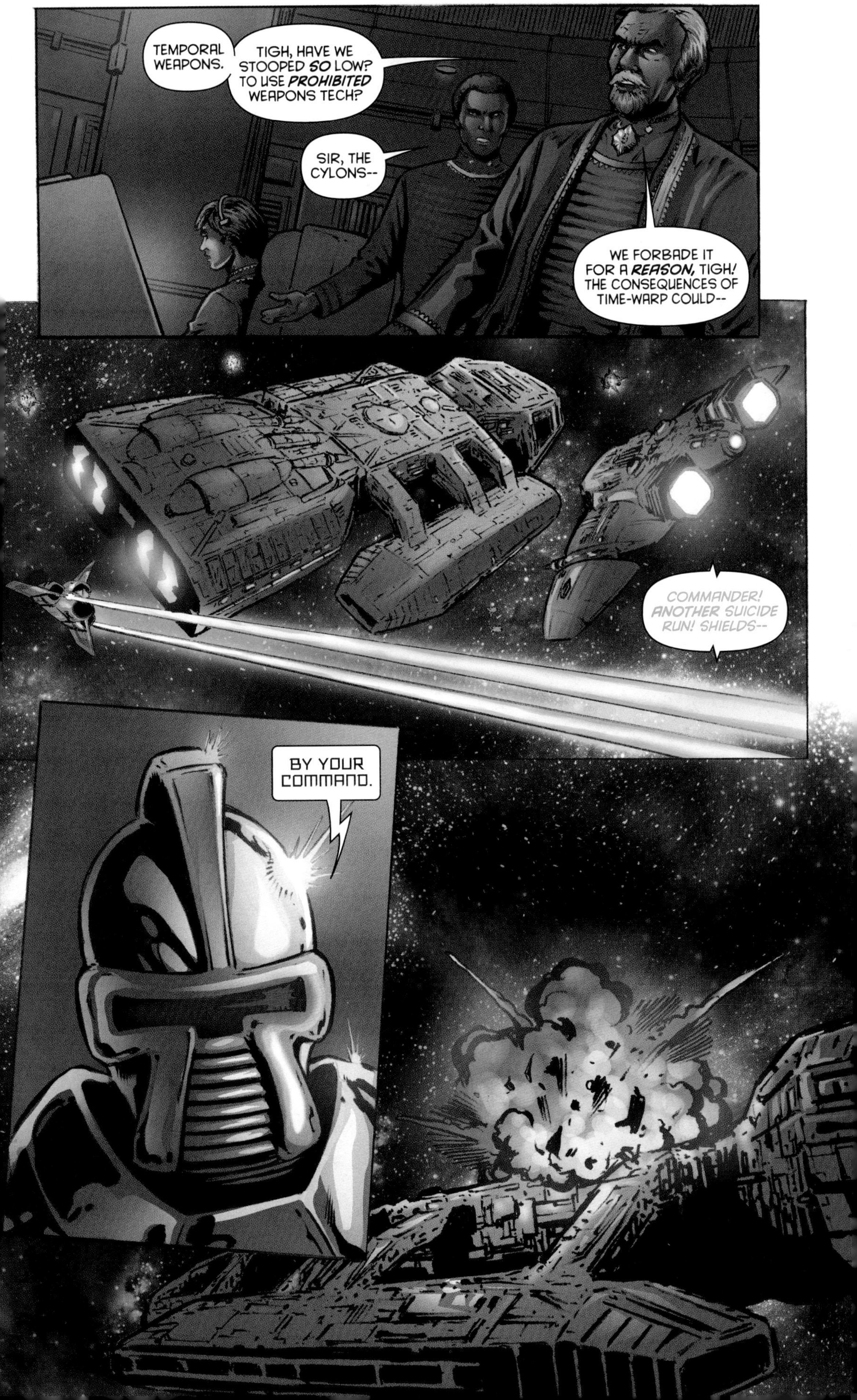
TEMPORAL WEAPONS.
TIGH, HAVE WE STOOPED SO LOW? TO USE PROHIBITED WEAPONS TECH?
SIR, THE CYLONS--
WE FORBADE IT FOR A REASON, TIGH! THE CONSEQUENCES OF TIME-WARP COULD--
COMMANDER! ANOTHER SUICIDE RUN! SHIELDS--
BY YOUR COMMAND.

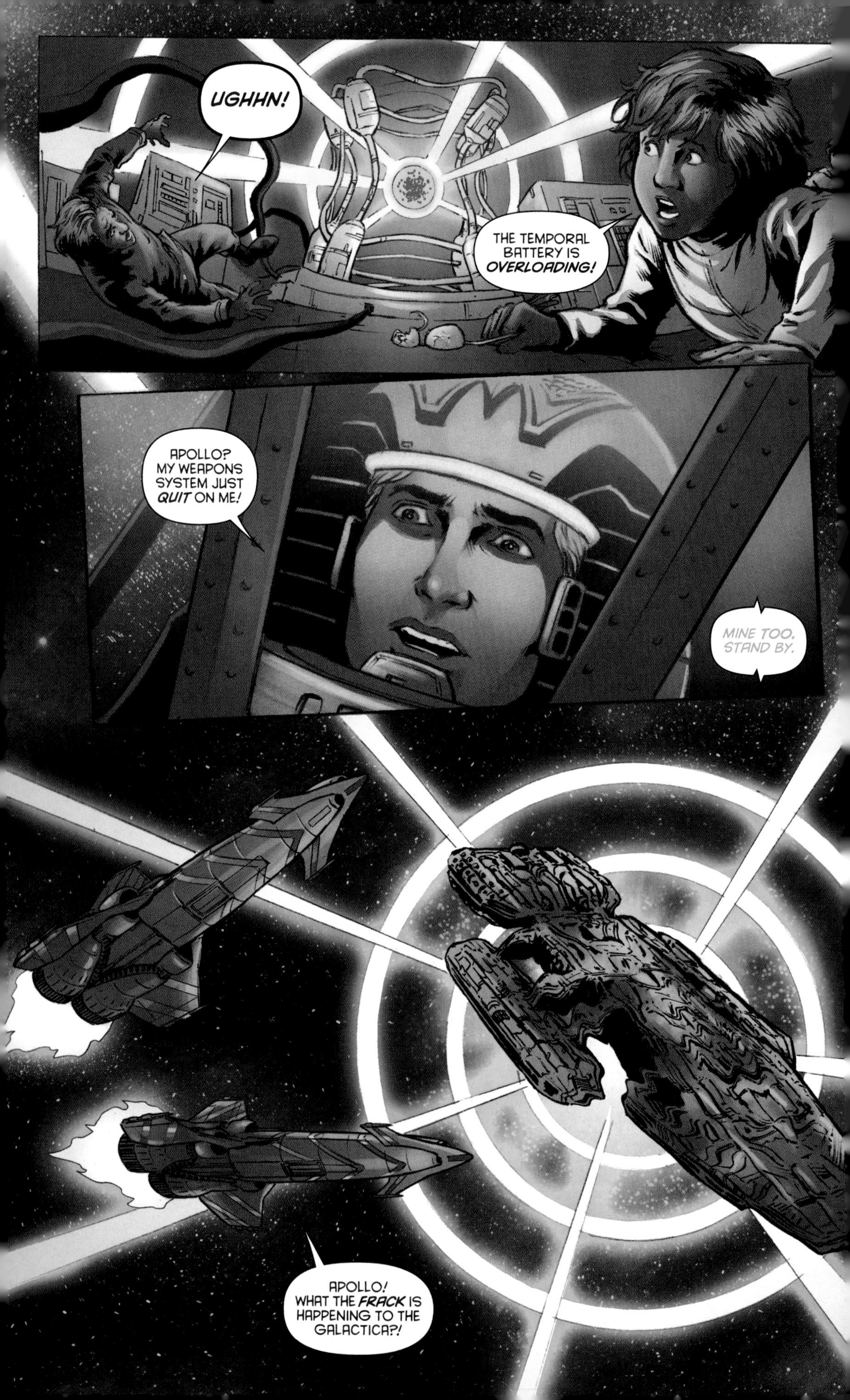
UGHHN!
THE TEMPORAL BATTERY IS *OVERLOADING!*
APOLLO? MY WEAPONS SYSTEM JUST *QUIT* ON ME!
MINE TOO. STAND BY.
APOLLO! WHAT THE *FRACK* IS HAPPENING TO THE GALACTICA?!

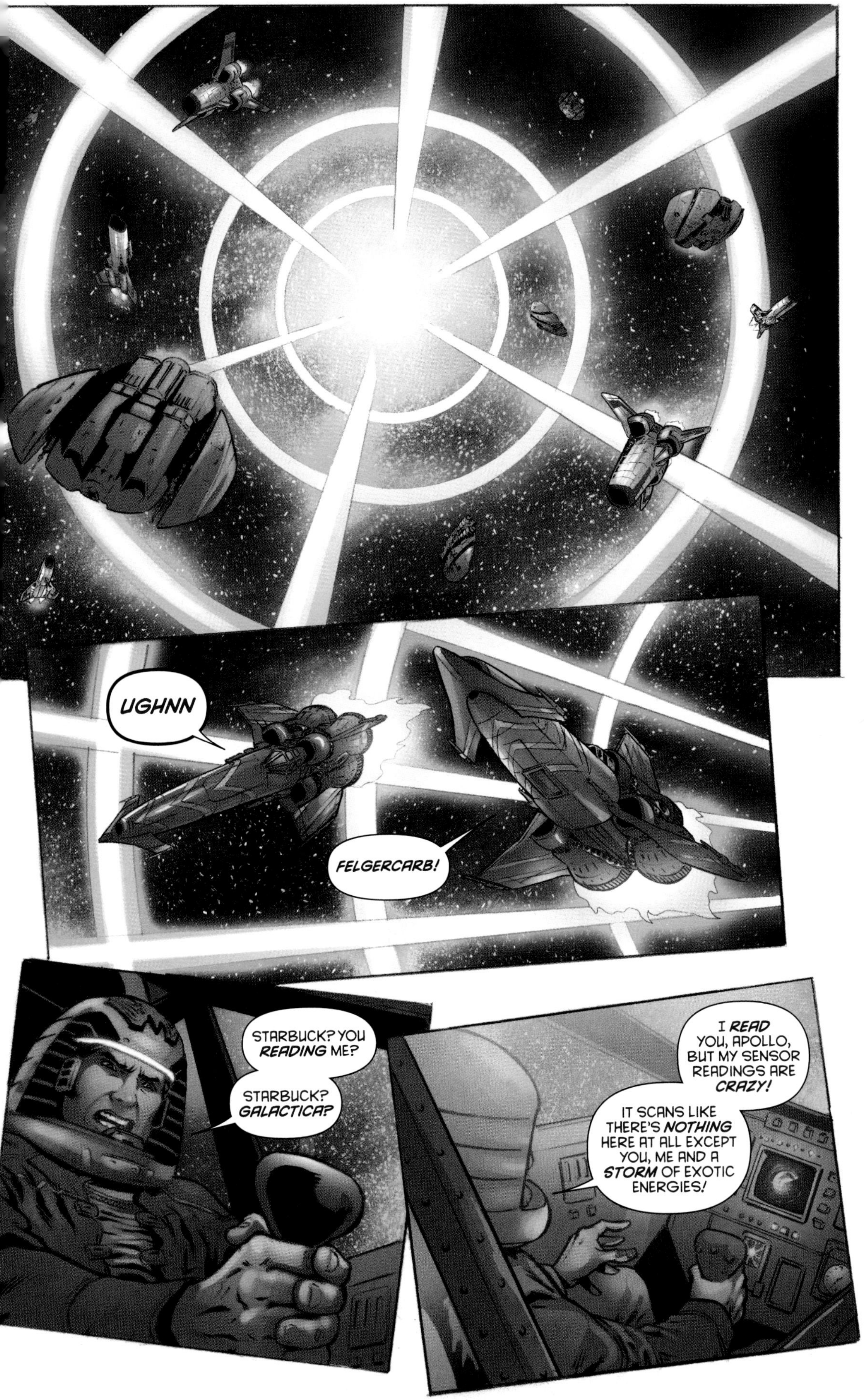
UGHNN
FELGERCARB!
STARBUCK? YOU *READING* ME?
STARBUCK? *GALACTICA?*
I *READ* YOU, APOLLO, BUT MY SENSOR READINGS ARE *CRAZY!*
IT SCANS LIKE THERE'S *NOTHING* HERE AT ALL EXCEPT YOU, ME AND A *STORM* OF EXOTIC ENERGIES!

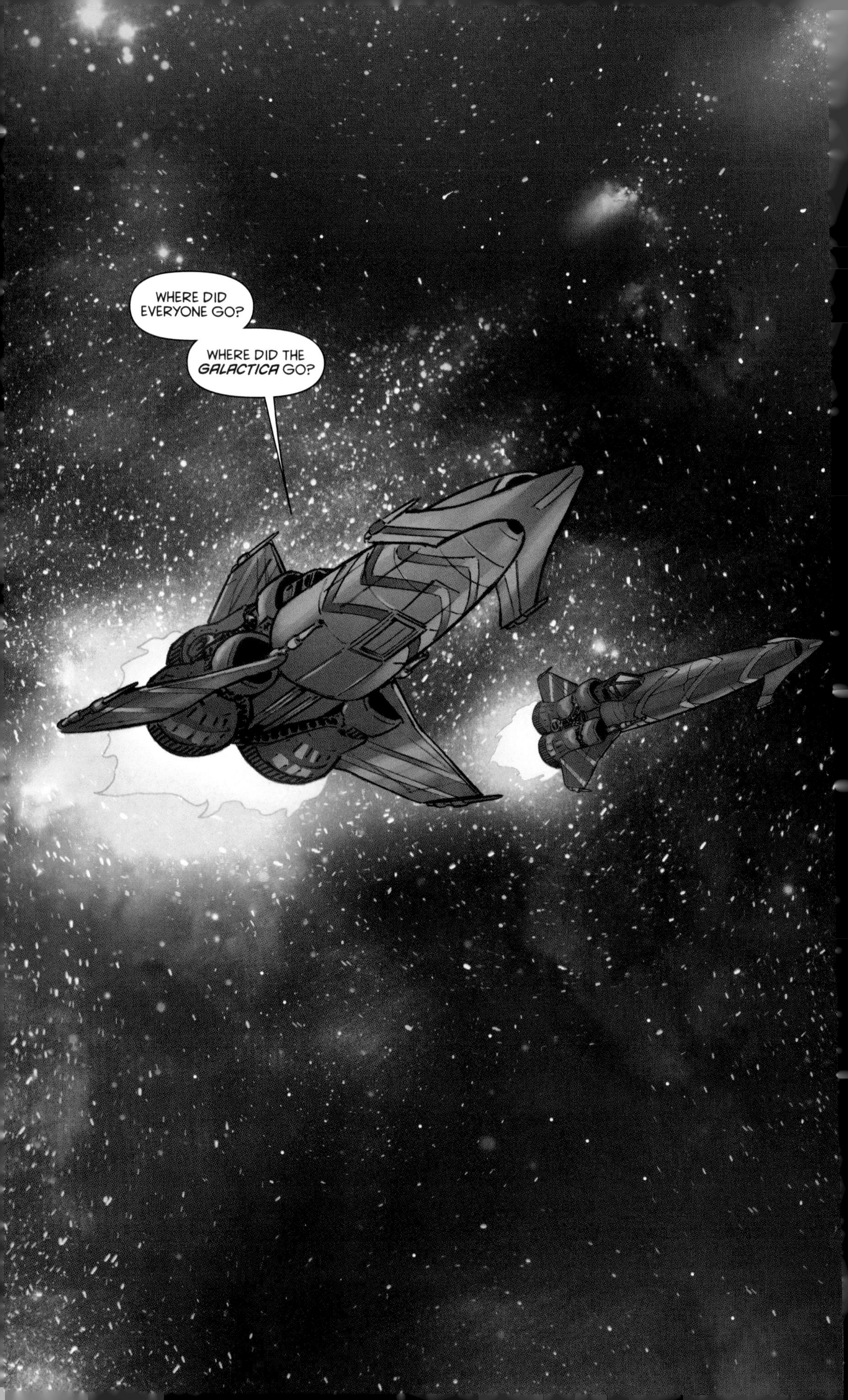
WHERE DID EVERYONE GO?
WHERE DID THE *GALACTICA* GO?

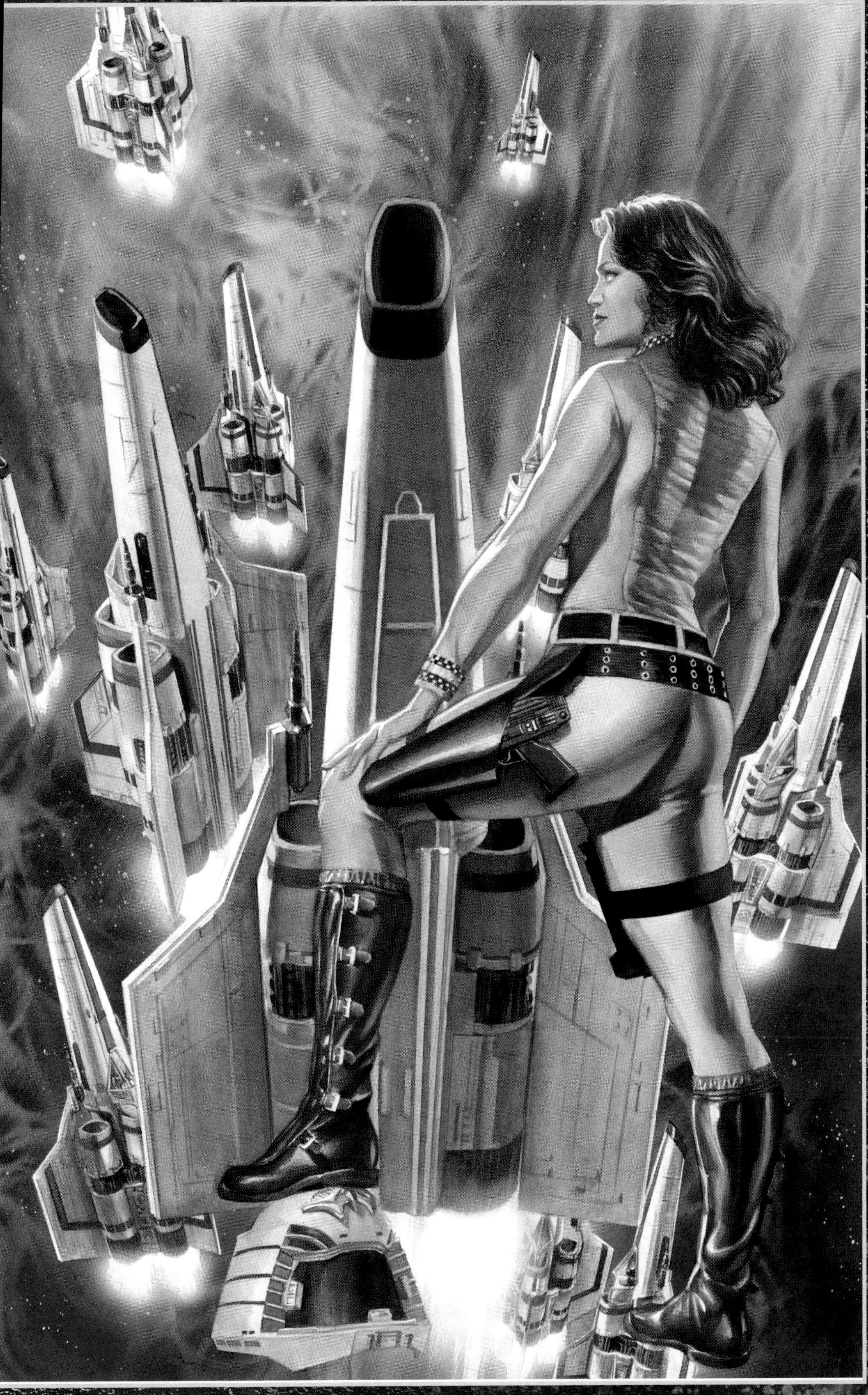

ISSUE 2

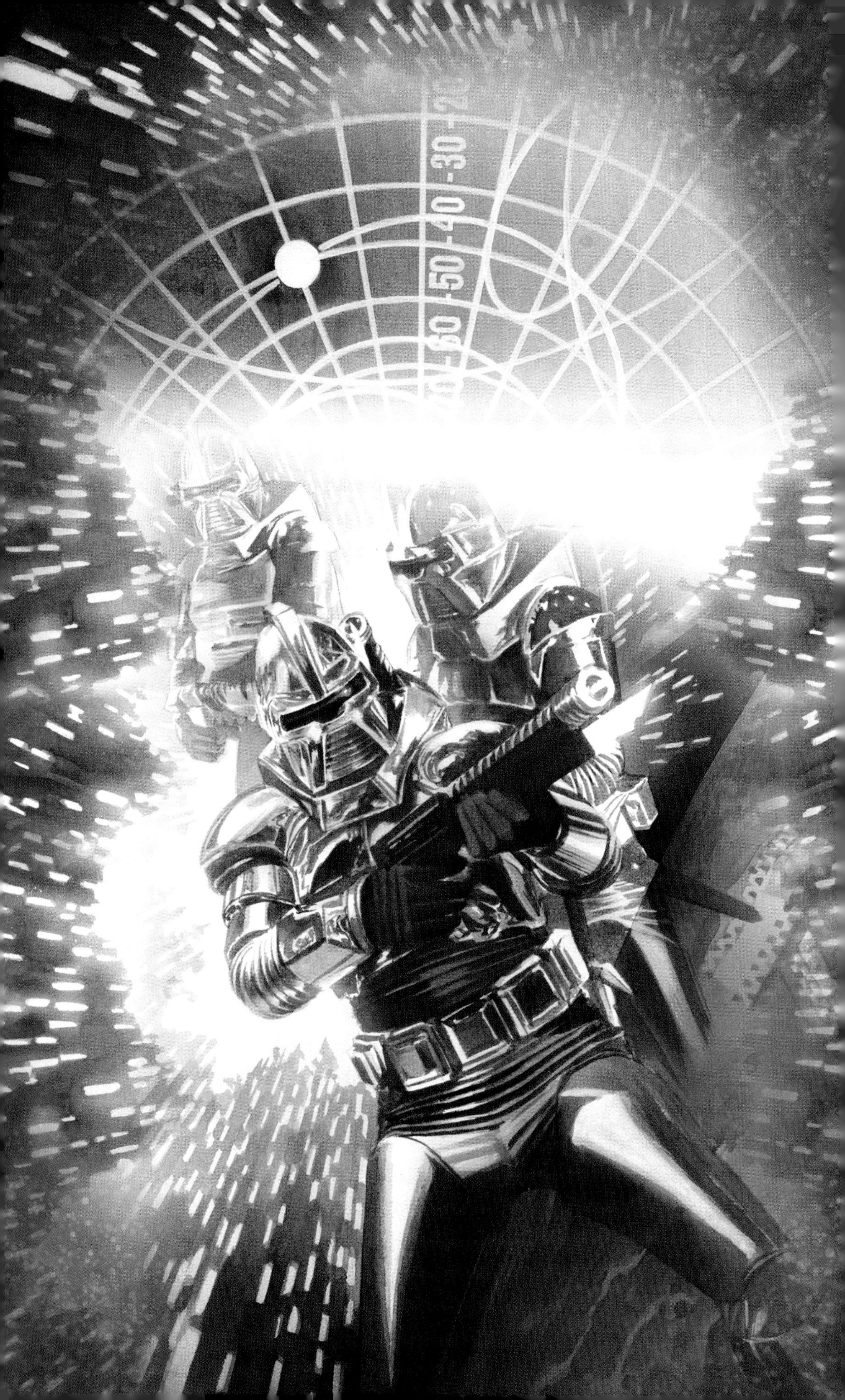

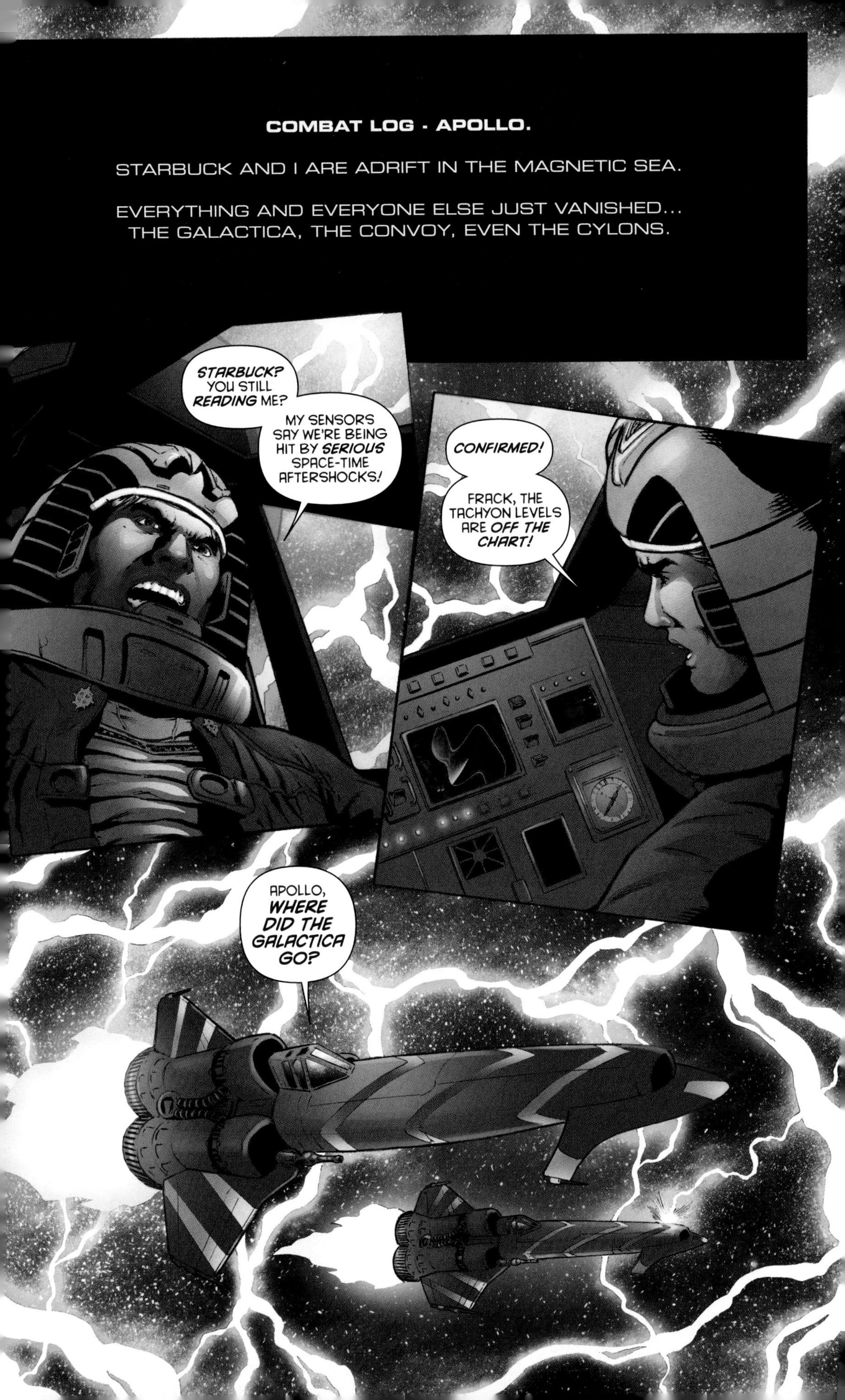
COMBAT LOG - APOLLO.
STARBUCK AND I ARE ADRIFT IN THE MAGNETIC SEA.
EVERYTHING AND EVERYONE ELSE JUST VANISHED... THE GALACTICA, THE CONVOY, EVEN THE CYLONS.
STARBUCK? YOU STILL READING ME?
MY SENSORS SAY WE'RE BEING HIT BY SERIOUS SPACE-TIME AFTERSHOCKS!
CONFIRMED!
FRACK, THE TACHYON LEVELS ARE OFF THE CHART!
APOLLO, WHERE DID THE GALACTICA GO?

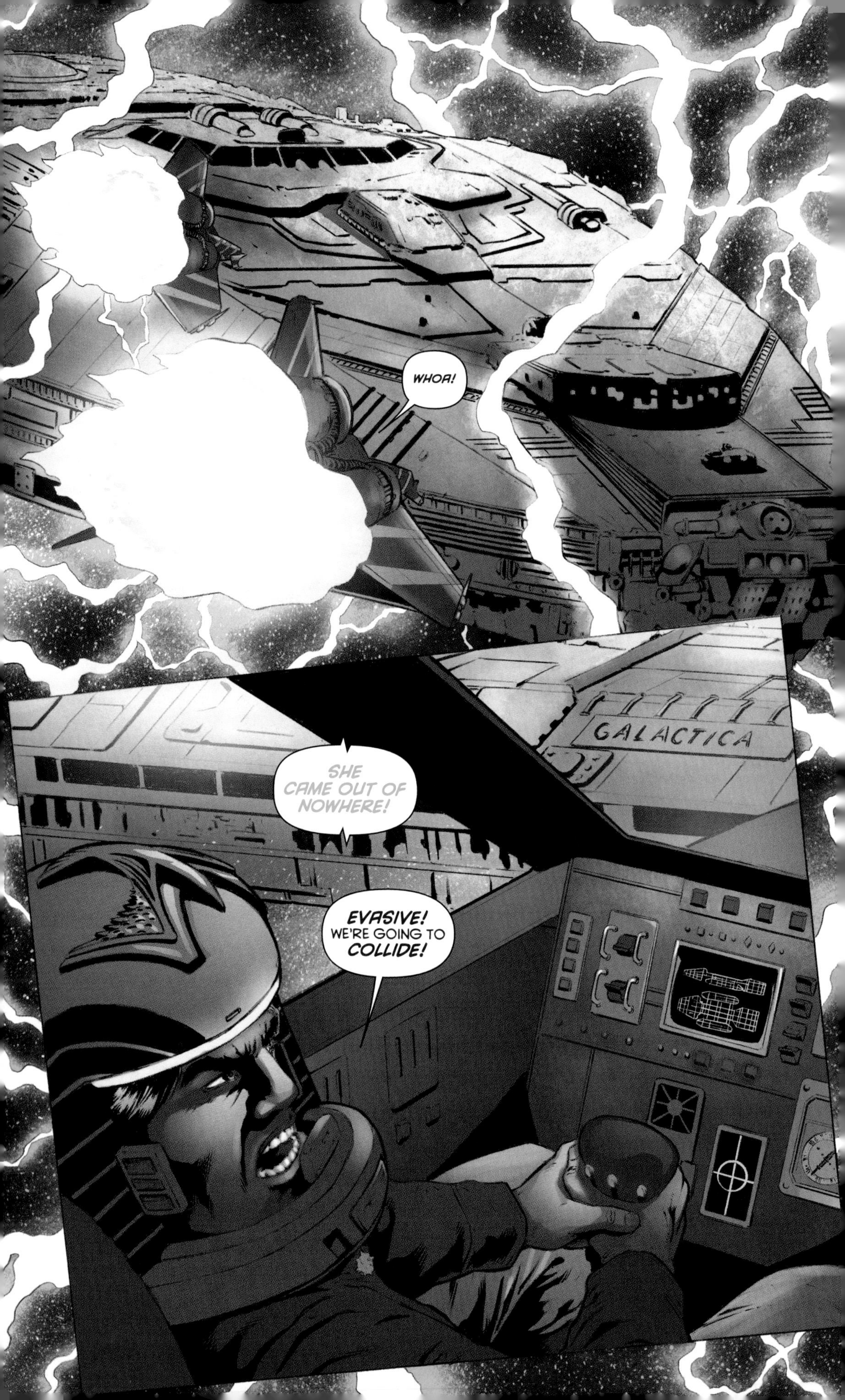
WHOA!
GALACTICA
SHE CAME OUT OF NOWHERE!
EVASIVE! WE'RE GOING TO COLLIDE!

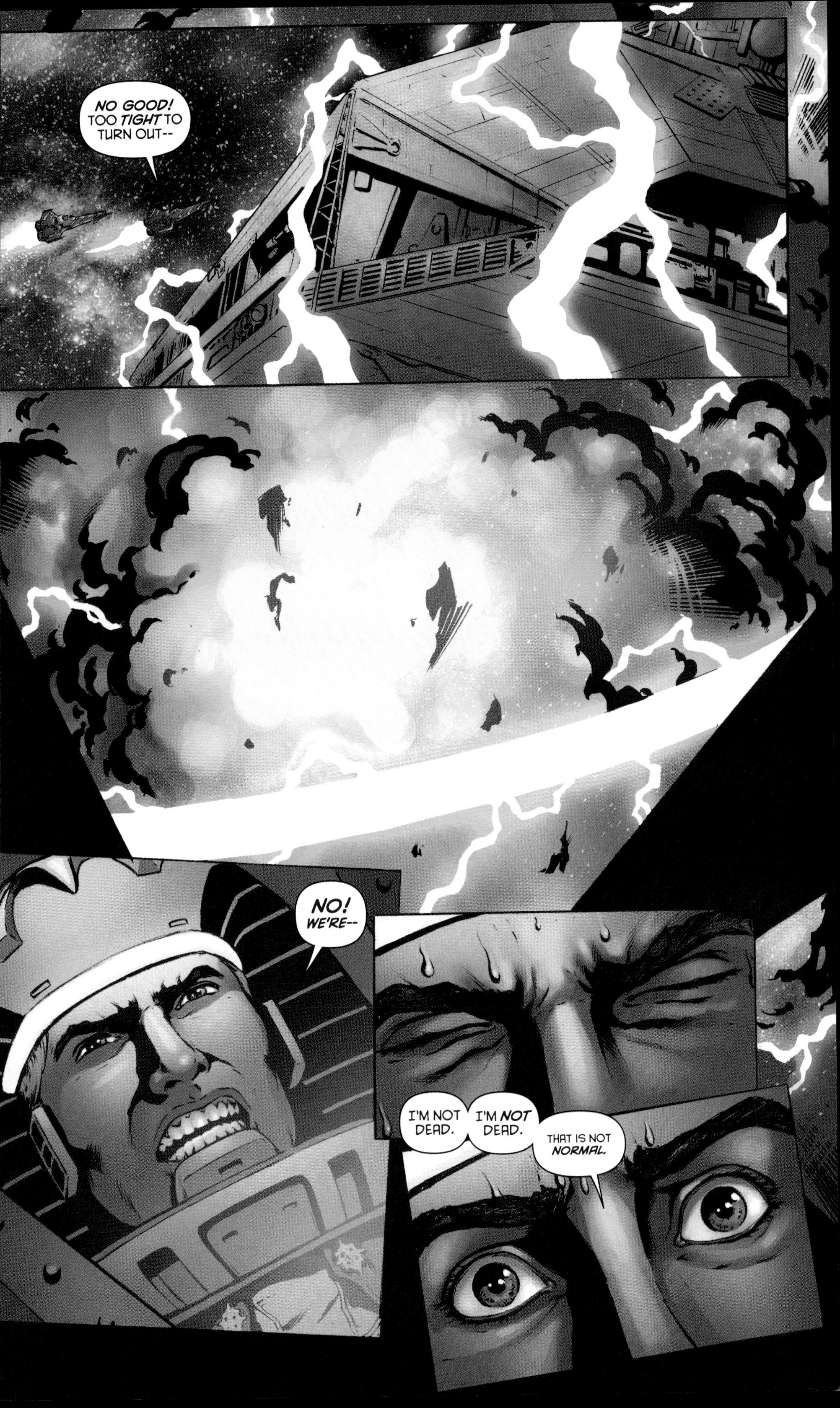
NO GOOD! TOO TIGHT TO TURN OUT--
NO! WE'RE--
I'M NOT DEAD.
I'M NOT DEAD.
THAT IS NOT NORMAL.

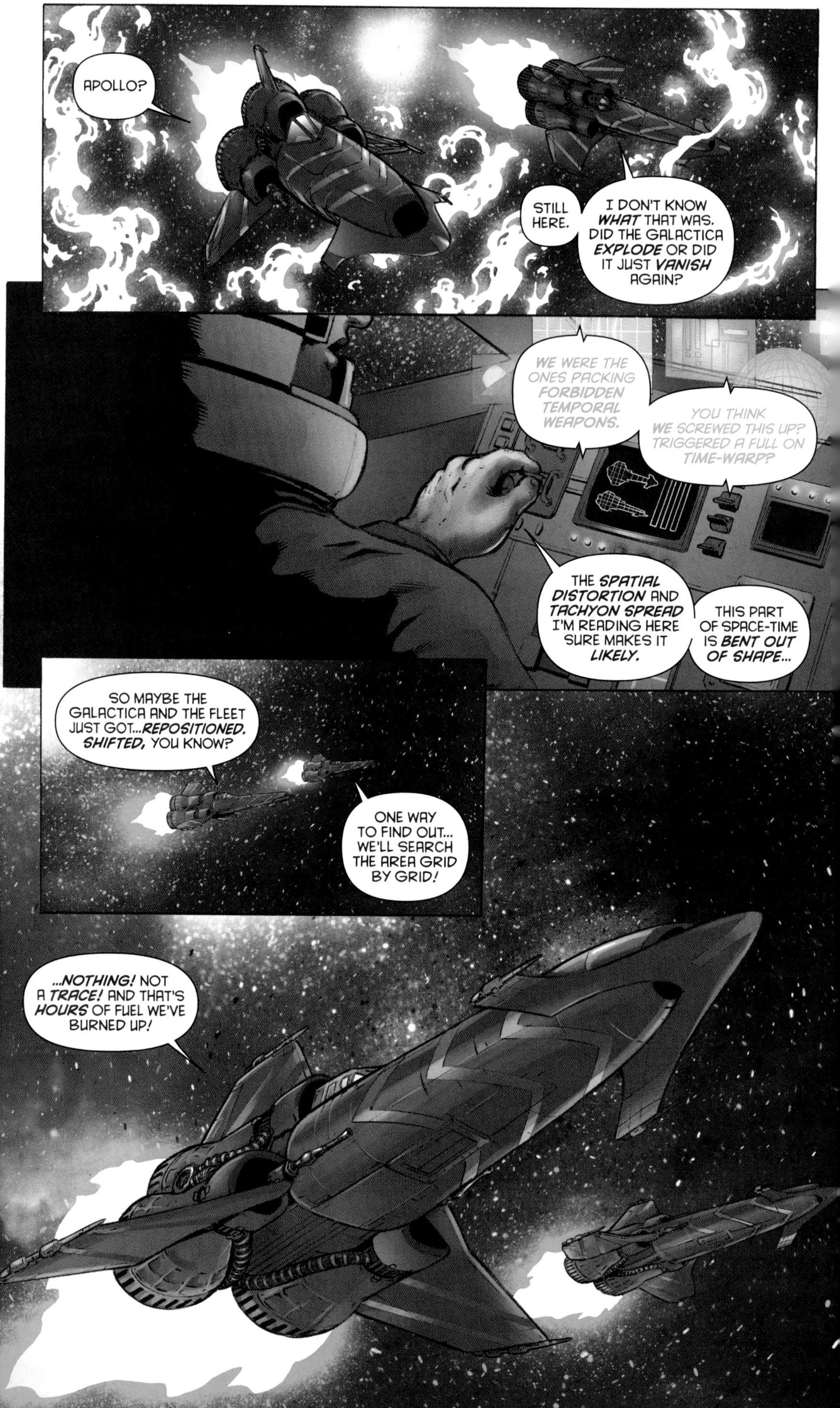
APOLLO?
STILL HERE.
I DON'T KNOW WHAT THAT WAS. DID THE GALACTICA EXPLODE OR DID IT JUST VANISH AGAIN?
WE WERE THE ONES PACKING FORBIDDEN TEMPORAL WEAPONS.
YOU THINK WE SCREWED THIS UP? TRIGGERED A FULL ON TIME-WARP?
THE SPATIAL DISTORTION AND TACHYON SPREAD I'M READING HERE SURE MAKES IT LIKELY.
THIS PART OF SPACE-TIME IS BENT OUT OF SHAPE...
SO MAYBE THE GALACTICA AND THE FLEET JUST GOT...REPOSITIONED. SHIFTED, YOU KNOW?
ONE WAY TO FIND OUT... WE'LL SEARCH THE AREA GRID BY GRID!
...NOTHING! NOT A TRACE! AND THAT'S HOURS OF FUEL WE'VE BURNED UP!

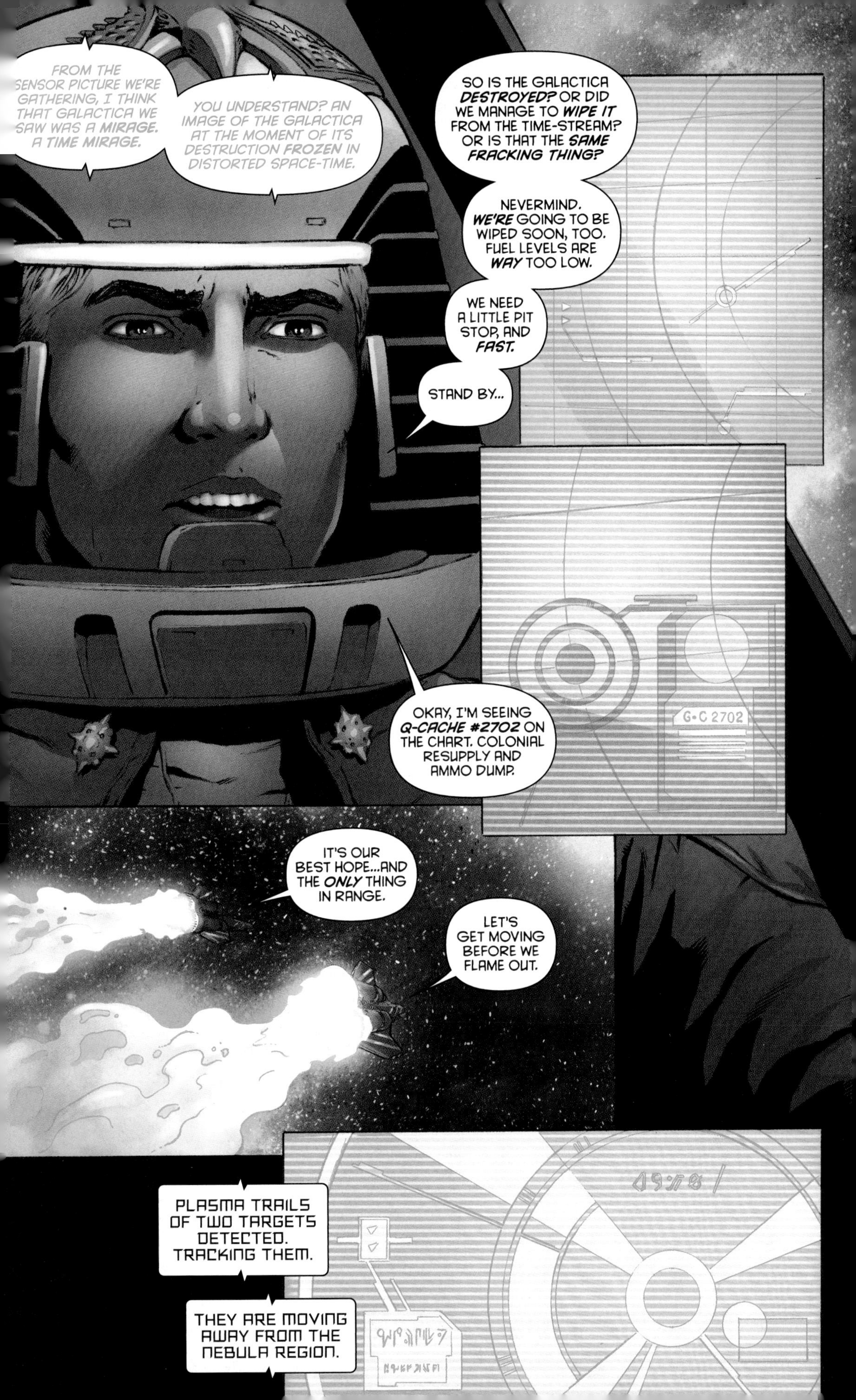

FROM THE SENSOR PICTURE WE'RE GATHERING, I THINK THAT GALACTICA WE SAW WAS A MIRAGE. A TIME MIRAGE.
YOU UNDERSTAND? AN IMAGE OF THE GALACTICA AT THE MOMENT OF ITS DESTRUCTION FROZEN IN DISTORTED SPACE-TIME.
SO IS THE GALACTICA DESTROYED? OR DID WE MANAGE TO WIPE IT FROM THE TIME-STREAM? OR IS THAT THE SAME FRACKING THING?
NEVERMIND. WE'RE GOING TO BE WIPED SOON, TOO. FUEL LEVELS ARE WAY TOO LOW.
WE NEED A LITTLE PIT STOP, AND FAST.
STAND BY...
OKAY, I'M SEEING Q-CACHE #2702 ON THE CHART. COLONIAL RESUPPLY AND AMMO DUMP.
G-C 2702
IT'S OUR BEST HOPE...AND THE ONLY THING IN RANGE.
LET'S GET MOVING BEFORE WE FLAME OUT.
PLASMA TRAILS OF TWO TARGETS DETECTED. TRACKING THEM.
THEY ARE MOVING AWAY FROM THE NEBULA REGION.

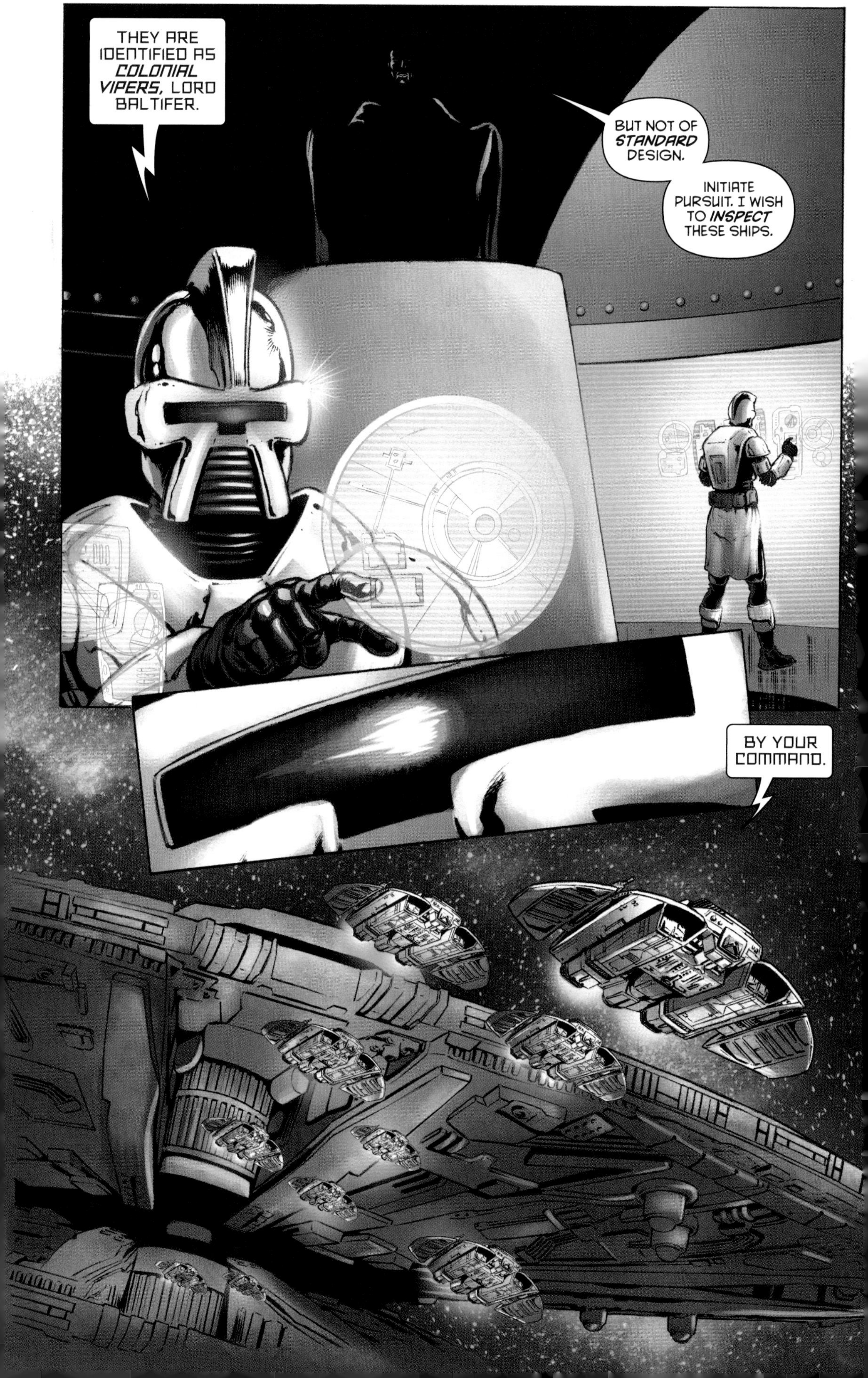
THEY ARE IDENTIFIED AS COLONIAL VIPERS, LORD BALTIFER.
BUT NOT OF STANDARD DESIGN.
INITIATE PURSUIT. I WISH TO INSPECT THESE SHIPS.
BY YOUR COMMAND.

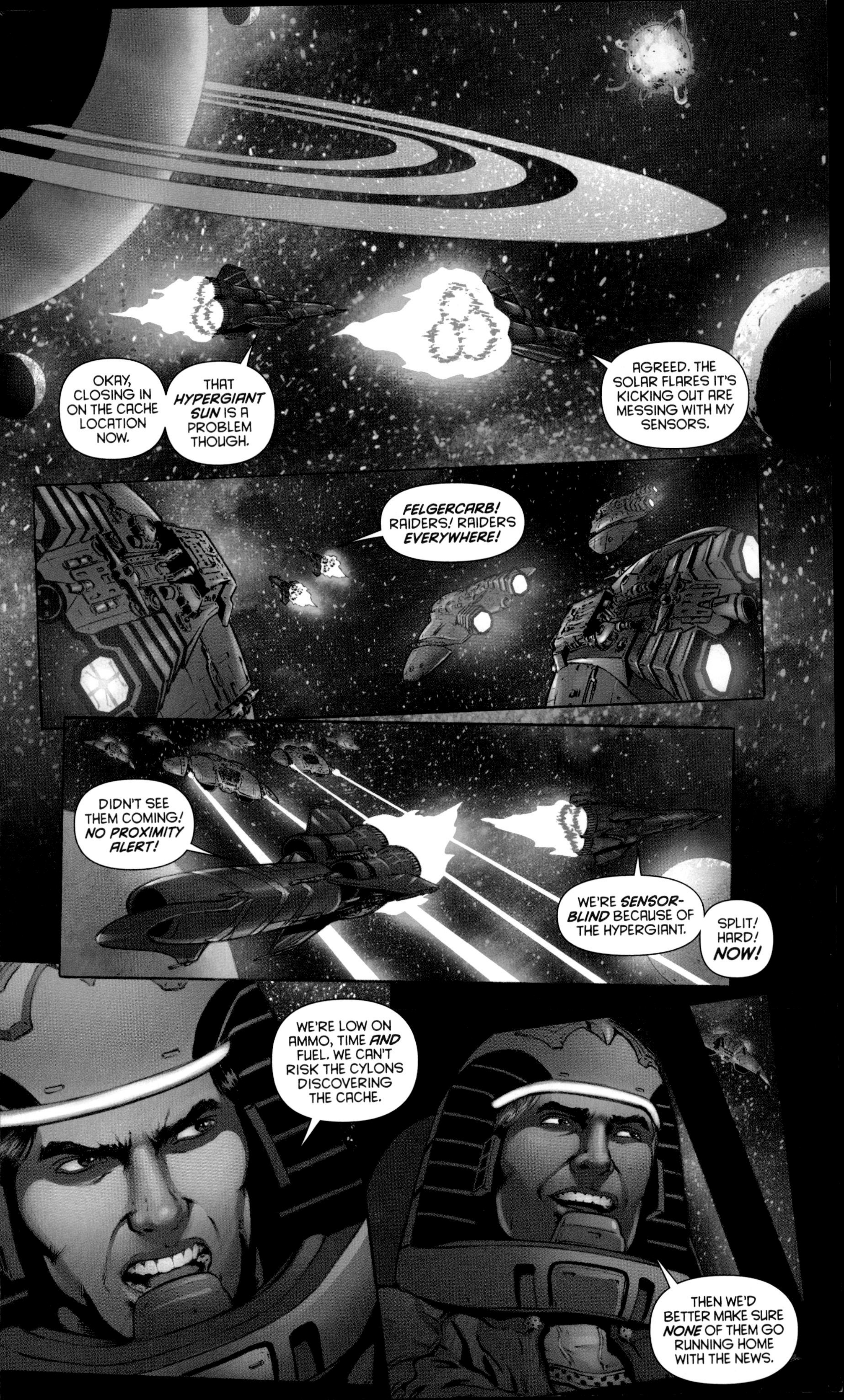
OKAY, CLOSING IN ON THE CACHE LOCATION NOW.
THAT HYPERGIANT SUN IS A PROBLEM THOUGH.
AGREED. THE SOLAR FLARES IT'S KICKING OUT ARE MESSING WITH MY SENSORS.
FELGERCARB! RAIDERS! RAIDERS EVERYWHERE!
DIDN'T SEE THEM COMING! NO PROXIMITY ALERT!
WE'RE SENSOR-BLIND BECAUSE OF THE HYPERGIANT.
SPLIT! HARD! NOW!
WE'RE LOW ON AMMO, TIME AND FUEL. WE CAN'T RISK THE CYLONS DISCOVERING THE CACHE.
THEN WE'D BETTER MAKE SURE NONE OF THEM GO RUNNING HOME WITH THE NEWS.

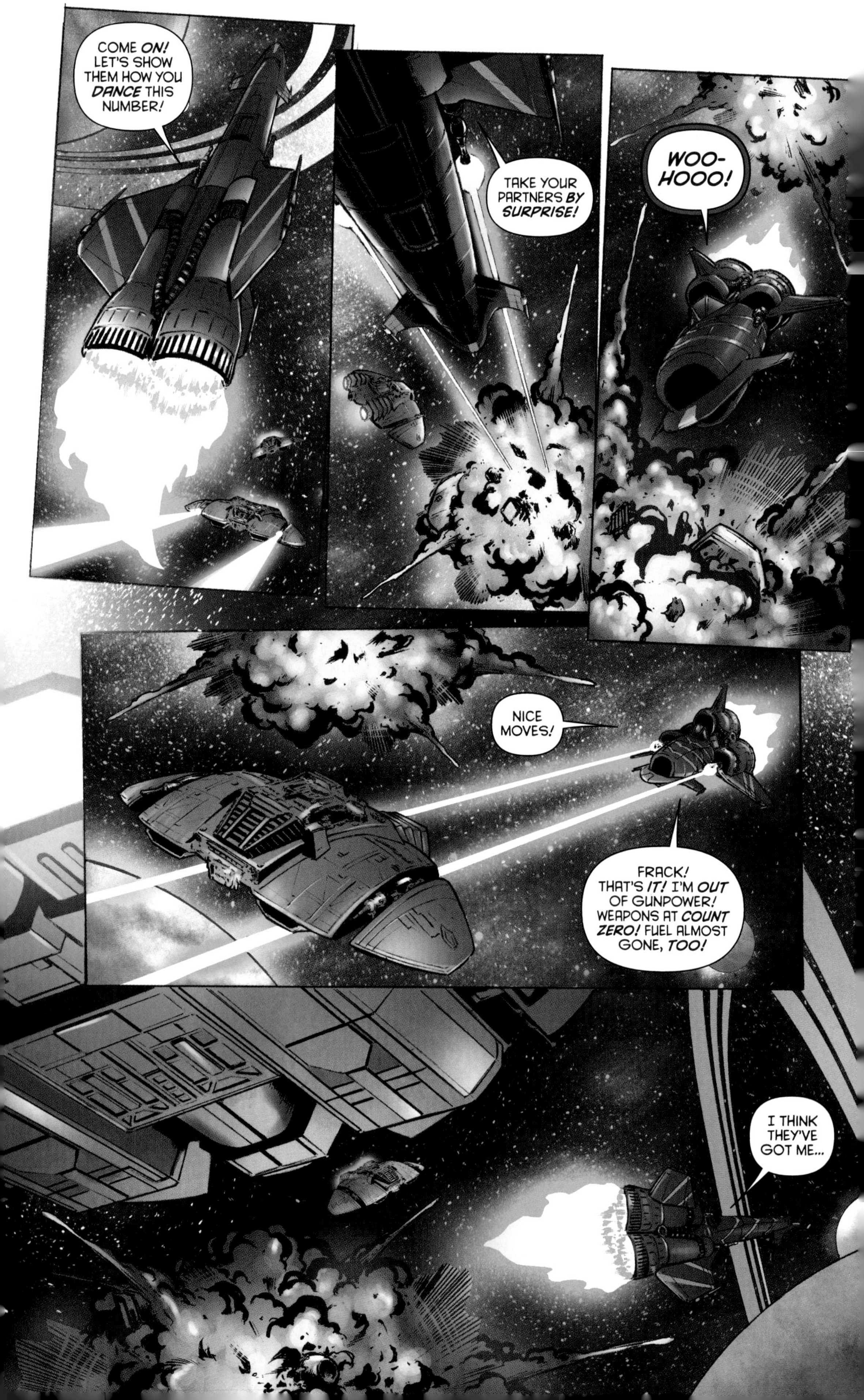
COME ON! LET'S SHOW THEM HOW YOU DANCE THIS NUMBER!
TAKE YOUR PARTNERS BY SURPRISE!
WOO-HOOO!
NICE MOVES!
FRACK! THAT'S IT! I'M OUT OF GUNPOWER! WEAPONS AT COUNT ZERO! FUEL ALMOST GONE, TOO!
I THINK THEY'VE GOT ME...

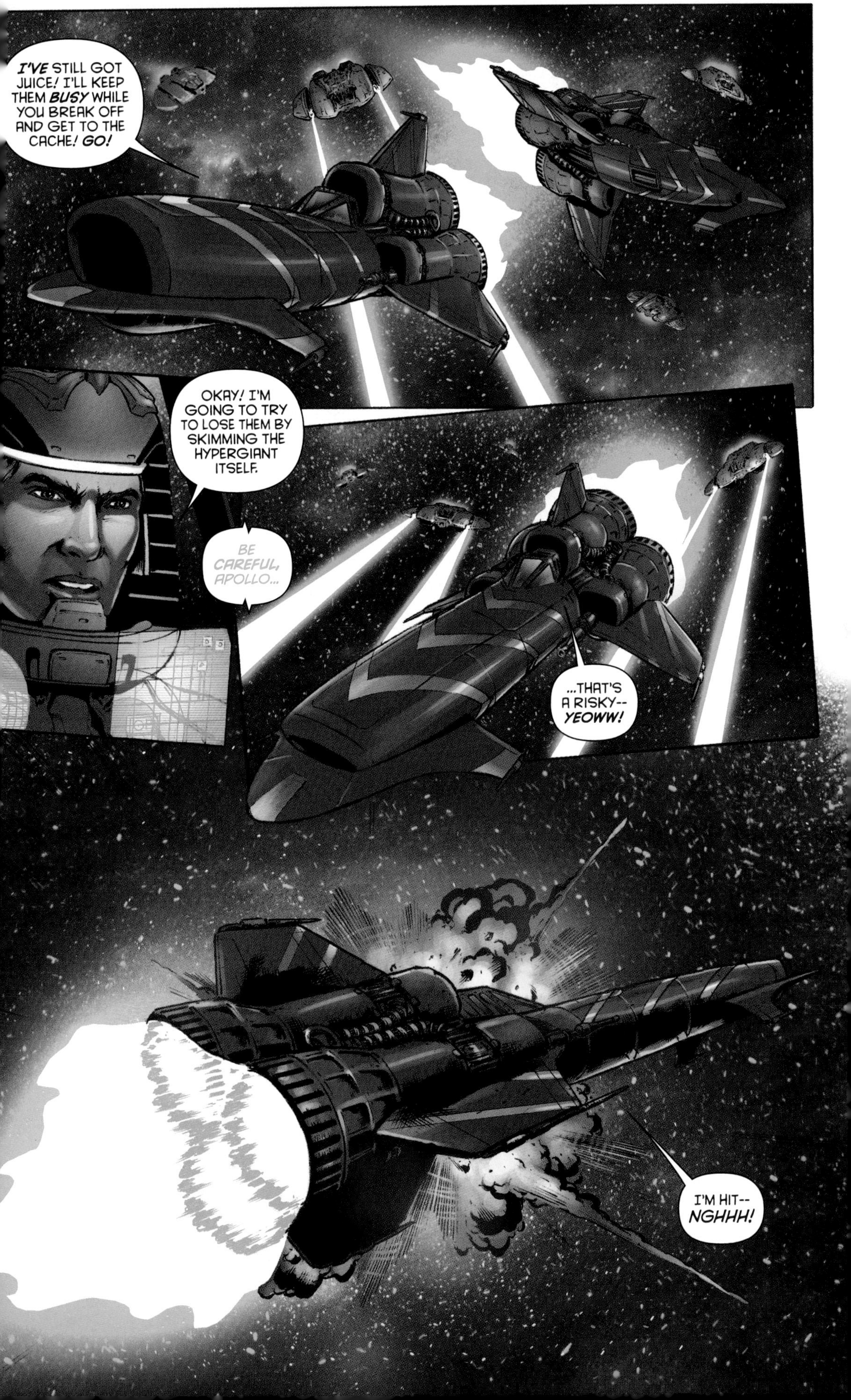

I'VE STILL GOT JUICE! I'LL KEEP THEM BUSY WHILE YOU BREAK OFF AND GET TO THE CACHE! GO!
OKAY! I'M GOING TO TRY TO LOSE THEM BY SKIMMING THE HYPERGIANT ITSELF.
BE CAREFUL, APOLLO...
...THAT'S A RISKY-- YEOWW!
I'M HIT-- NGHHH!

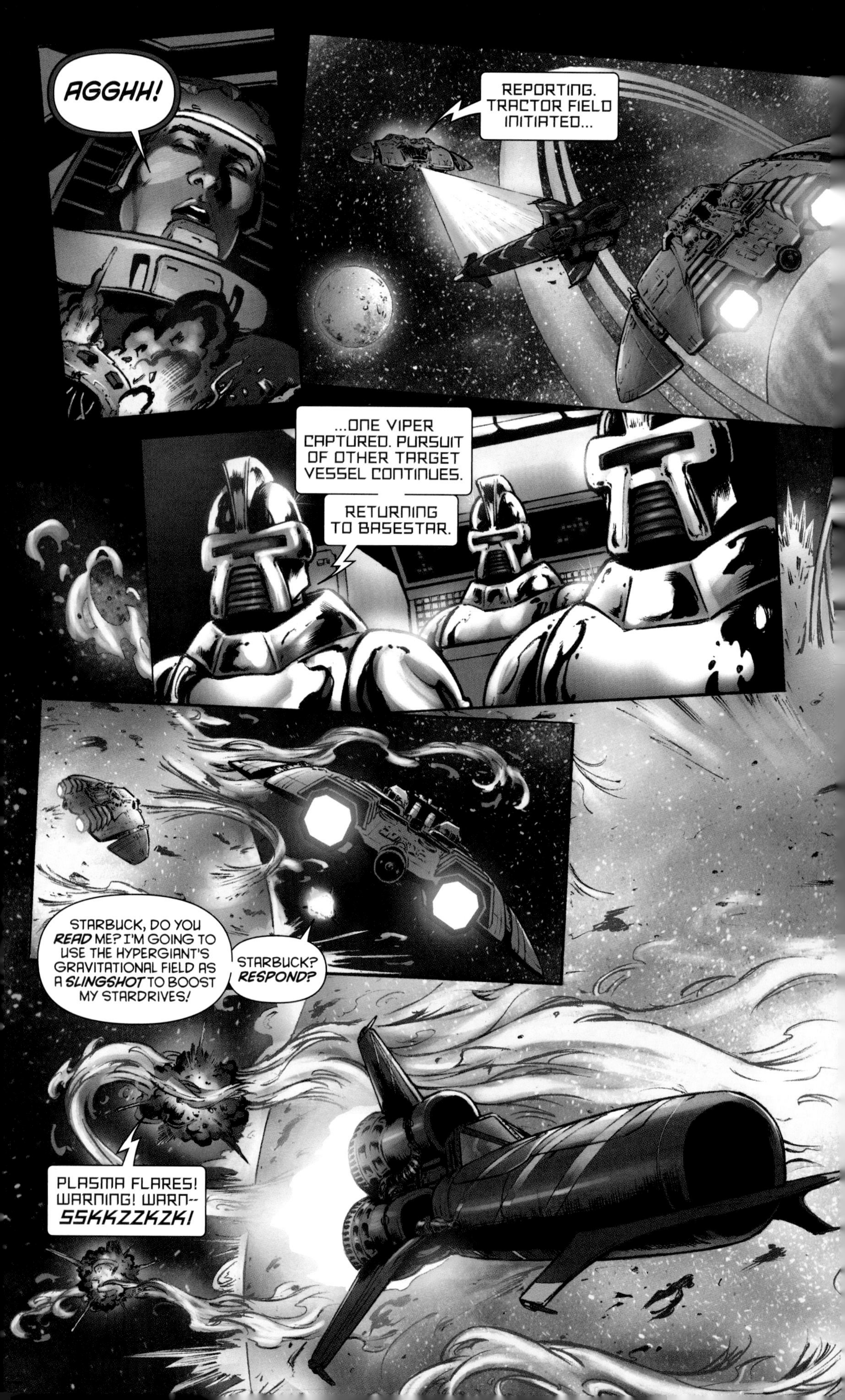
AGGHH!
REPORTING. TRACTOR FIELD INITIATED...
...ONE VIPER CAPTURED. PURSUIT OF OTHER TARGET VESSEL CONTINUES.
RETURNING TO BASESTAR.
STARBUCK, DO YOU READ ME? I'M GOING TO USE THE HYPERGIANT'S GRAVITATIONAL FIELD AS A SLINGSHOT TO BOOST MY STARDRIVES!
STARBUCK? RESPOND?
PLASMA FLARES! WARNING! WARN-- SSKKZZKZK!

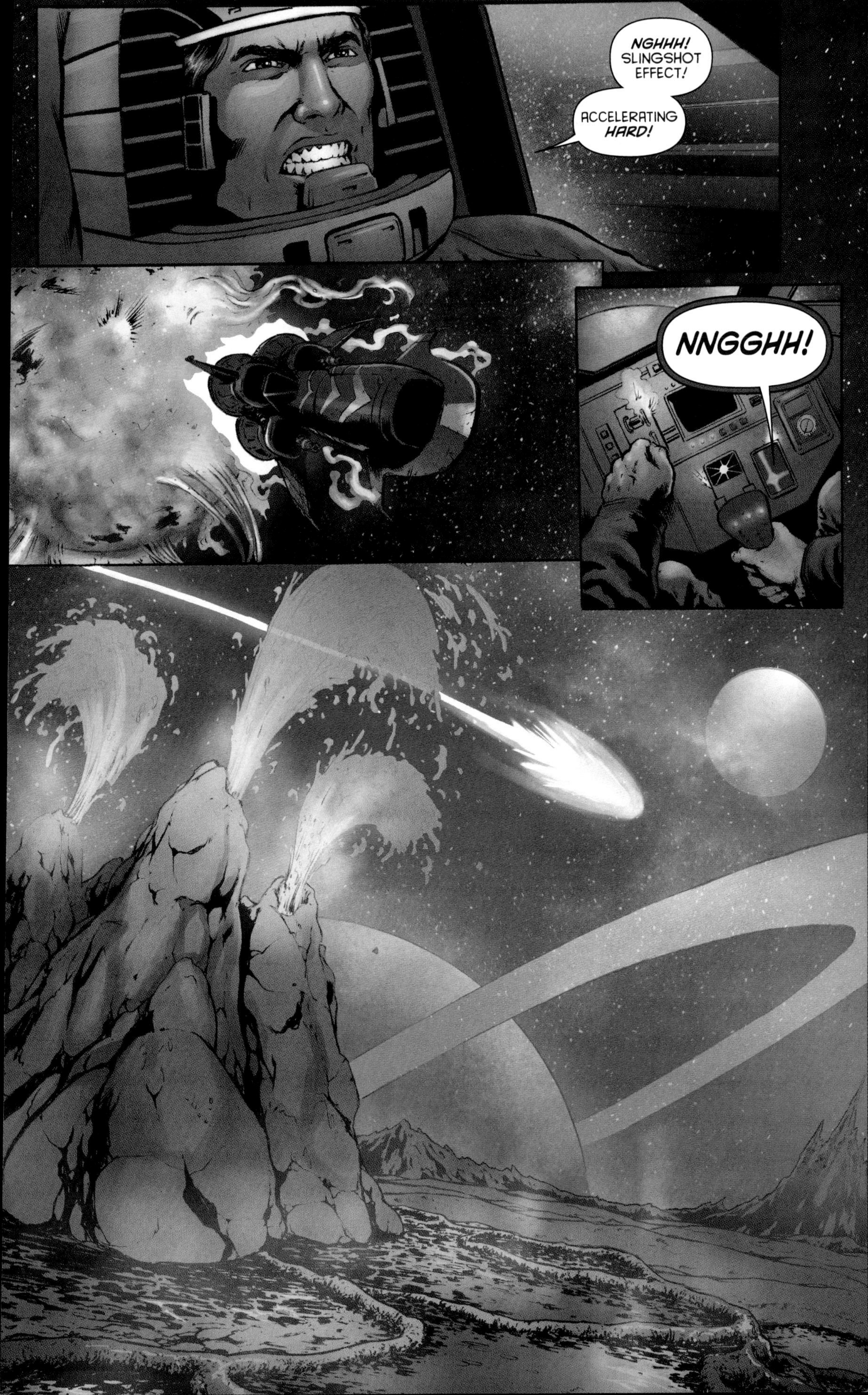
NGHHH! SLINGSHOT EFFECT!
ACCELERATING HARD!
NNGGHH!

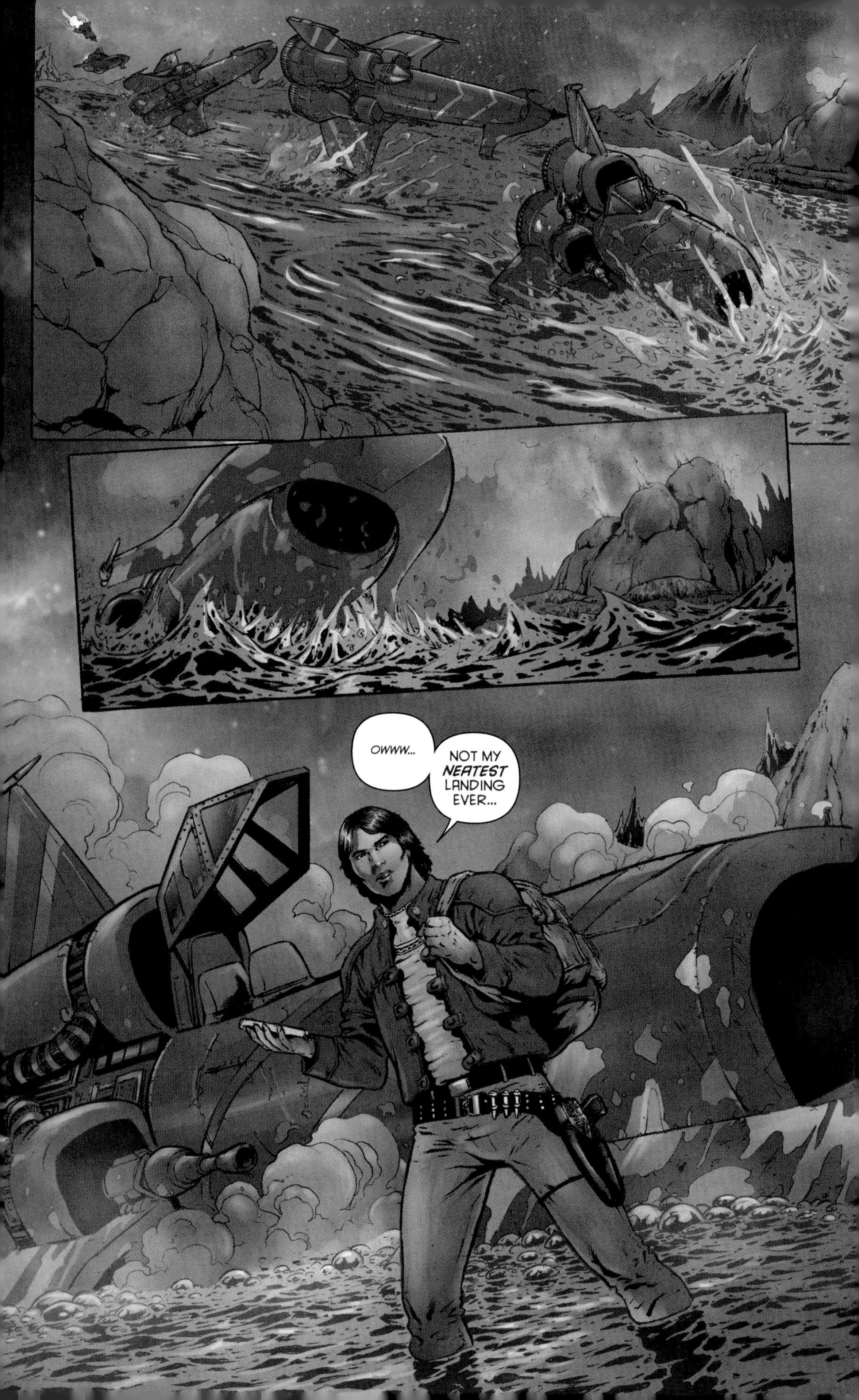
OWWW...
NOT MY NEATEST LANDING EVER...

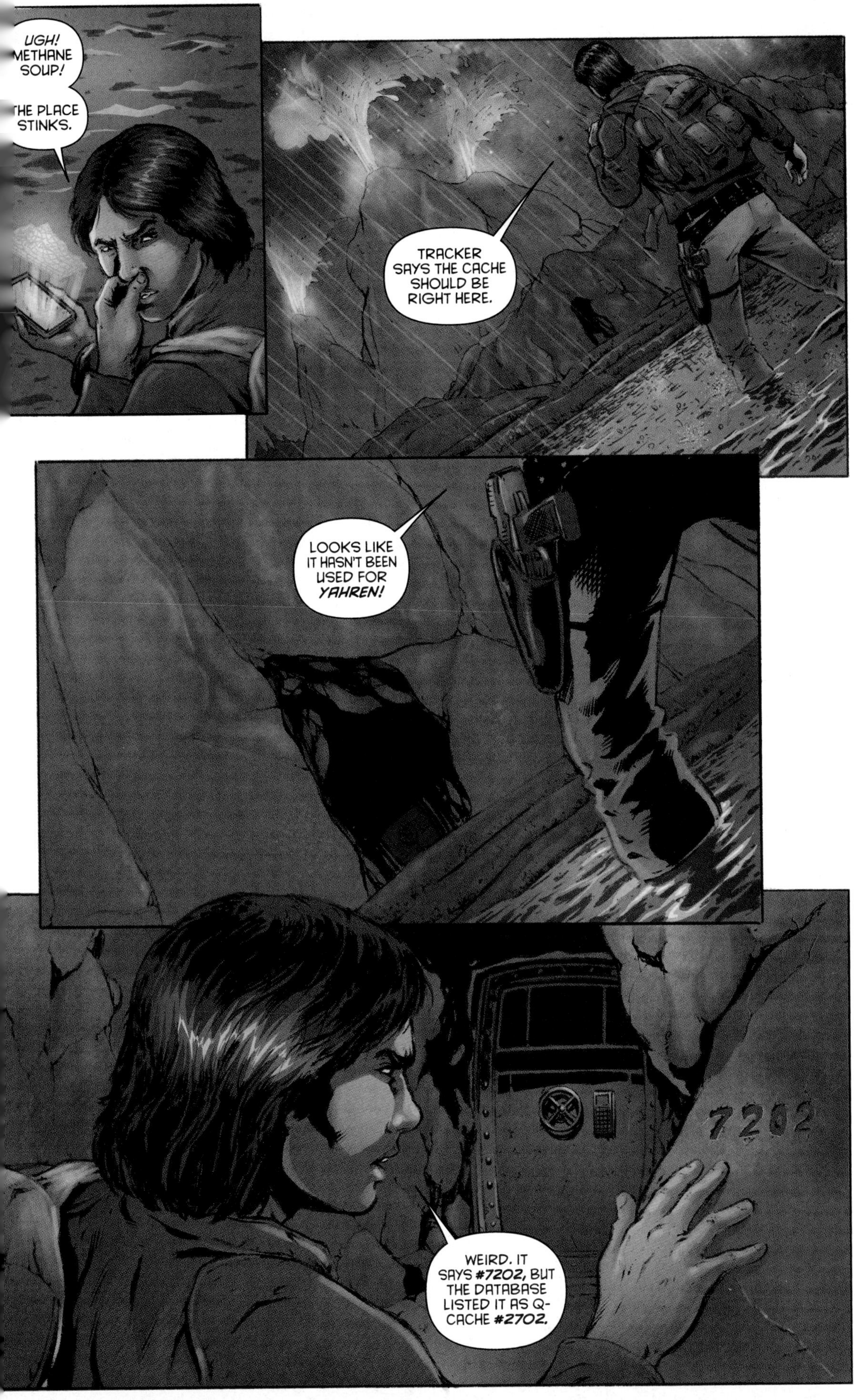
UGH! METHANE SOUP!
THE PLACE STINKS.
TRACKER SAYS THE CACHE SHOULD BE RIGHT HERE.
LOOKS LIKE IT HASN'T BEEN USED FOR *YAHREN!*
7202
WEIRD. IT SAYS ***#7202,*** BUT THE DATABASE LISTED IT AS Q-CACHE ***#2702.***

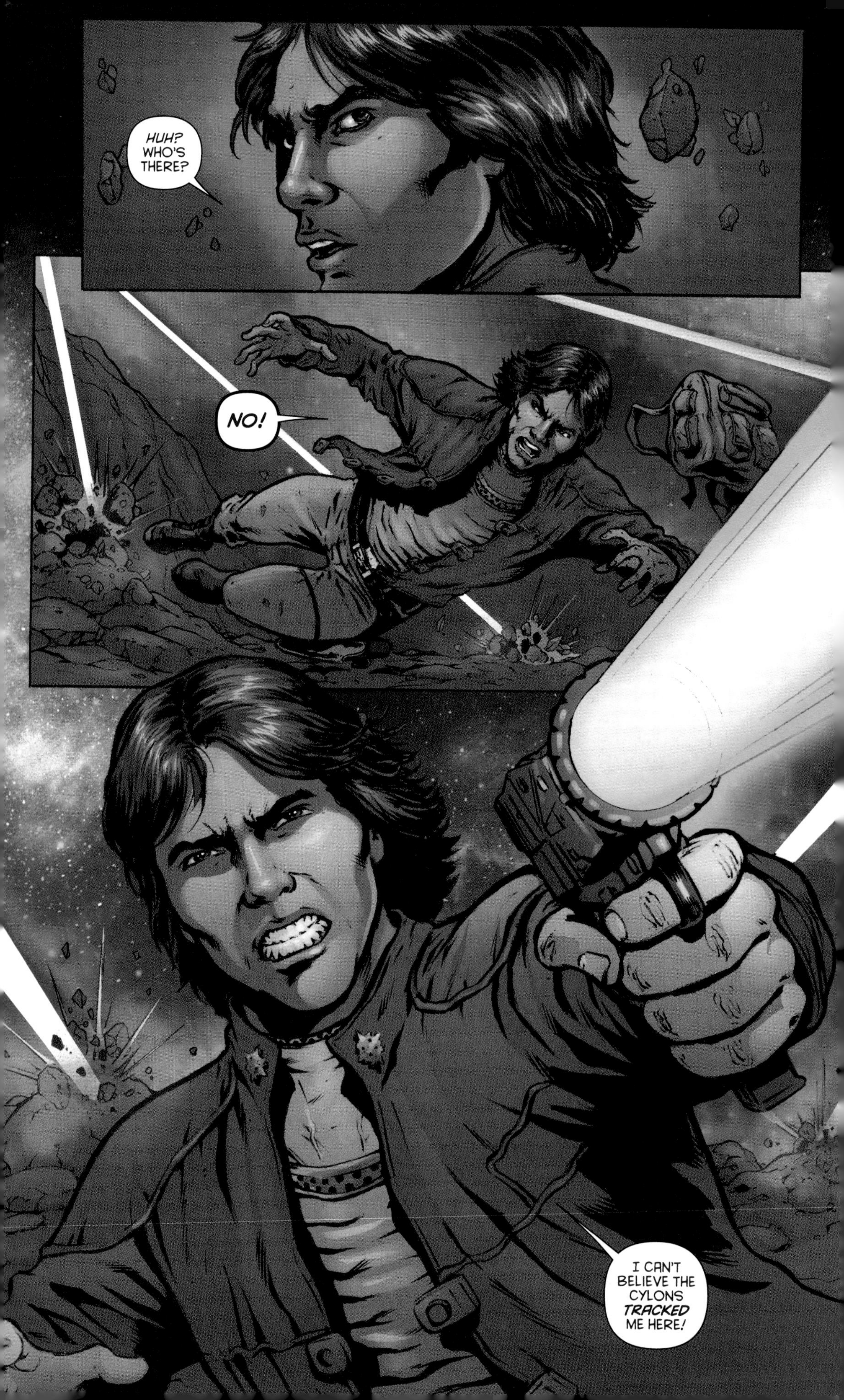
HUH? WHO'S THERE?
NO!
I CAN'T BELIEVE THE CYLONS *TRACKED* ME HERE!

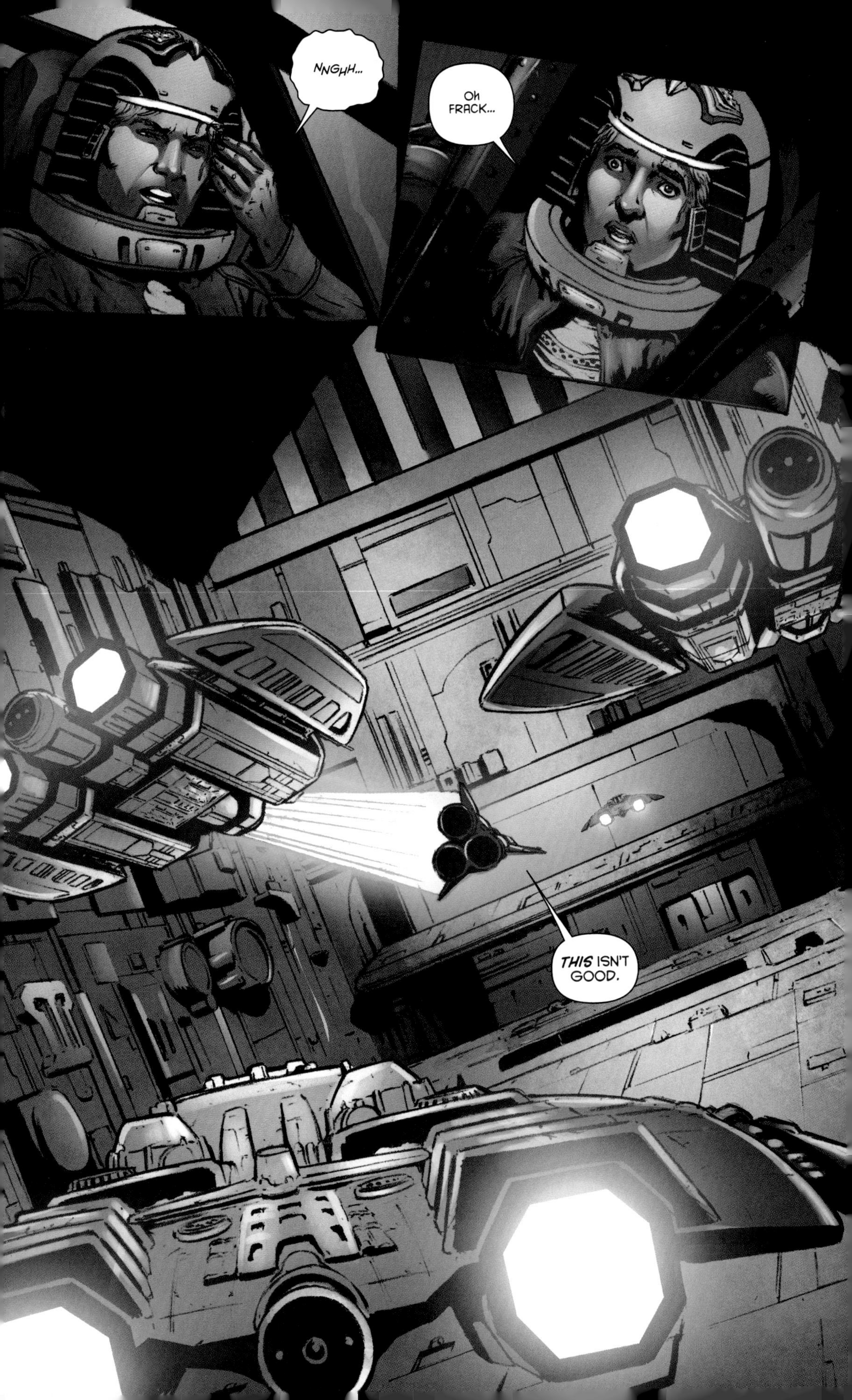
NNGHH...
Oh FRACK...
THIS ISN'T GOOD.

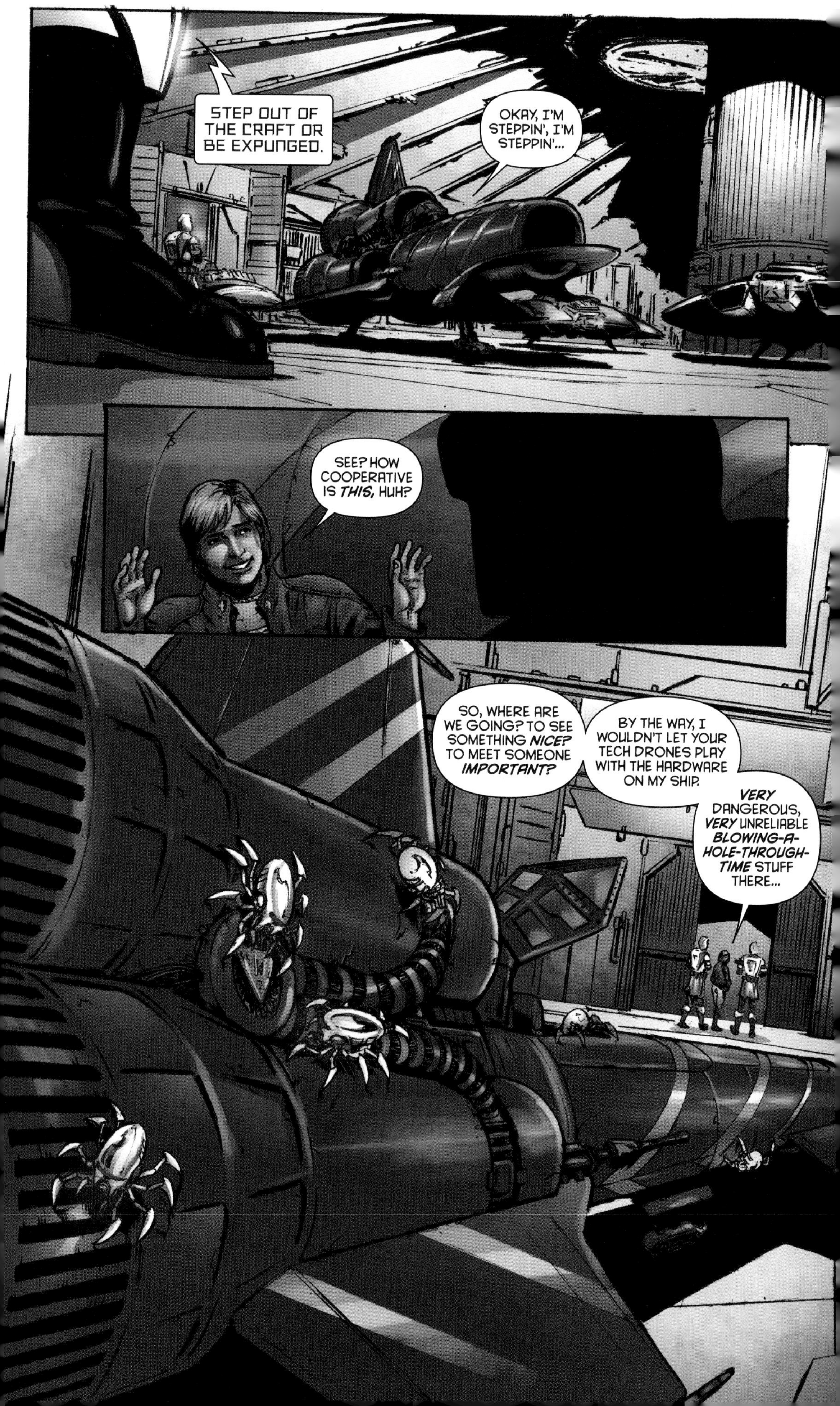
STEP OUT OF THE CRAFT OR BE EXPUNGED.
OKAY, I'M STEPPIN', I'M STEPPIN'...
SEE? HOW COOPERATIVE IS THIS, HUH?
SO, WHERE ARE WE GOING? TO SEE SOMETHING NICE? TO MEET SOMEONE IMPORTANT?
BY THE WAY, I WOULDN'T LET YOUR TECH DRONES PLAY WITH THE HARDWARE ON MY SHIP.
VERY DANGEROUS, VERY UNRELIABLE BLOWING-A-HOLE-THROUGH-TIME STUFF THERE...

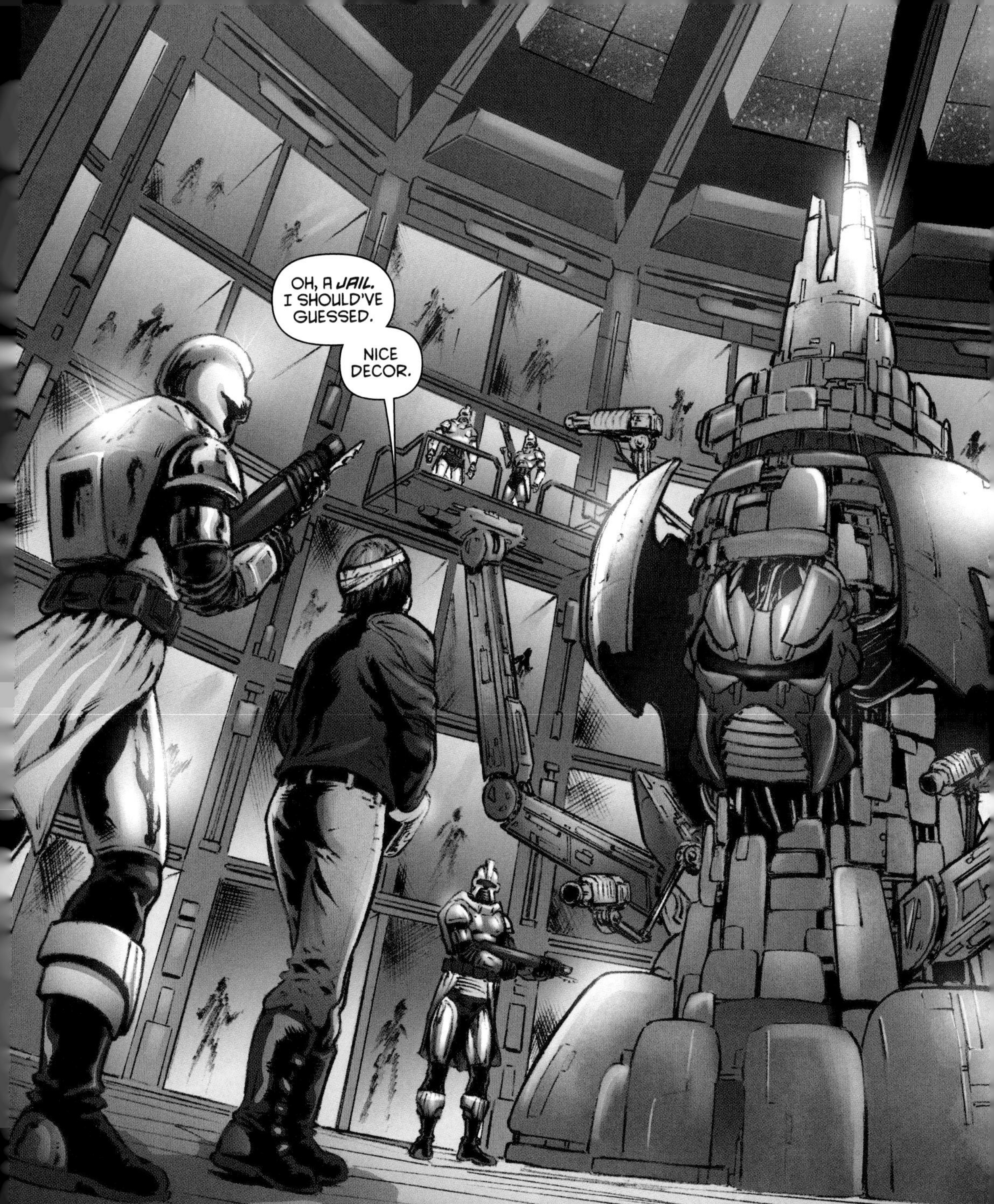
OH, A JAIL. I SHOULD'VE GUESSED.
NICE DECOR.

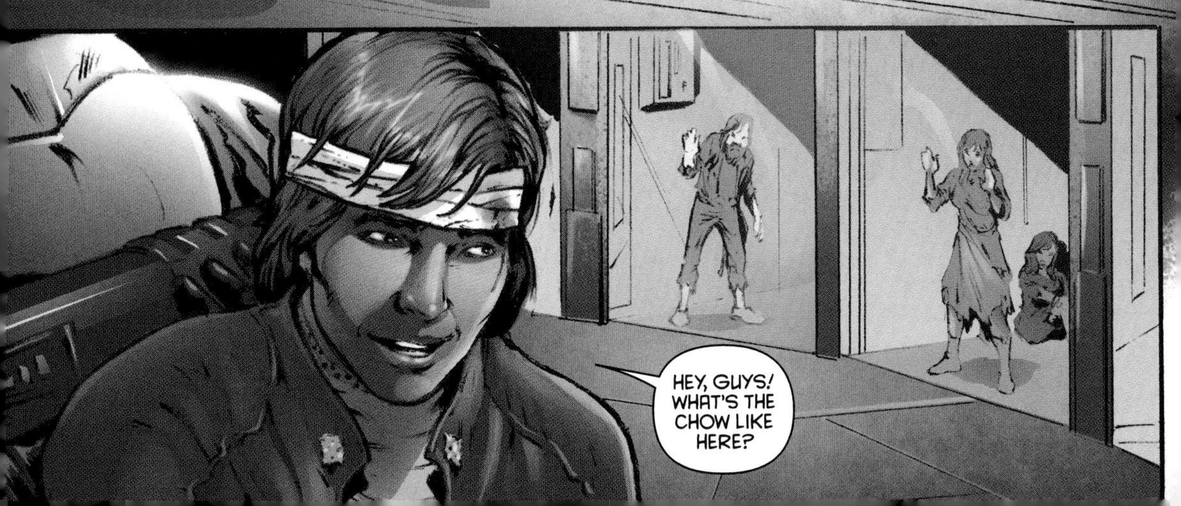
HEY, GUYS! WHAT'S THE CHOW LIKE HERE?

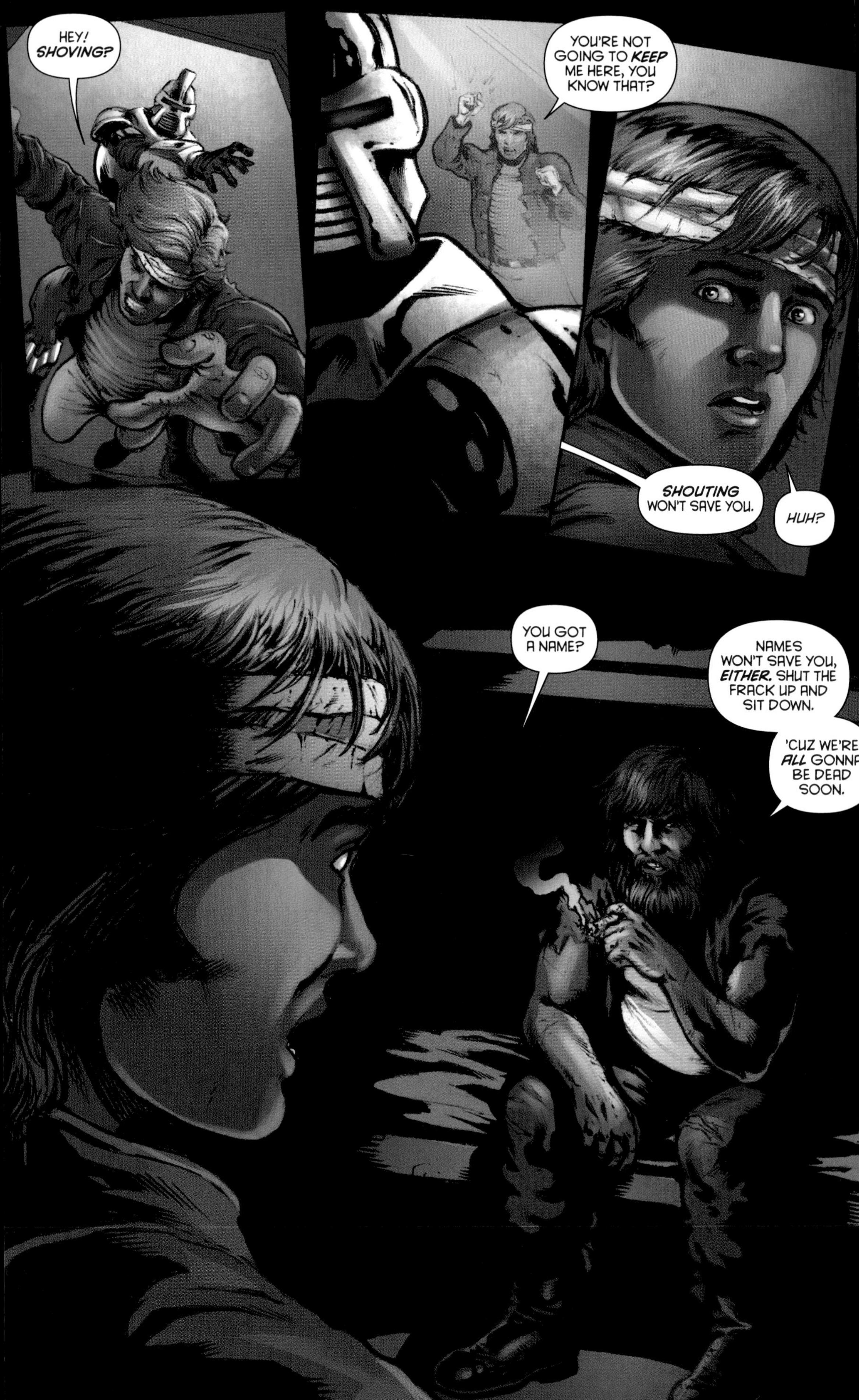
HEY! *SHOVING?*
YOU'RE NOT GOING TO *KEEP* ME HERE, YOU KNOW THAT?
SHOUTING WON'T SAVE YOU.
HUH?
YOU GOT A NAME?
NAMES WON'T SAVE YOU, *EITHER.* SHUT THE FRACK UP AND SIT DOWN.
'CUZ WE'RE *ALL* GONNA BE DEAD SOON.

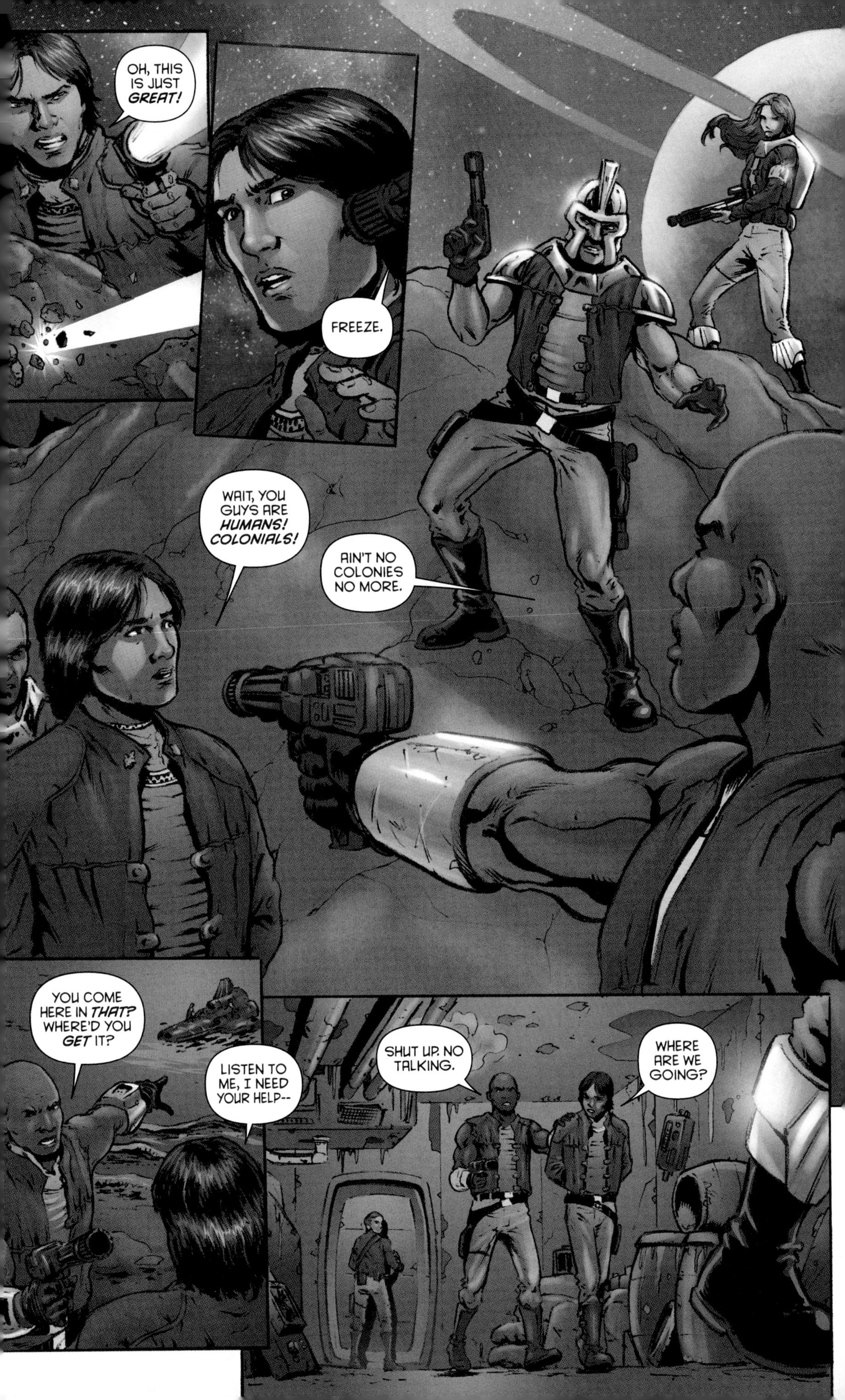

OH, THIS IS JUST *GREAT!*
FREEZE.
WAIT, YOU GUYS ARE *HUMANS! COLONIALS!*
AIN'T NO COLONIES NO MORE.
YOU COME HERE IN *THAT?* WHERE'D YOU *GET* IT?
LISTEN TO ME, I NEED YOUR HELP--
SHUT UP. NO TALKING.
WHERE ARE WE GOING?

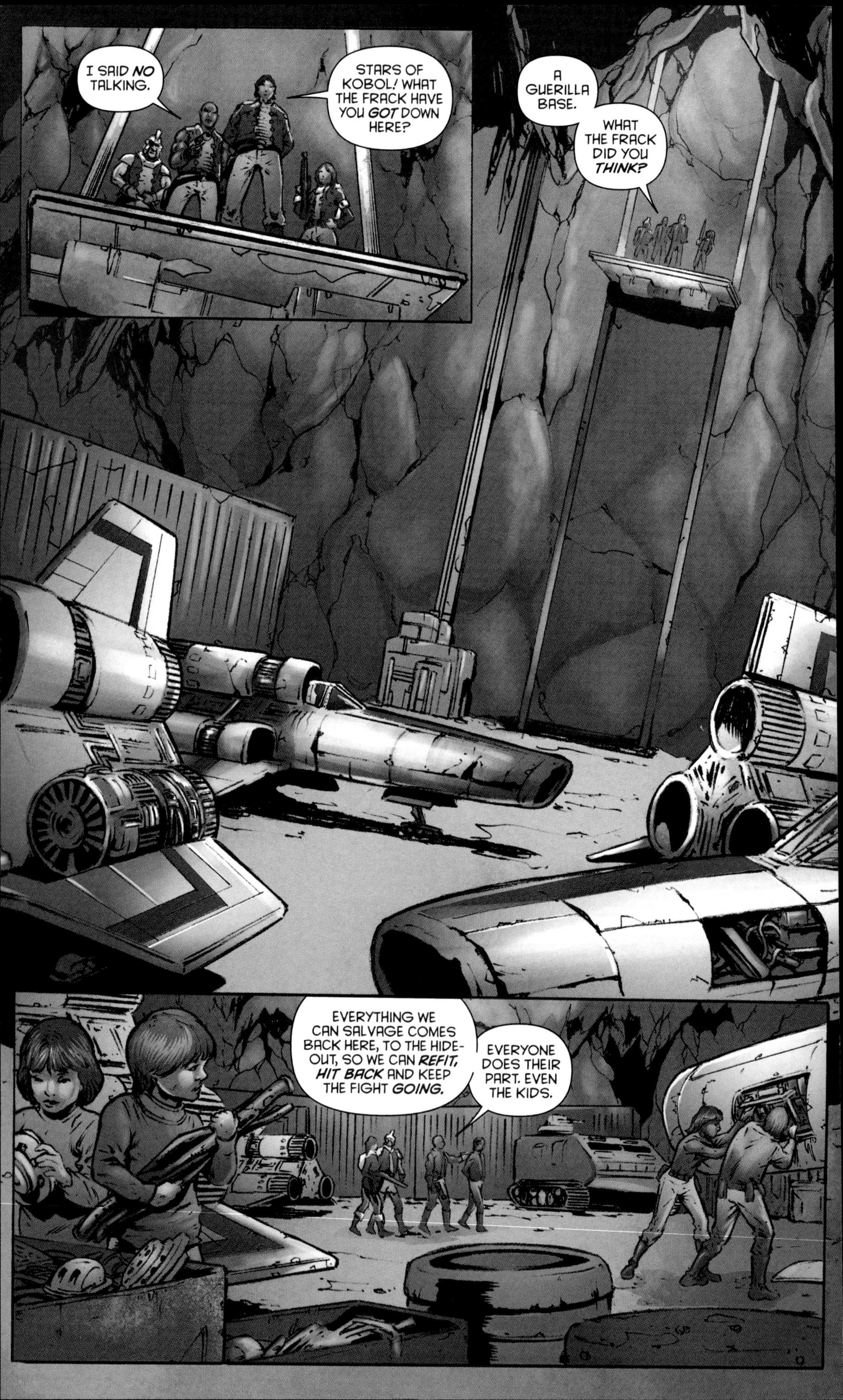
I SAID *NO* TALKING.
STARS OF KOBOL! WHAT THE FRACK HAVE YOU *GOT* DOWN HERE?
A GUERILLA BASE.
WHAT THE FRACK DID YOU *THINK?*
EVERYTHING WE CAN SALVAGE COMES BACK HERE, TO THE HIDE-OUT, SO WE CAN *REFIT, HIT BACK* AND KEEP THE FIGHT *GOING.*
EVERYONE DOES THEIR PART. EVEN THE KIDS.

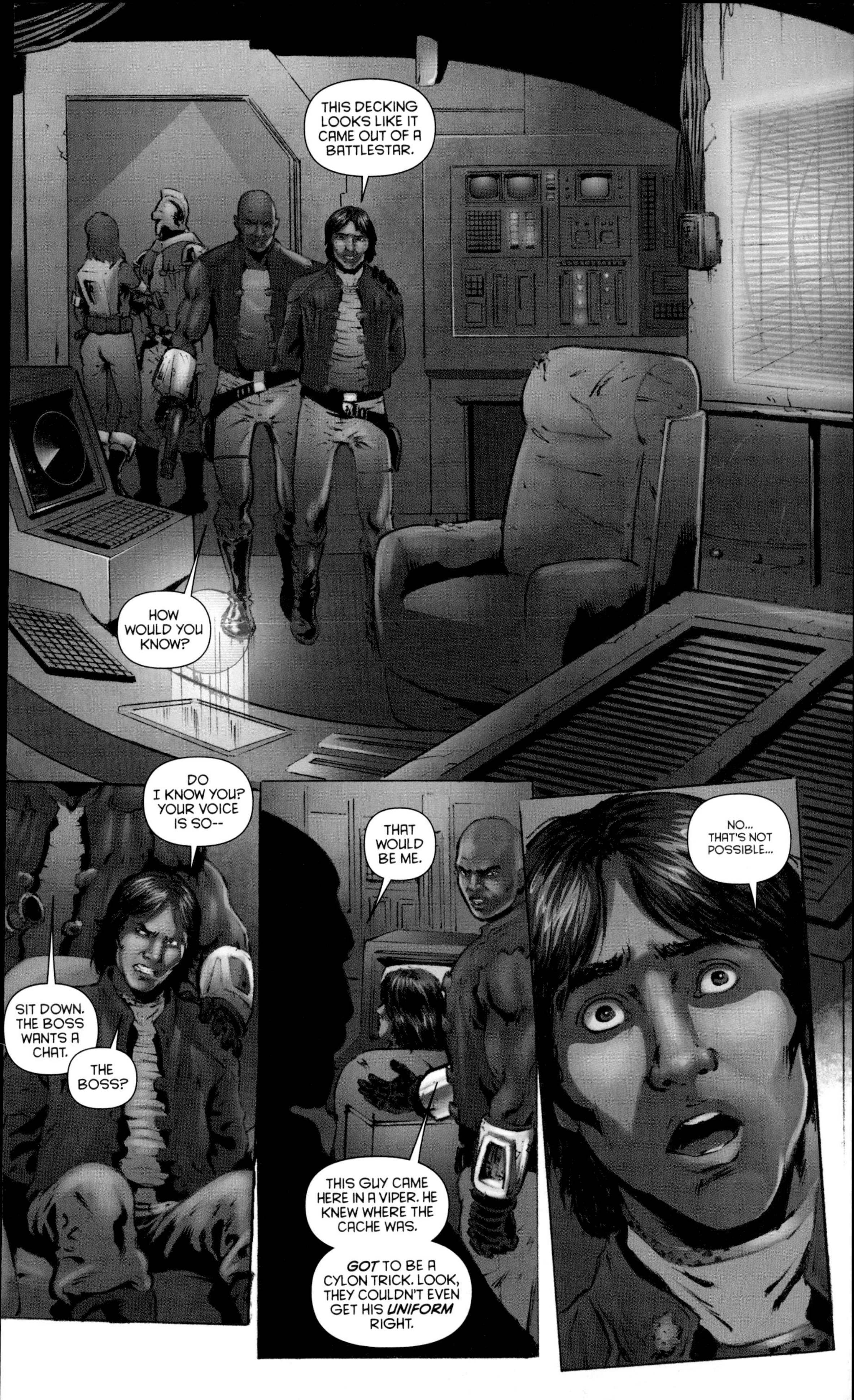
THIS DECKING LOOKS LIKE IT CAME OUT OF A BATTLESTAR.
HOW WOULD YOU KNOW?
DO I KNOW YOU? YOUR VOICE IS SO--
SIT DOWN. THE BOSS WANTS A CHAT.
THE BOSS?
THAT WOULD BE ME.
THIS GUY CAME HERE IN A VIPER. HE KNEW WHERE THE CACHE WAS.
GOT TO BE A CYLON TRICK. LOOK, THEY COULDN'T EVEN GET HIS *UNIFORM* RIGHT.
NO... THAT'S NOT POSSIBLE...

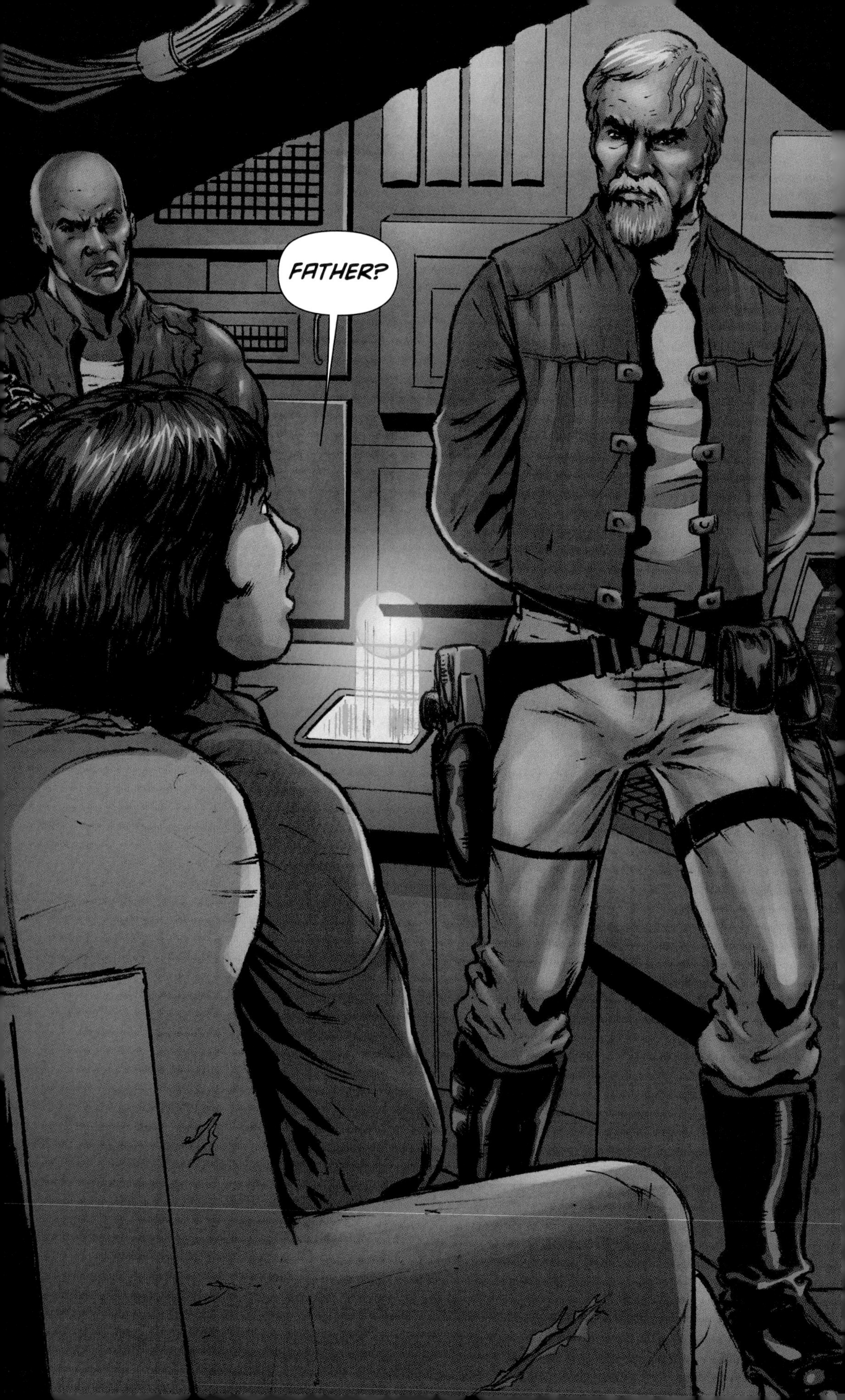
FATHER?

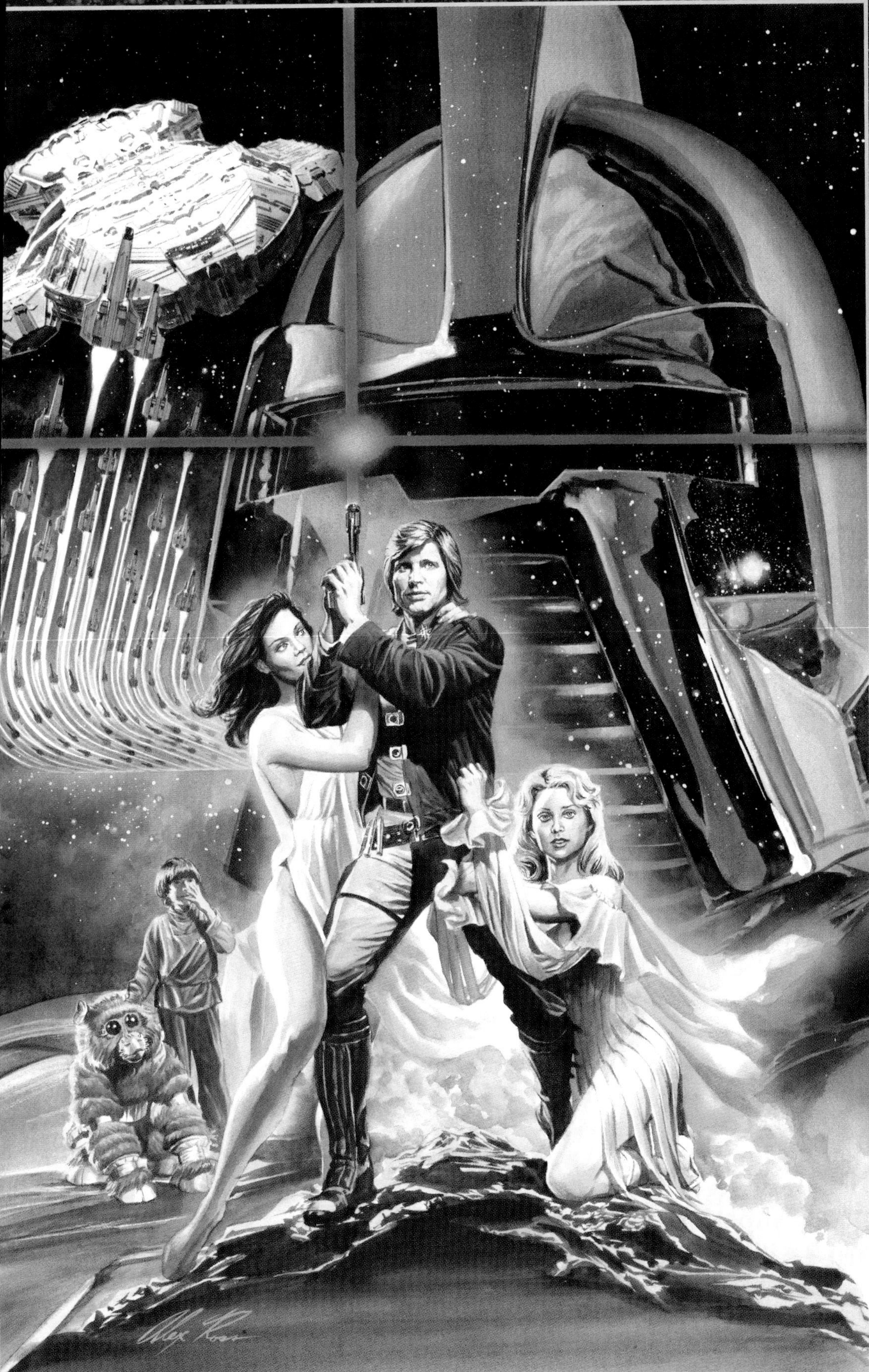

ISSUE 3

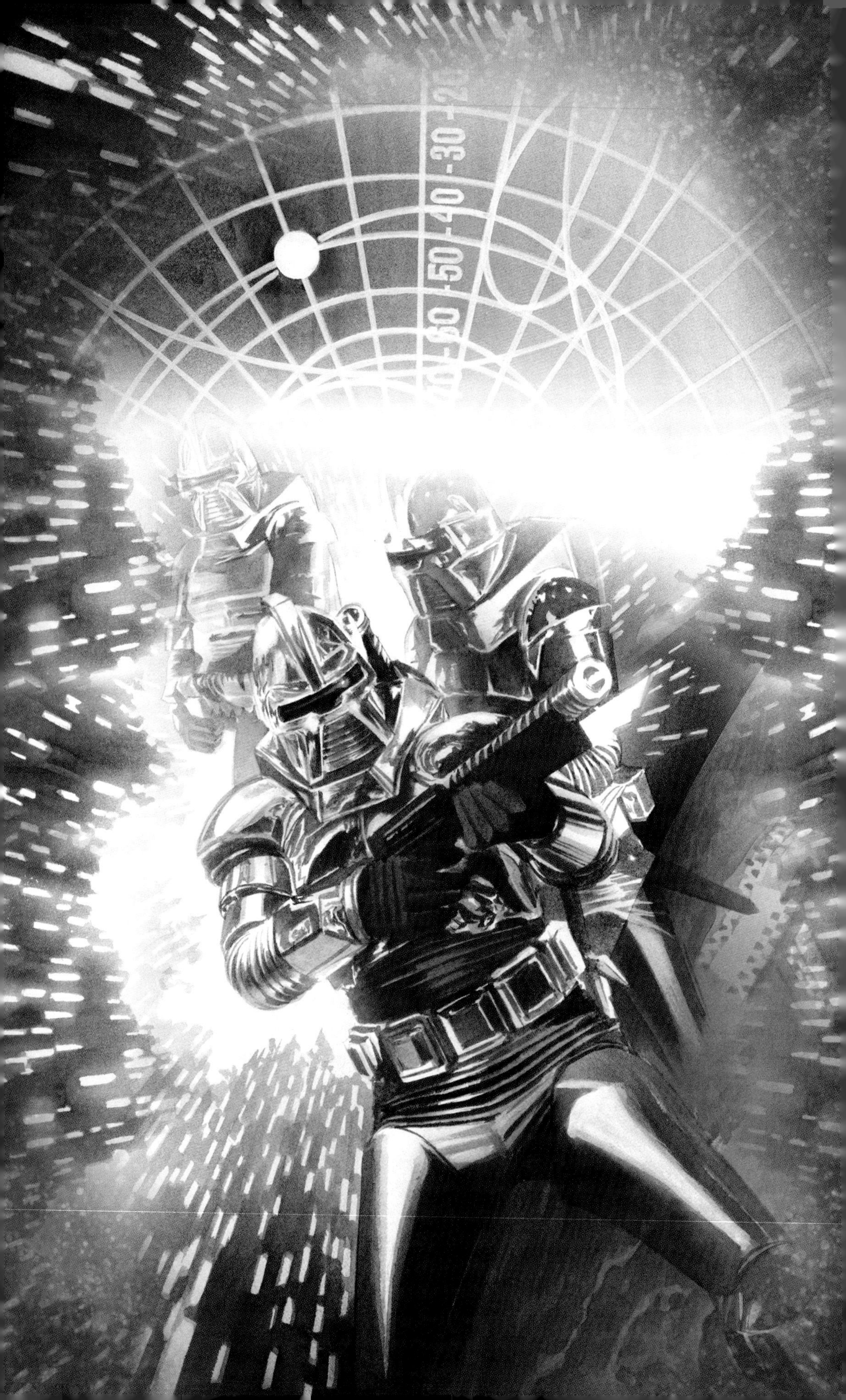

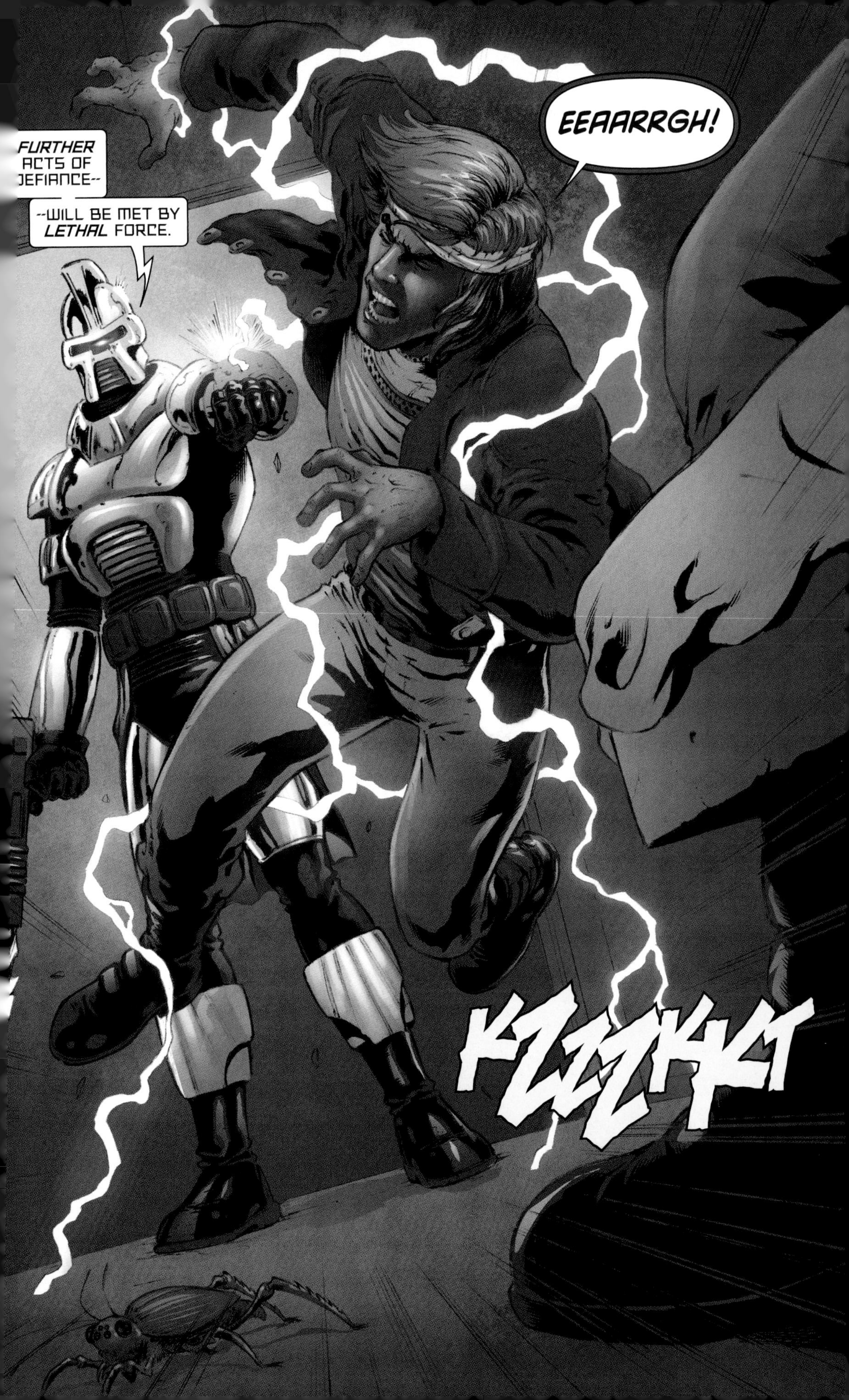
FURTHER ACTS OF DEFIANCE--
--WILL BE MET BY LETHAL FORCE.
EEAARRGH!
KZZZKKT

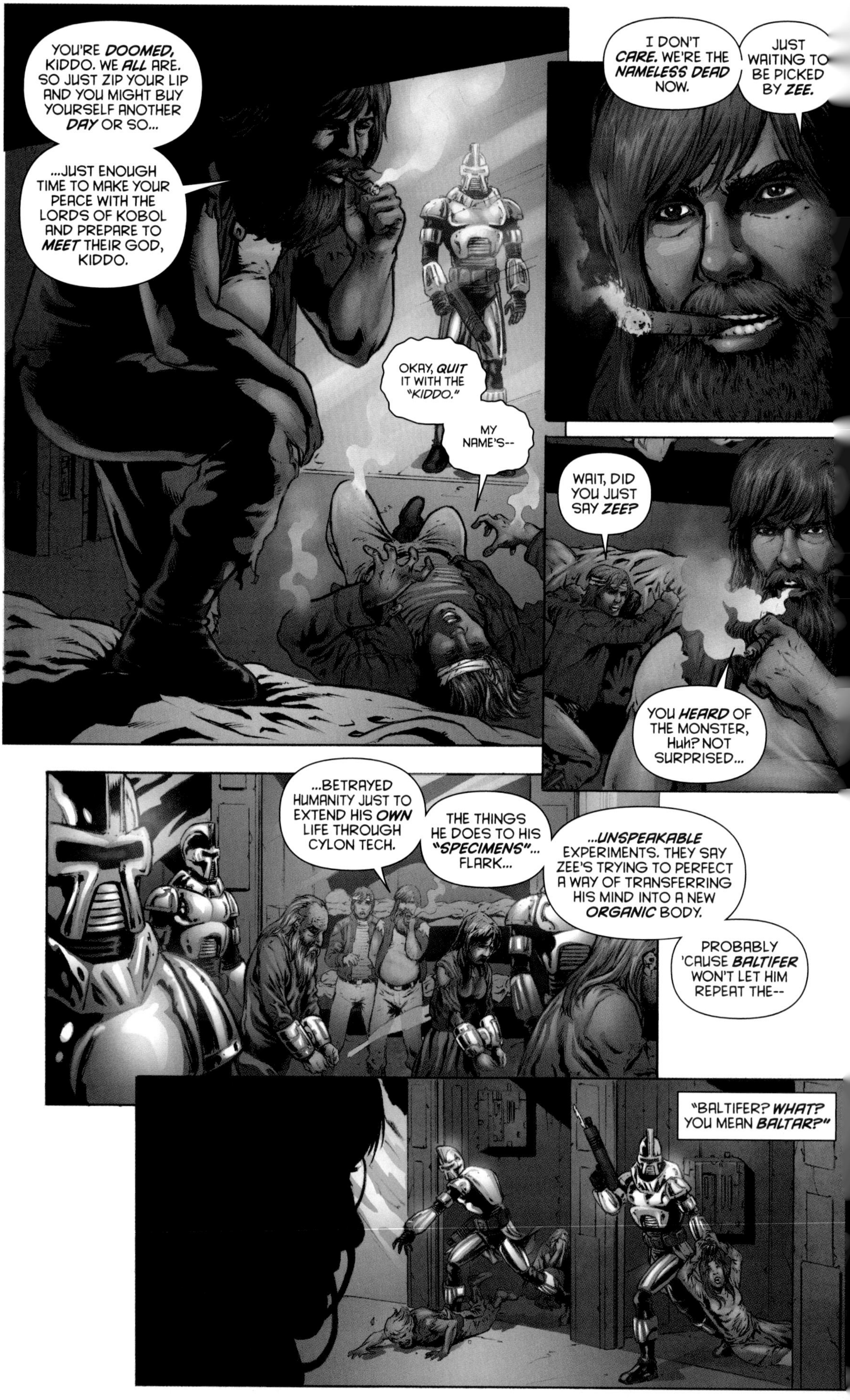
YOU'RE DOOMED, KIDDO. WE ALL ARE. SO JUST ZIP YOUR LIP AND YOU MIGHT BUY YOURSELF ANOTHER DAY OR SO...
...JUST ENOUGH TIME TO MAKE YOUR PEACE WITH THE LORDS OF KOBOL AND PREPARE TO MEET THEIR GOD, KIDDO.
OKAY, QUIT IT WITH THE "KIDDO."
MY NAME'S--
I DON'T CARE. WE'RE THE NAMELESS DEAD NOW.
JUST WAITING TO BE PICKED BY ZEE.
WAIT, DID YOU JUST SAY ZEE?
YOU HEARD OF THE MONSTER, Huh? NOT SURPRISED...
...BETRAYED HUMANITY JUST TO EXTEND HIS OWN LIFE THROUGH CYLON TECH.
THE THINGS HE DOES TO HIS "SPECIMENS"... FLARK...
...UNSPEAKABLE EXPERIMENTS. THEY SAY ZEE'S TRYING TO PERFECT A WAY OF TRANSFERRING HIS MIND INTO A NEW ORGANIC BODY.
PROBABLY 'CAUSE BALTIFER WON'T LET HIM REPEAT THE--
"BALTIFER? WHAT? YOU MEAN BALTAR?"

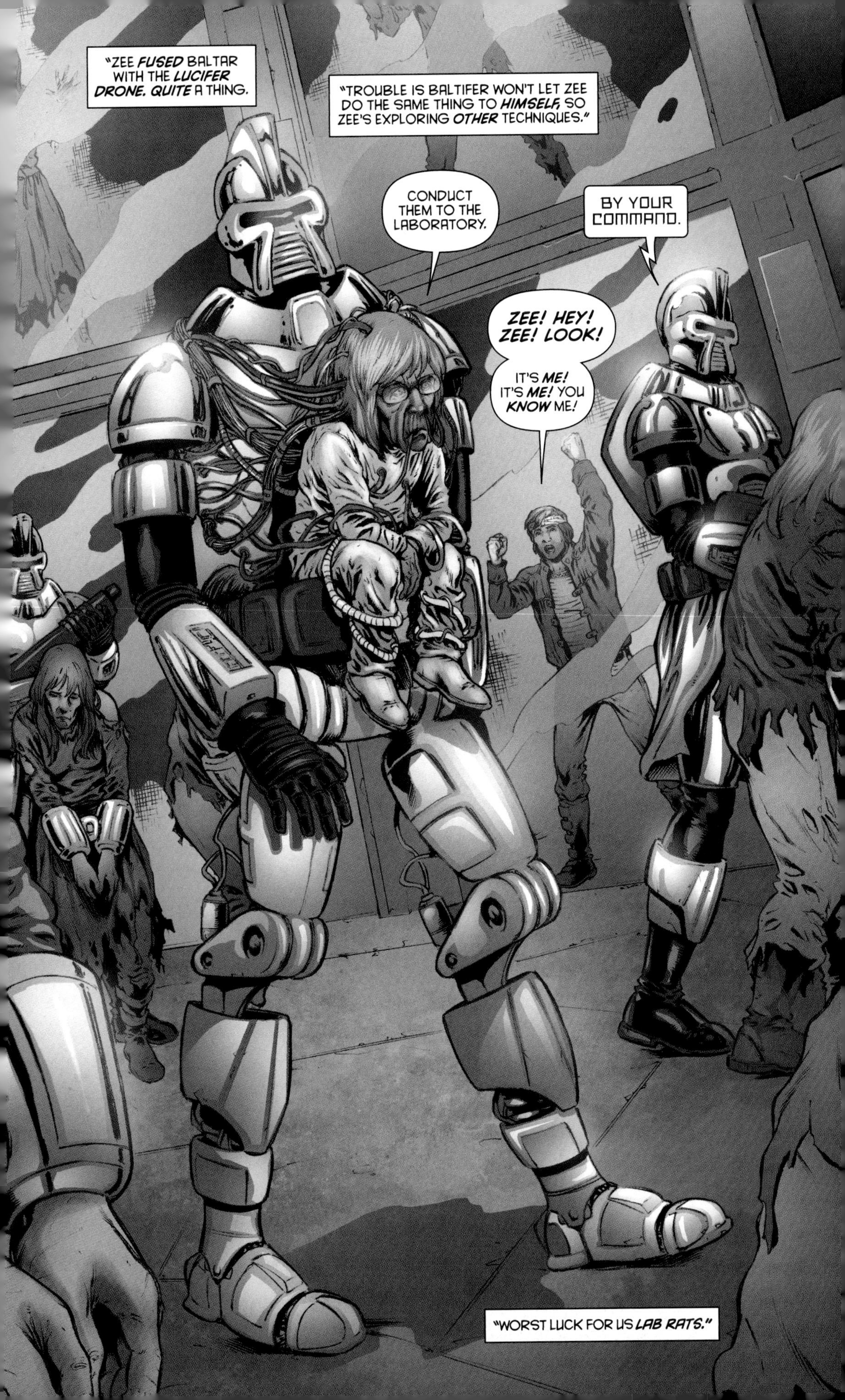
"ZEE FUSED BALTAR WITH THE LUCIFER DRONE. QUITE A THING.
"TROUBLE IS BALTIFER WON'T LET ZEE DO THE SAME THING TO HIMSELF, SO ZEE'S EXPLORING OTHER TECHNIQUES."
CONDUCT THEM TO THE LABORATORY.
BY YOUR COMMAND.
ZEE! HEY! ZEE! LOOK!
IT'S ME! IT'S ME! YOU KNOW ME!
"WORST LUCK FOR US LAB RATS."

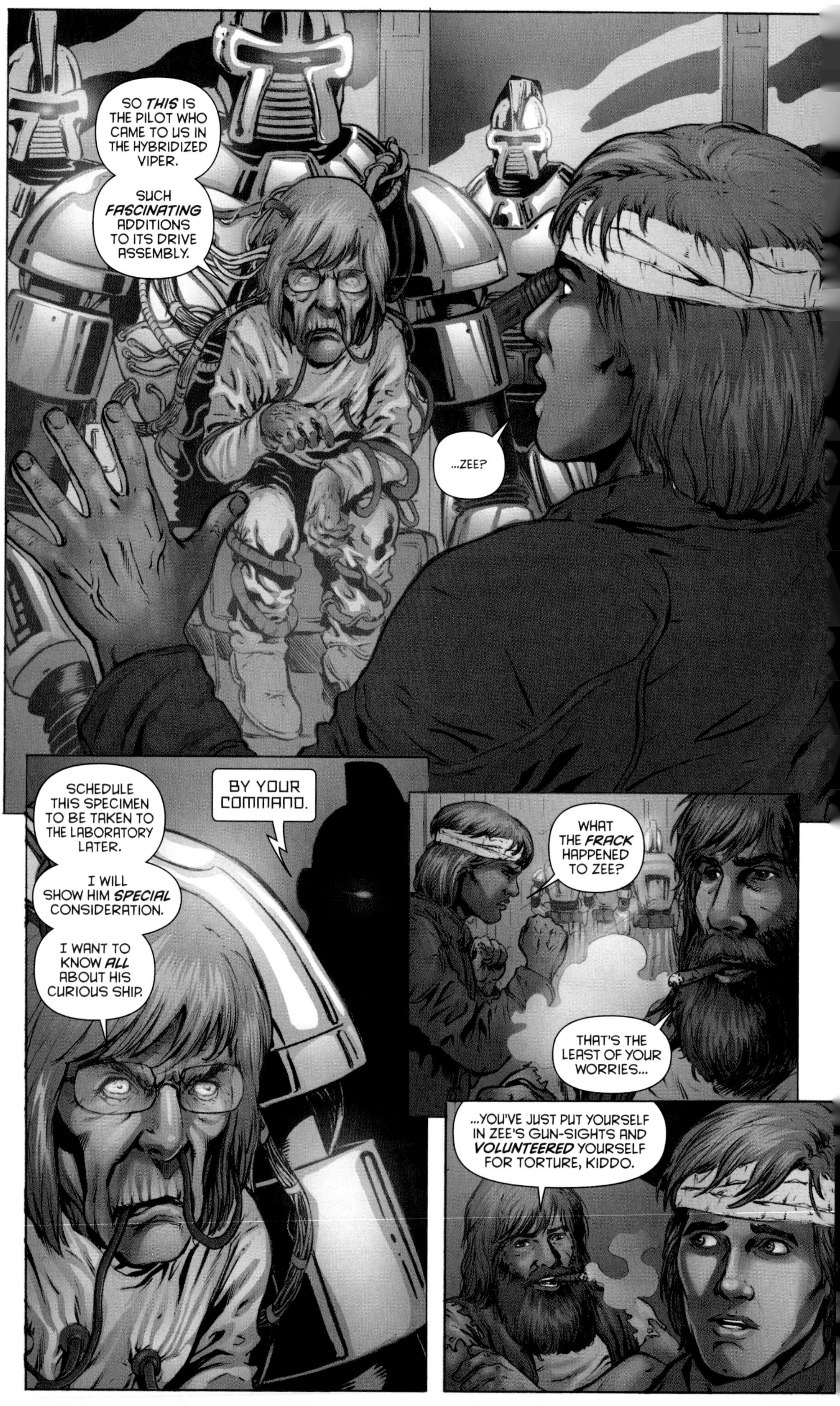
SO THIS IS THE PILOT WHO CAME TO US IN THE HYBRIDIZED VIPER.
SUCH FASCINATING ADDITIONS TO ITS DRIVE ASSEMBLY.
...ZEE?
SCHEDULE THIS SPECIMEN TO BE TAKEN TO THE LABORATORY LATER.
I WILL SHOW HIM SPECIAL CONSIDERATION.
I WANT TO KNOW ALL ABOUT HIS CURIOUS SHIP.
BY YOUR COMMAND.
WHAT THE FRACK HAPPENED TO ZEE?
THAT'S THE LEAST OF YOUR WORRIES...
...YOU'VE JUST PUT YOURSELF IN ZEE'S GUN-SIGHTS AND VOLUNTEERED YOURSELF FOR TORTURE, KIDDO.

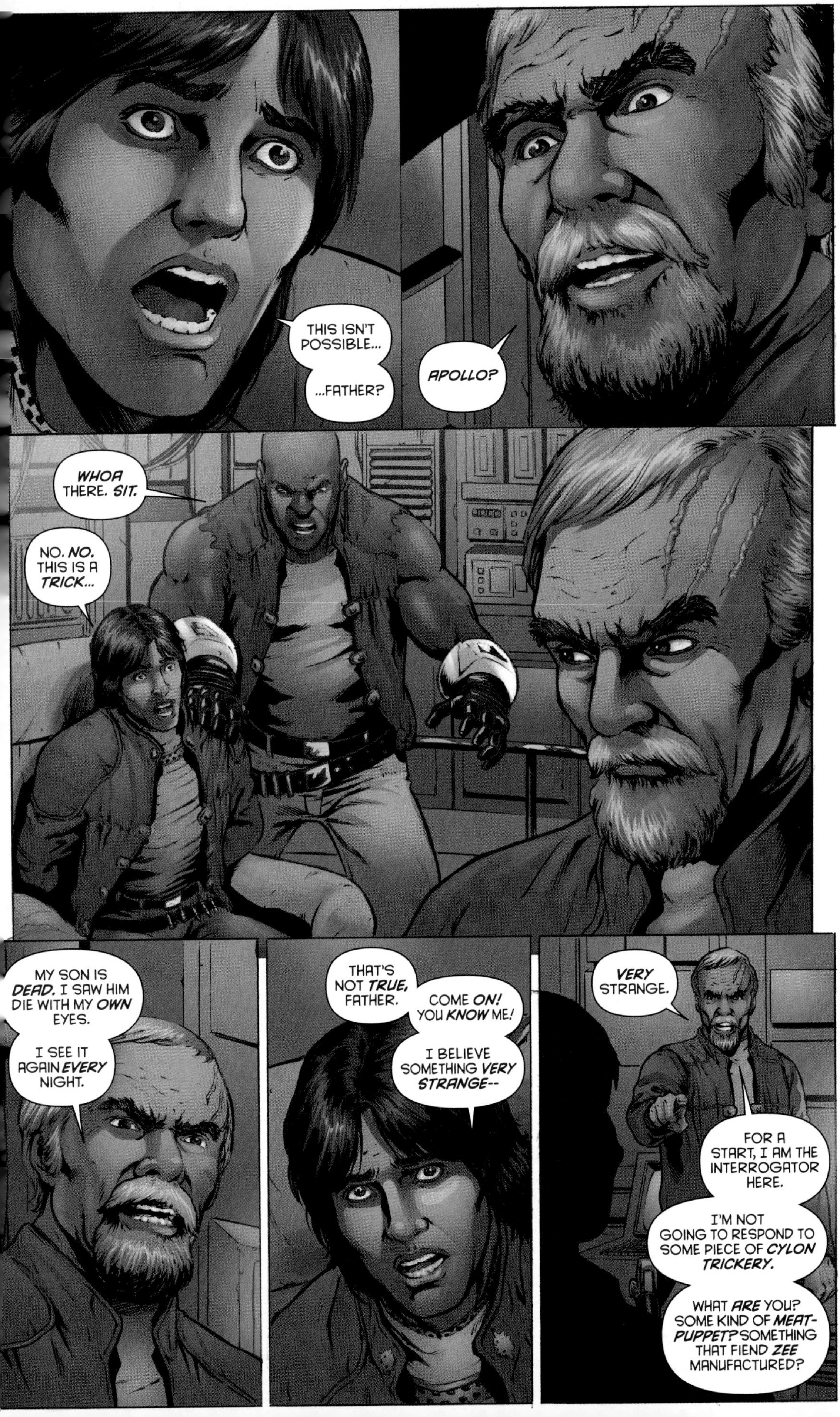
THIS ISN'T POSSIBLE...
...FATHER?
APOLLO?
WHOA THERE. SIT.
NO. NO. THIS IS A TRICK...
MY SON IS DEAD. I SAW HIM DIE WITH MY OWN EYES.
I SEE IT AGAIN EVERY NIGHT.
THAT'S NOT TRUE, FATHER.
COME ON! YOU KNOW ME!
I BELIEVE SOMETHING VERY STRANGE--
VERY STRANGE.
FOR A START, I AM THE INTERROGATOR HERE.
I'M NOT GOING TO RESPOND TO SOME PIECE OF CYLON TRICKERY.
WHAT ARE YOU? SOME KIND OF MEAT-PUPPET? SOMETHING THAT FIEND ZEE MANUFACTURED?

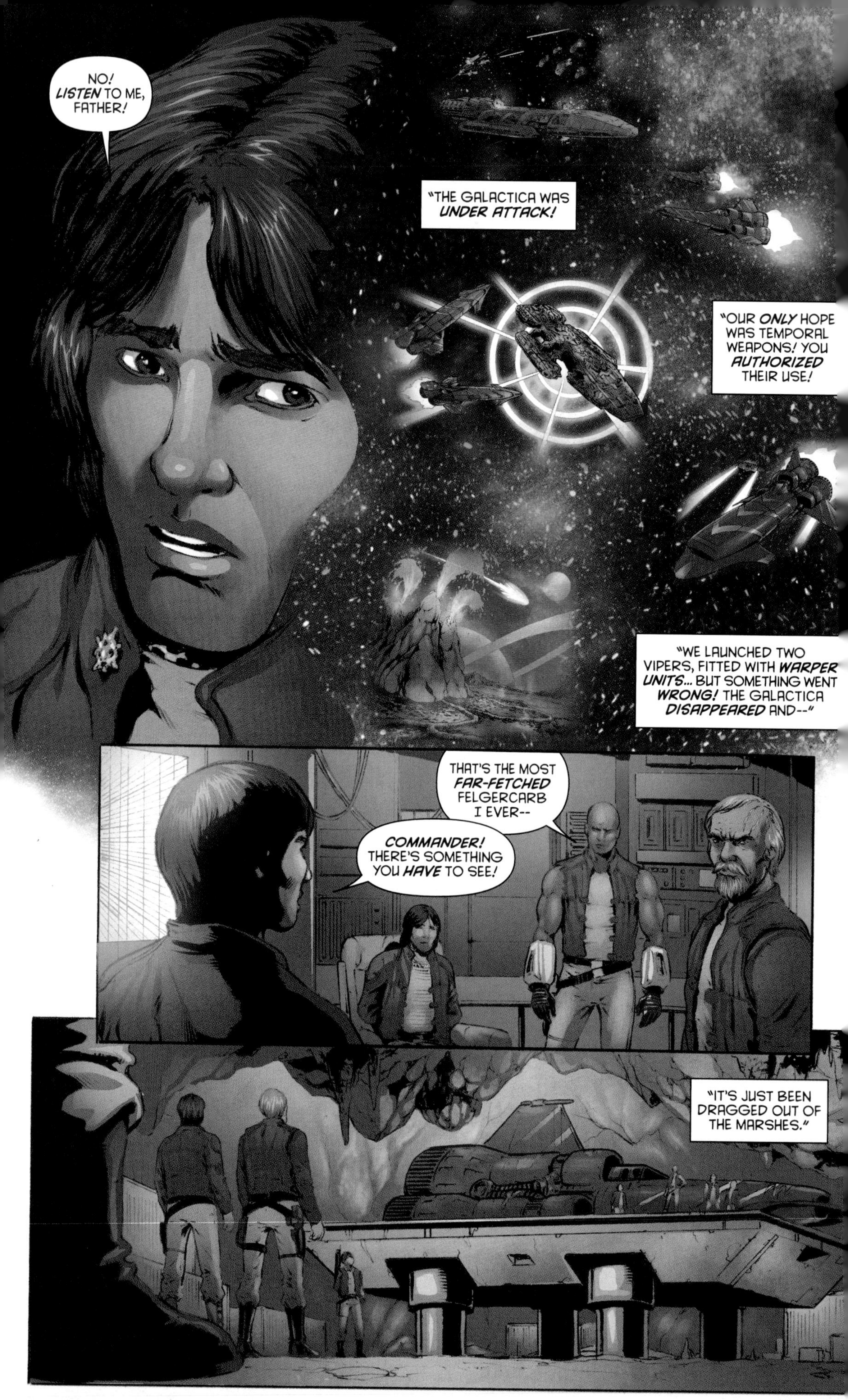
NO! LISTEN TO ME, FATHER!
"THE GALACTICA WAS UNDER ATTACK!
"OUR ONLY HOPE WAS TEMPORAL WEAPONS! YOU AUTHORIZED THEIR USE!
"WE LAUNCHED TWO VIPERS, FITTED WITH WARPER UNITS... BUT SOMETHING WENT WRONG! THE GALACTICA DISAPPEARED AND--"
THAT'S THE MOST FAR-FETCHED FELGERCARB I EVER--
COMMANDER! THERE'S SOMETHING YOU HAVE TO SEE!
"IT'S JUST BEEN DRAGGED OUT OF THE MARSHES."

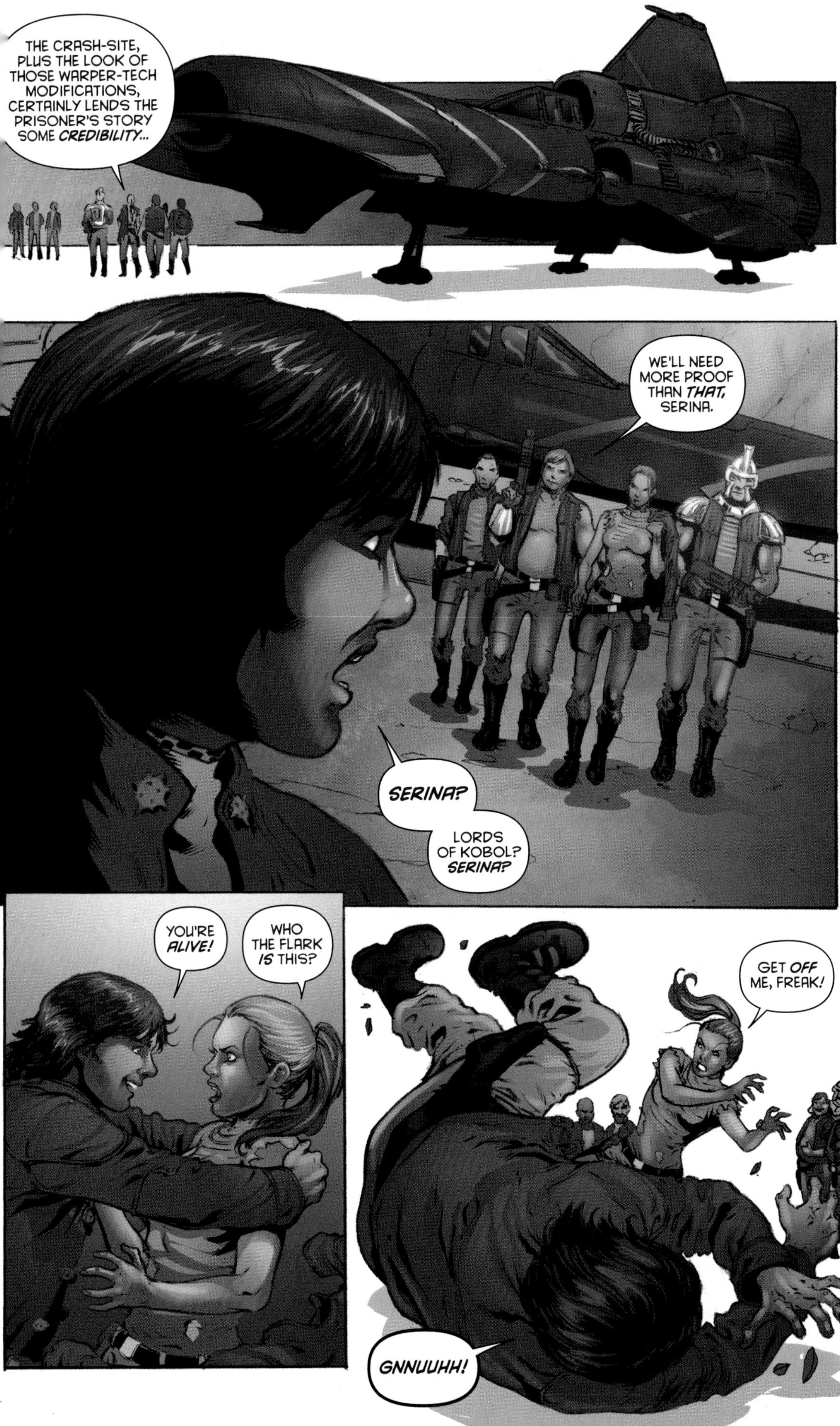
THE CRASH-SITE, PLUS THE LOOK OF THOSE WARPER-TECH MODIFICATIONS, CERTAINLY LENDS THE PRISONER'S STORY SOME *CREDIBILITY*...
WE'LL NEED MORE PROOF THAN *THAT,* SERINA.
SERINA?
LORDS OF KOBOL? *SERINA?*
YOU'RE *ALIVE!*
WHO THE FLARK *IS* THIS?
GET *OFF* ME, FREAK!
GNNUUHH!

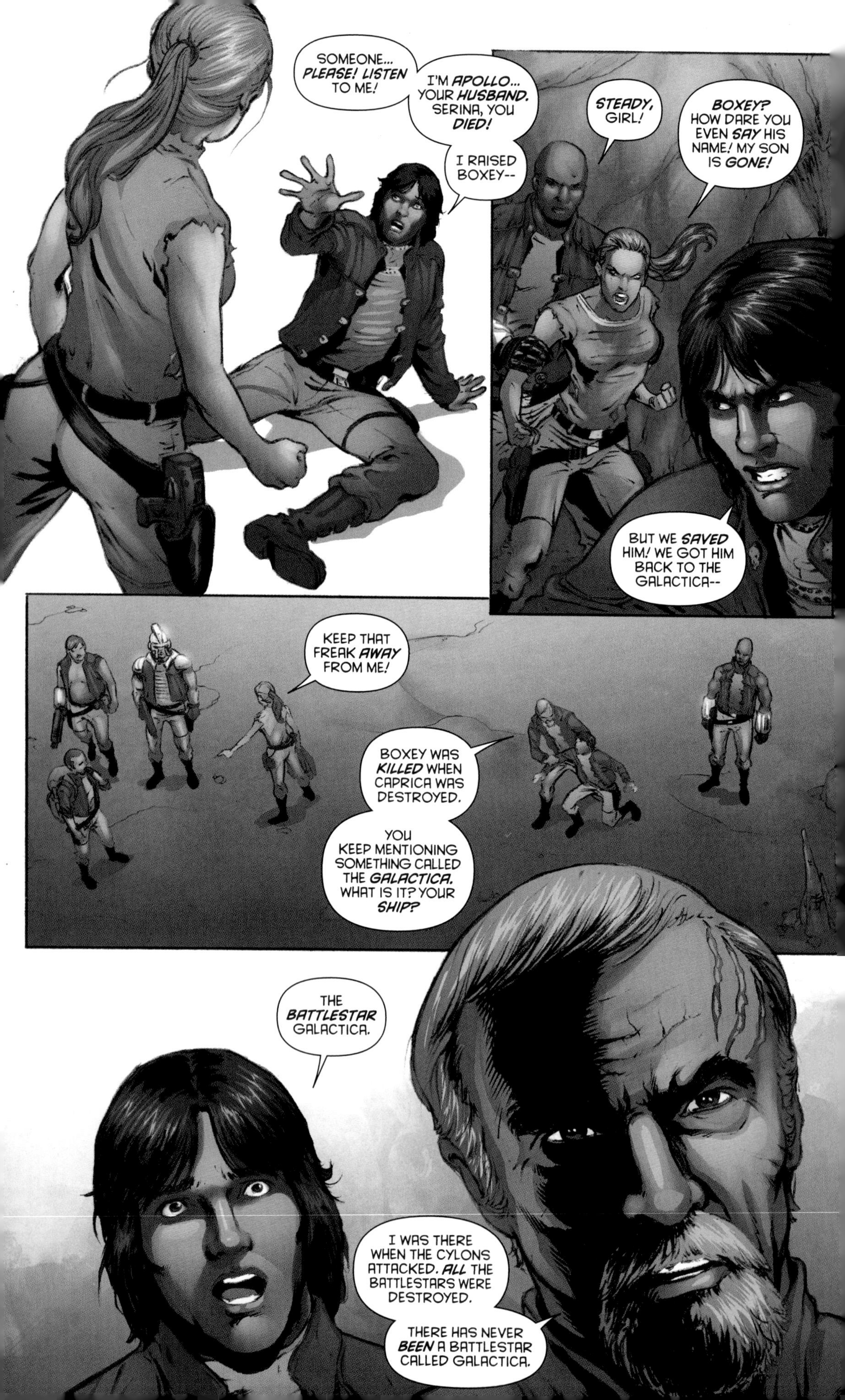
SOMEONE... PLEASE! LISTEN TO ME!
I'M APOLLO... YOUR HUSBAND. SERINA, YOU DIED!
I RAISED BOXEY--
STEADY, GIRL!
BOXEY? HOW DARE YOU EVEN SAY HIS NAME! MY SON IS GONE!
BUT WE SAVED HIM! WE GOT HIM BACK TO THE GALACTICA--
KEEP THAT FREAK AWAY FROM ME!
BOXEY WAS KILLED WHEN CAPRICA WAS DESTROYED.
YOU KEEP MENTIONING SOMETHING CALLED THE GALACTICA. WHAT IS IT? YOUR SHIP?
THE BATTLESTAR GALACTICA.
I WAS THERE WHEN THE CYLONS ATTACKED. ALL THE BATTLESTARS WERE DESTROYED.
THERE HAS NEVER BEEN A BATTLESTAR CALLED GALACTICA.

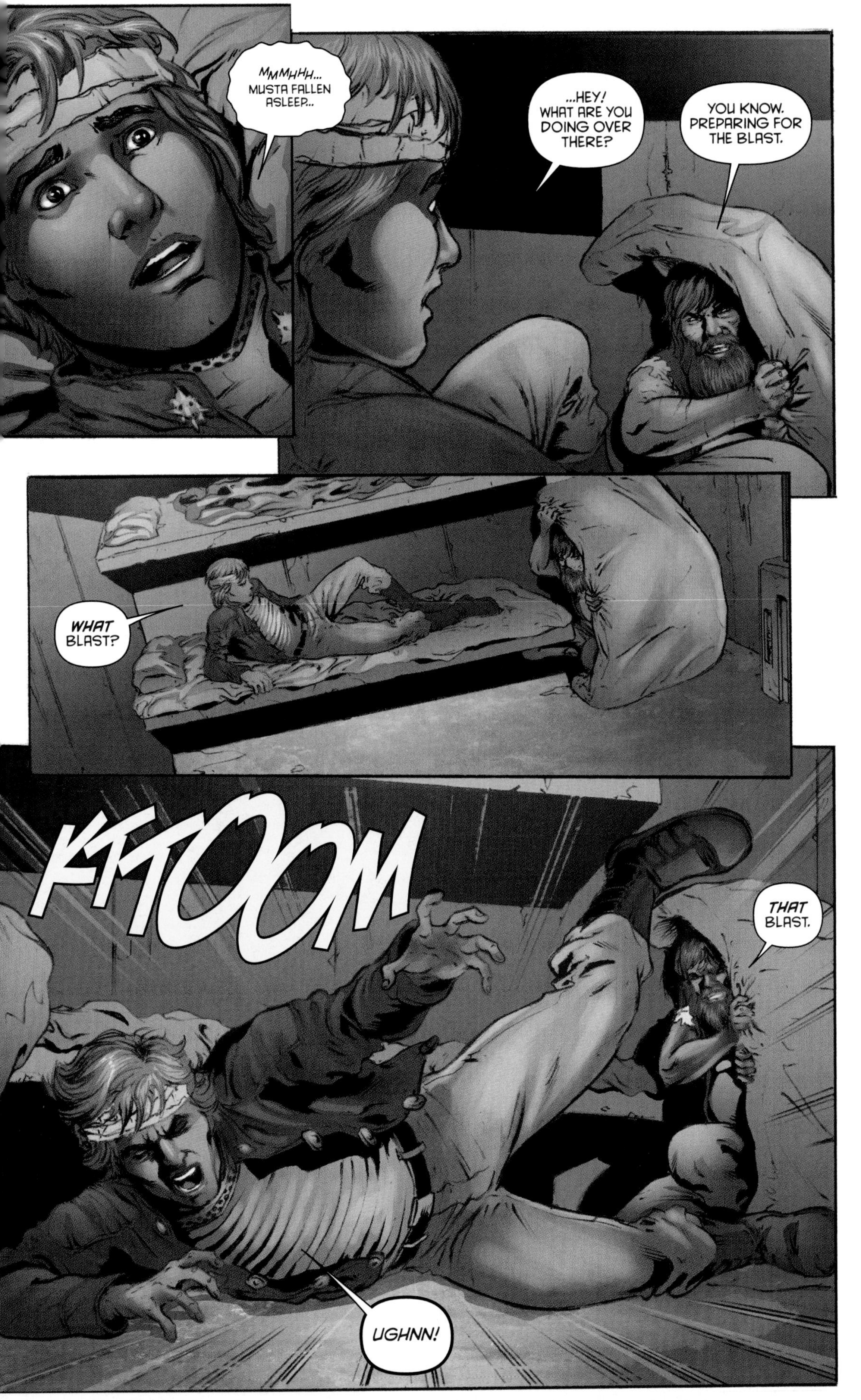
MMMHHH...
MUSTA FALLEN ASLEEP...
...HEY! WHAT ARE YOU DOING OVER THERE?
YOU KNOW. PREPARING FOR THE BLAST.
WHAT BLAST?
KTTOOM
THAT BLAST.
UGHNN!

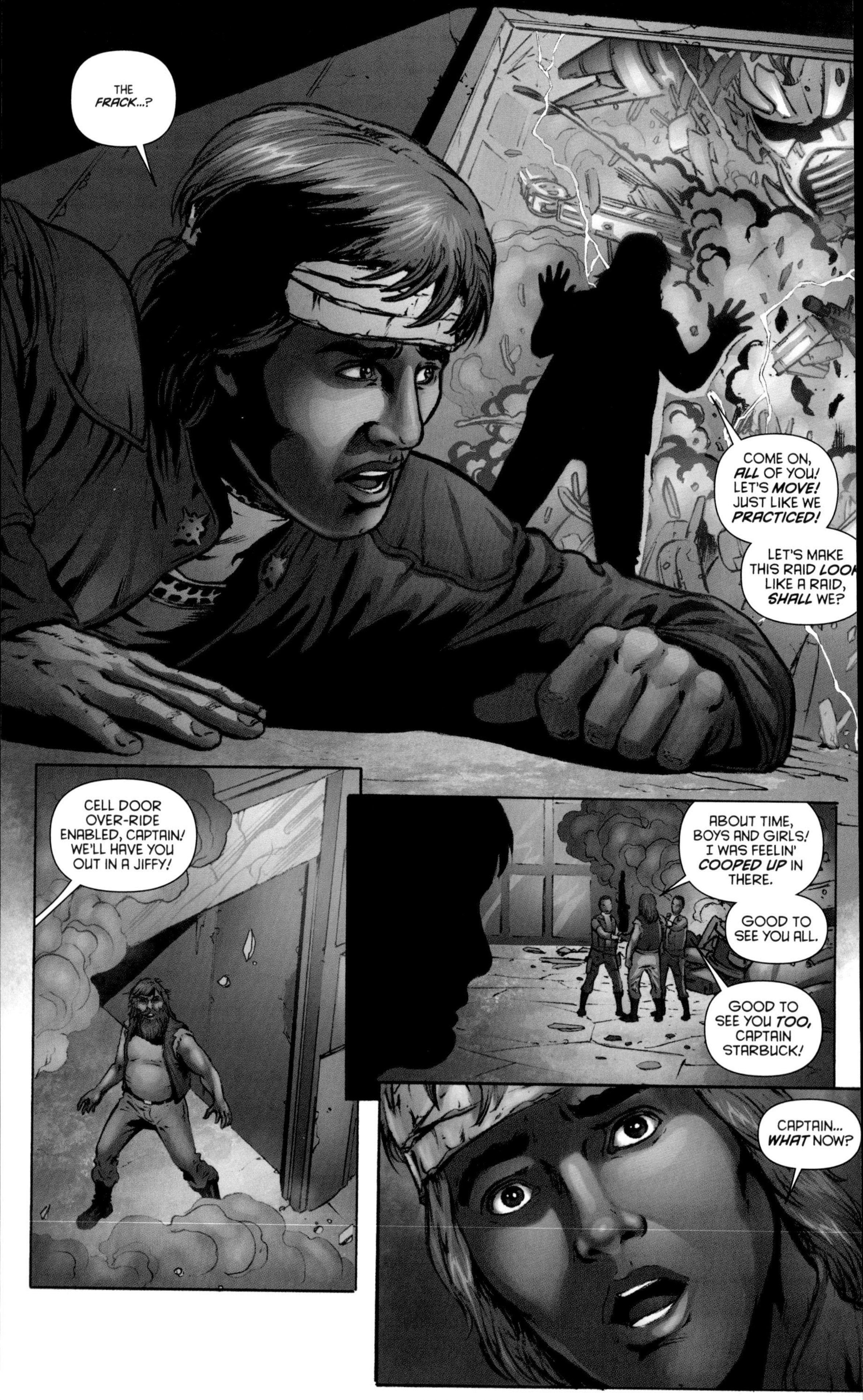
THE *FRACK*...?
COME ON, *ALL* OF YOU! LET'S *MOVE!* JUST LIKE WE *PRACTICED!*
LET'S MAKE THIS RAID *LOOK* LIKE A RAID, *SHALL* WE?
CELL DOOR OVER-RIDE ENABLED, CAPTAIN! WE'LL HAVE YOU OUT IN A JIFFY!
ABOUT TIME, BOYS AND GIRLS! I WAS FEELIN' *COOPED UP* IN THERE.
GOOD TO SEE YOU ALL.
GOOD TO SEE YOU *TOO,* CAPTAIN STARBUCK!
CAPTAIN... *WHAT* NOW?

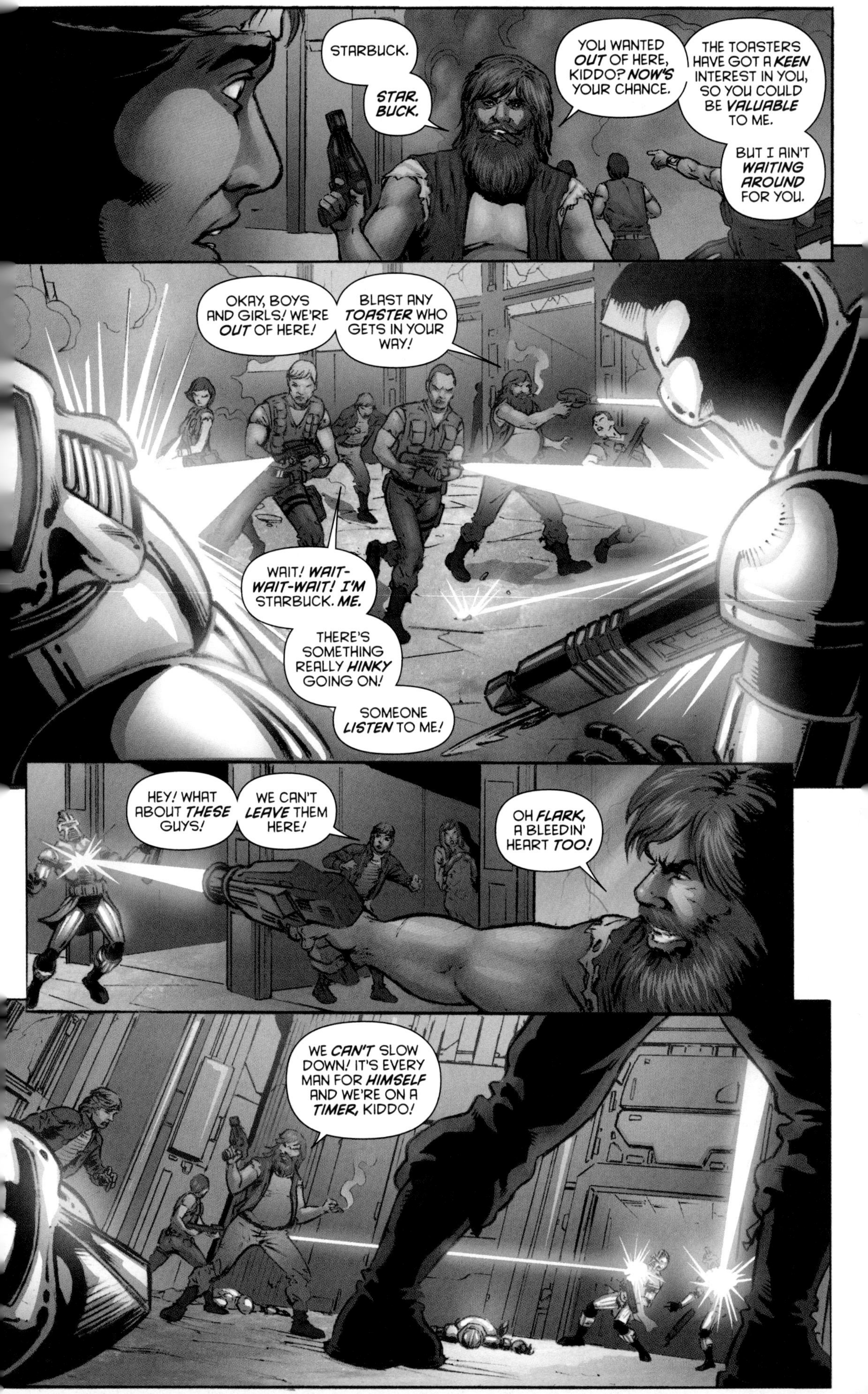

STARBUCK.
STAR. BUCK.
YOU WANTED OUT OF HERE, KIDDO? NOW'S YOUR CHANCE.
THE TOASTERS HAVE GOT A KEEN INTEREST IN YOU, SO YOU COULD BE VALUABLE TO ME.
BUT I AIN'T WAITING AROUND FOR YOU.
OKAY, BOYS AND GIRLS! WE'RE OUT OF HERE!
BLAST ANY TOASTER WHO GETS IN YOUR WAY!
WAIT! WAIT-WAIT-WAIT! I'M STARBUCK. ME.
THERE'S SOMETHING REALLY HINKY GOING ON!
SOMEONE LISTEN TO ME!
HEY! WHAT ABOUT THESE GUYS!
WE CAN'T LEAVE THEM HERE!
OH FLARK, A BLEEDIN' HEART TOO!
WE CAN'T SLOW DOWN! IT'S EVERY MAN FOR HIMSELF AND WE'RE ON A TIMER, KIDDO!

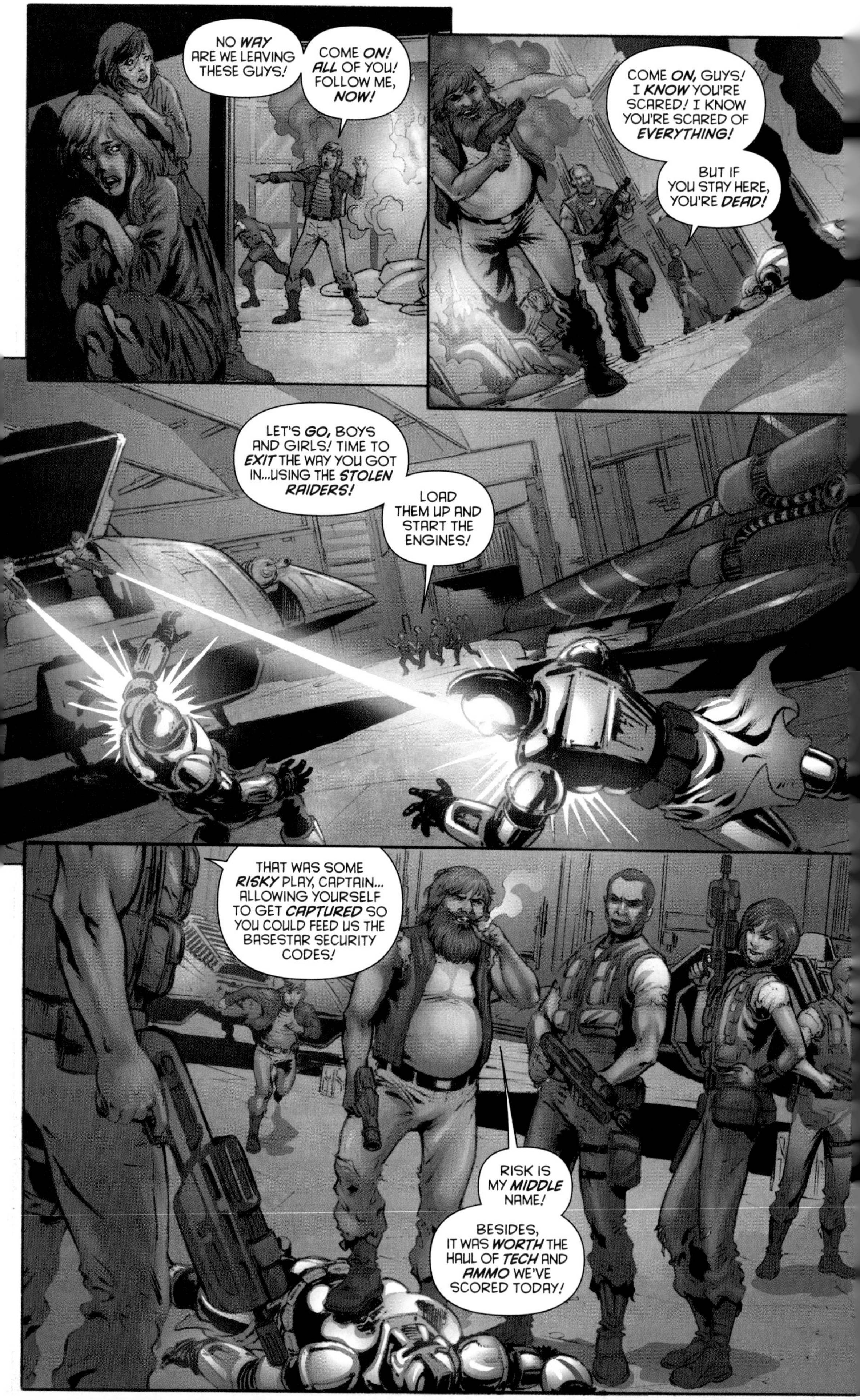

NO WAY ARE WE LEAVING THESE GUYS!
COME ON! ALL OF YOU! FOLLOW ME, NOW!
COME ON, GUYS! I KNOW YOU'RE SCARED! I KNOW YOU'RE SCARED OF EVERYTHING!
BUT IF YOU STAY HERE, YOU'RE DEAD!
LET'S GO, BOYS AND GIRLS! TIME TO EXIT THE WAY YOU GOT IN...USING THE STOLEN RAIDERS!
LOAD THEM UP AND START THE ENGINES!
THAT WAS SOME RISKY PLAY, CAPTAIN... ALLOWING YOURSELF TO GET CAPTURED SO YOU COULD FEED US THE BASESTAR SECURITY CODES!
RISK IS MY MIDDLE NAME!
BESIDES, IT WAS WORTH THE HAUL OF TECH AND AMMO WE'VE SCORED TODAY!

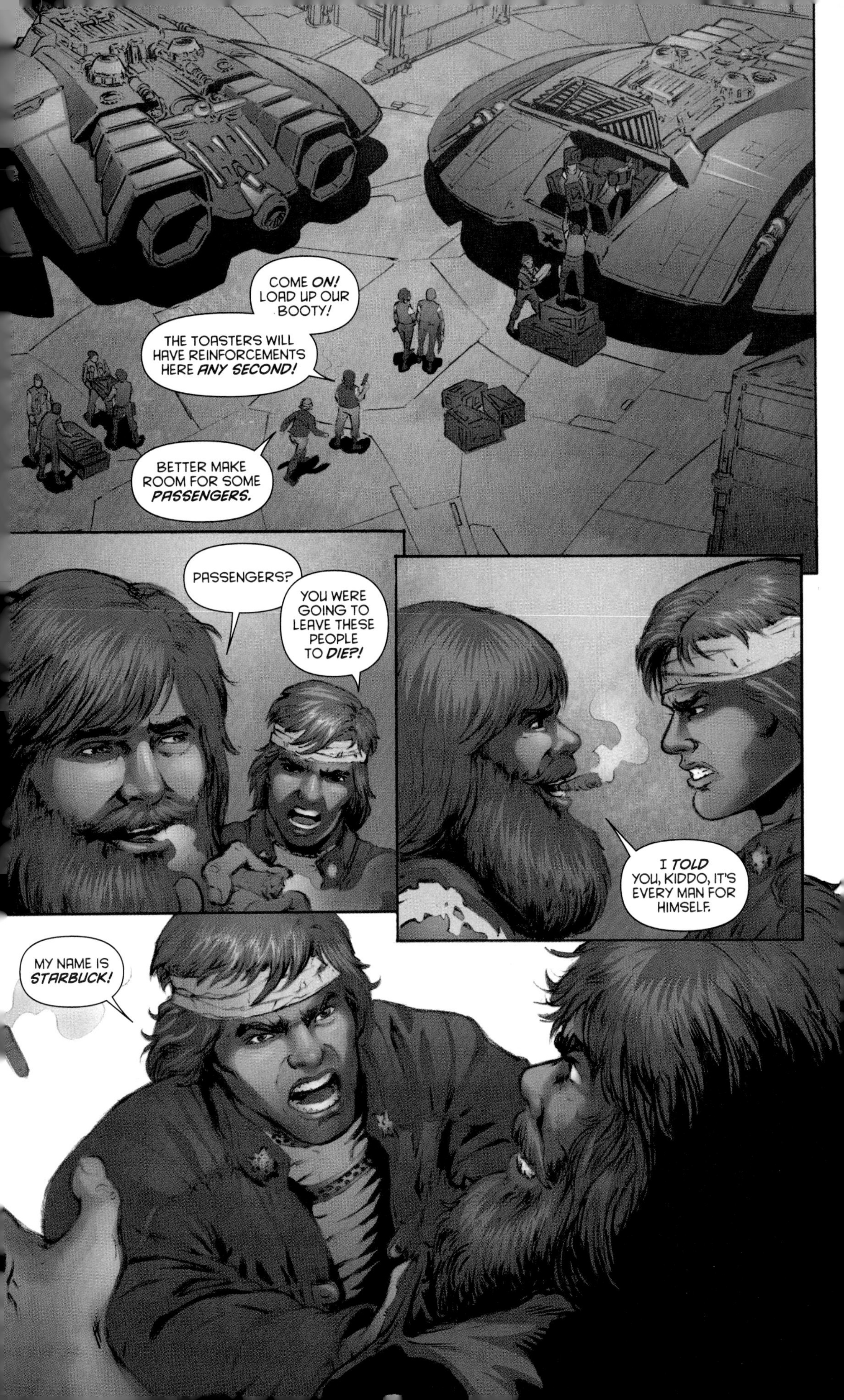
COME ON! LOAD UP OUR BOOTY!
THE TOASTERS WILL HAVE REINFORCEMENTS HERE ANY SECOND!
BETTER MAKE ROOM FOR SOME PASSENGERS.
PASSENGERS?
YOU WERE GOING TO LEAVE THESE PEOPLE TO DIE?!
I TOLD YOU, KIDDO, IT'S EVERY MAN FOR HIMSELF.
MY NAME IS STARBUCK!

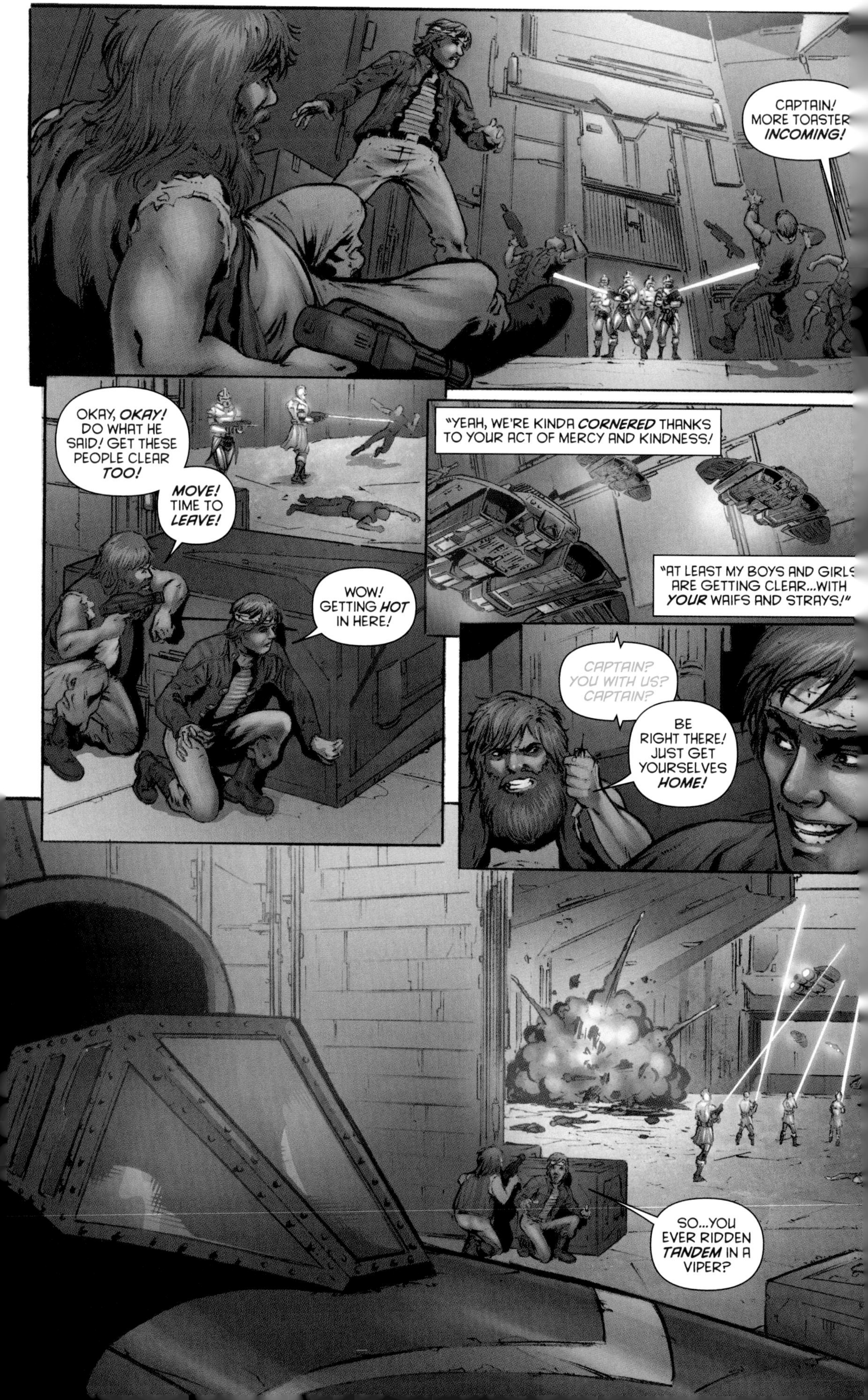

CAPTAIN! MORE TOASTER INCOMING!
OKAY, OKAY! DO WHAT HE SAID! GET THESE PEOPLE CLEAR TOO!
MOVE! TIME TO LEAVE!
WOW! GETTING HOT IN HERE!
"YEAH, WE'RE KINDA CORNERED THANKS TO YOUR ACT OF MERCY AND KINDNESS!
"AT LEAST MY BOYS AND GIRLS ARE GETTING CLEAR...WITH YOUR WAIFS AND STRAYS!"
CAPTAIN? YOU WITH US? CAPTAIN?
BE RIGHT THERE! JUST GET YOURSELVES HOME!
SO...YOU EVER RIDDEN TANDEM IN A VIPER?

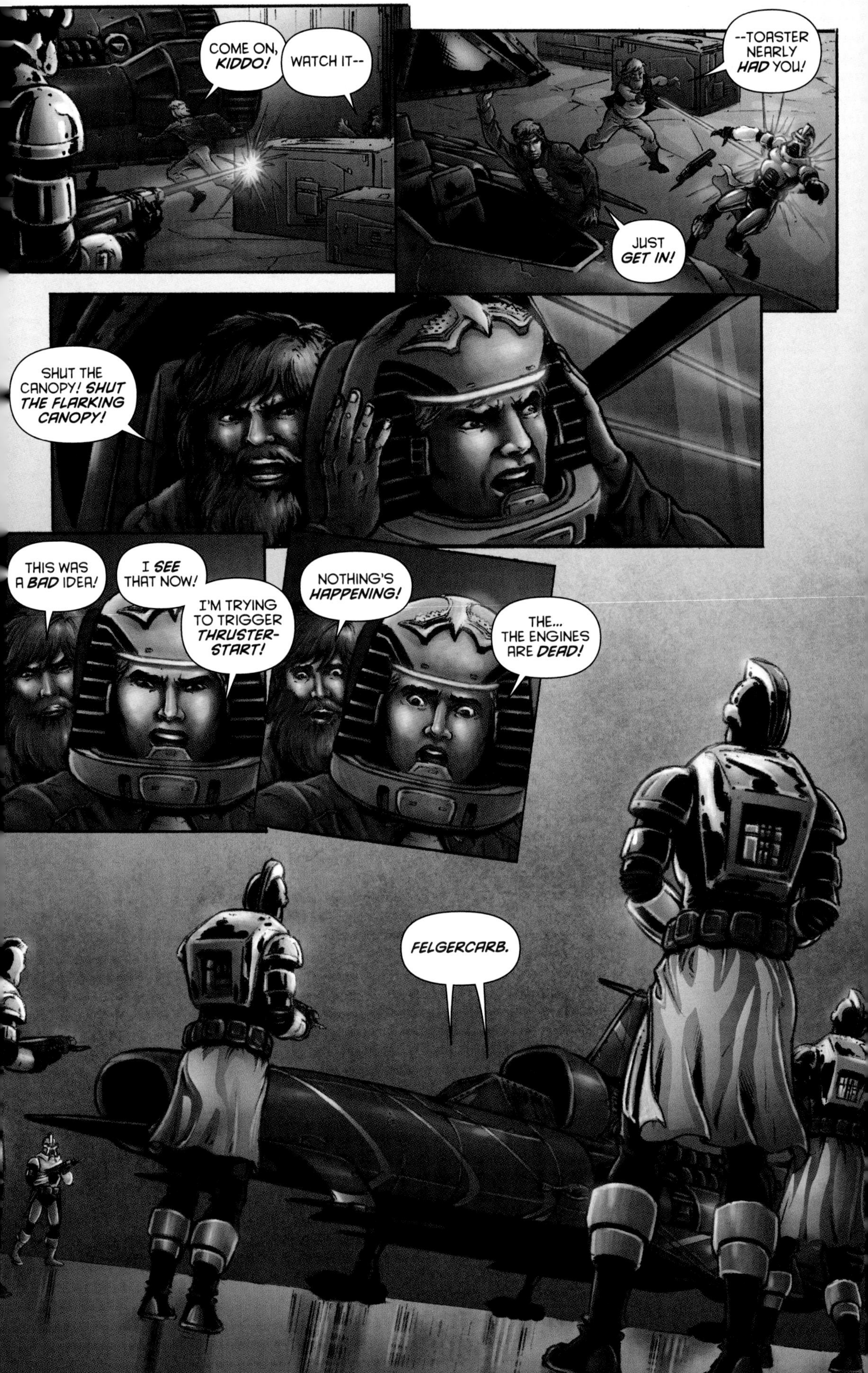
COME ON, *KIDDO!*
WATCH IT--
--TOASTER NEARLY *HAD* YOU!
JUST *GET IN!*
SHUT THE CANOPY! *SHUT THE FLARKING CANOPY!*
THIS WAS A *BAD* IDEA!
I *SEE* THAT NOW!
I'M TRYING TO TRIGGER *THRUSTER-START!*
NOTHING'S *HAPPENING!*
THE... THE ENGINES ARE *DEAD!*
FELGERCARB.

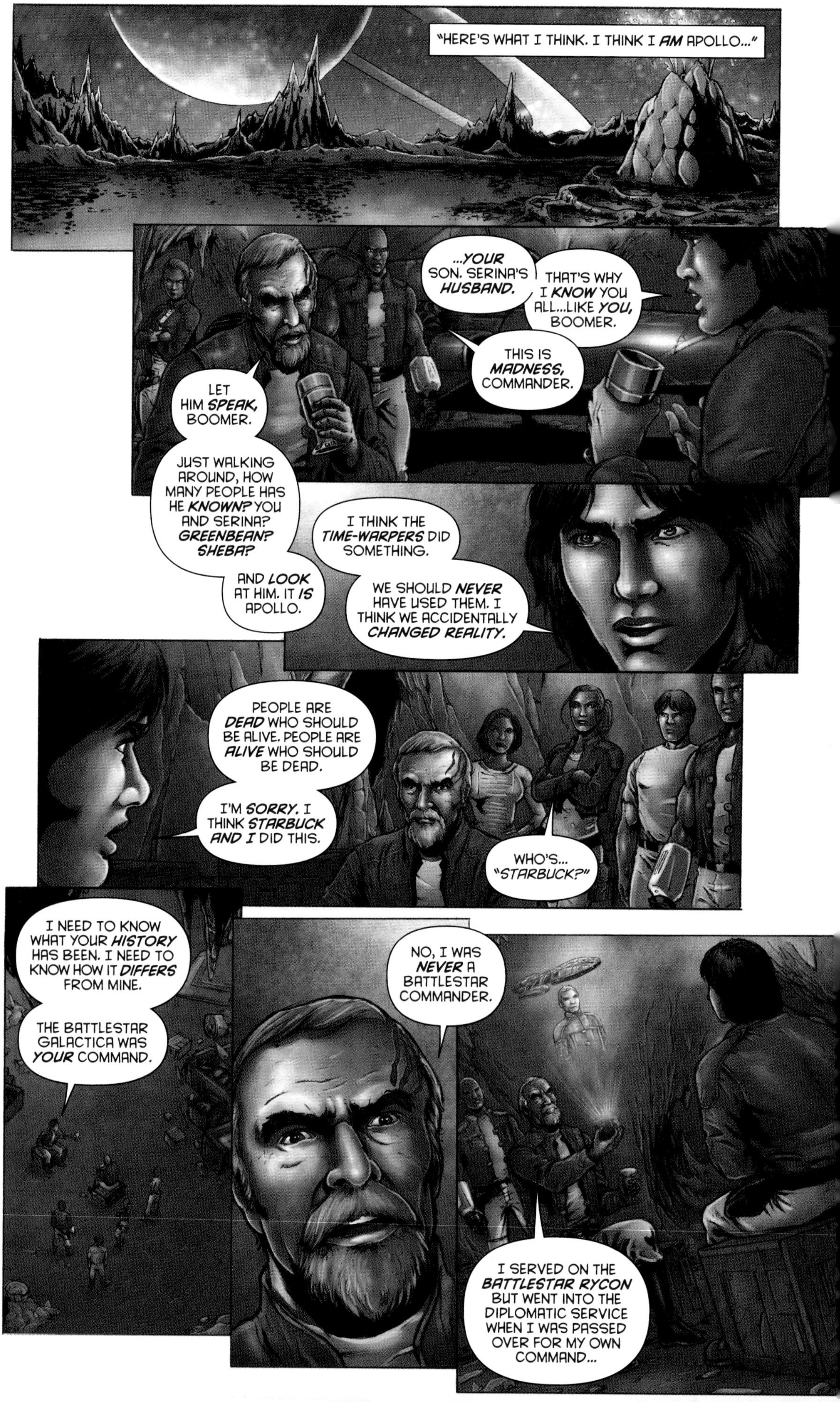
"HERE'S WHAT I THINK. I THINK I AM APOLLO..."
...YOUR SON. SERINA'S HUSBAND.
THAT'S WHY I KNOW YOU ALL...LIKE YOU, BOOMER.
THIS IS MADNESS, COMMANDER.
LET HIM SPEAK, BOOMER.
JUST WALKING AROUND, HOW MANY PEOPLE HAS HE KNOWN? YOU AND SERINA? GREENBEAN? SHEBA?
AND LOOK AT HIM. IT IS APOLLO.
I THINK THE TIME-WARPERS DID SOMETHING.
WE SHOULD NEVER HAVE USED THEM. I THINK WE ACCIDENTALLY CHANGED REALITY.
PEOPLE ARE DEAD WHO SHOULD BE ALIVE. PEOPLE ARE ALIVE WHO SHOULD BE DEAD.
I'M SORRY. I THINK STARBUCK AND I DID THIS.
WHO'S... "STARBUCK?"
I NEED TO KNOW WHAT YOUR HISTORY HAS BEEN. I NEED TO KNOW HOW IT DIFFERS FROM MINE.
THE BATTLESTAR GALACTICA WAS YOUR COMMAND.
NO, I WAS NEVER A BATTLESTAR COMMANDER.
I SERVED ON THE BATTLESTAR RYCON BUT WENT INTO THE DIPLOMATIC SERVICE WHEN I WAS PASSED OVER FOR MY OWN COMMAND...

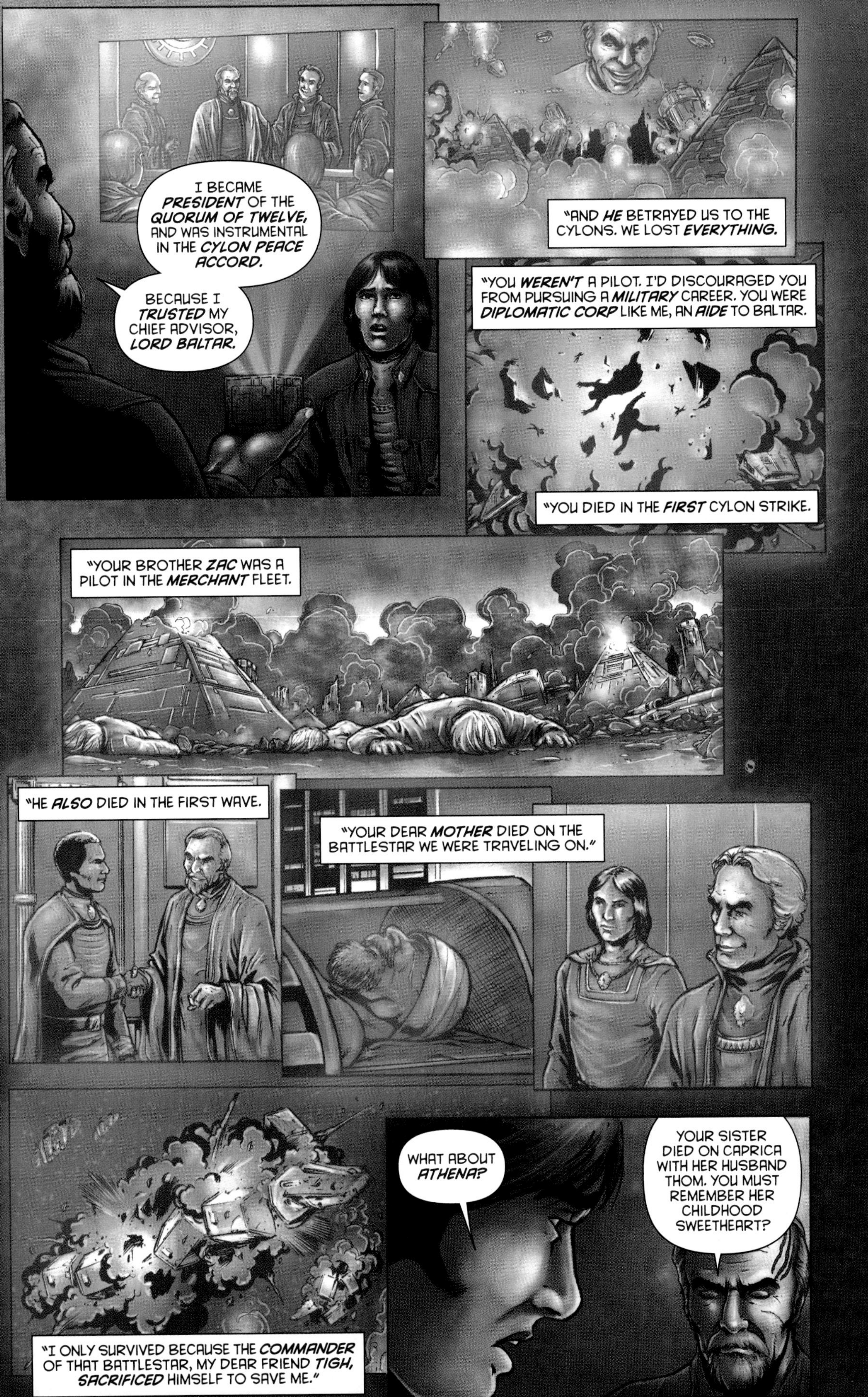

I BECAME PRESIDENT OF THE QUORUM OF TWELVE, AND WAS INSTRUMENTAL IN THE CYLON PEACE ACCORD.
BECAUSE I TRUSTED MY CHIEF ADVISOR, LORD BALTAR.
"AND HE BETRAYED US TO THE CYLONS. WE LOST EVERYTHING.
"YOU WEREN'T A PILOT. I'D DISCOURAGED YOU FROM PURSUING A MILITARY CAREER. YOU WERE DIPLOMATIC CORP LIKE ME, AN AIDE TO BALTAR.
"YOU DIED IN THE FIRST CYLON STRIKE.
"YOUR BROTHER ZAC WAS A PILOT IN THE MERCHANT FLEET.
"HE ALSO DIED IN THE FIRST WAVE.
"YOUR DEAR MOTHER DIED ON THE BATTLESTAR WE WERE TRAVELING ON."
"I ONLY SURVIVED BECAUSE THE COMMANDER OF THAT BATTLESTAR, MY DEAR FRIEND TIGH, SACRIFICED HIMSELF TO SAVE ME."
WHAT ABOUT ATHENA?
YOUR SISTER DIED ON CAPRICA WITH HER HUSBAND THOM. YOU MUST REMEMBER HER CHILDHOOD SWEETHEART?

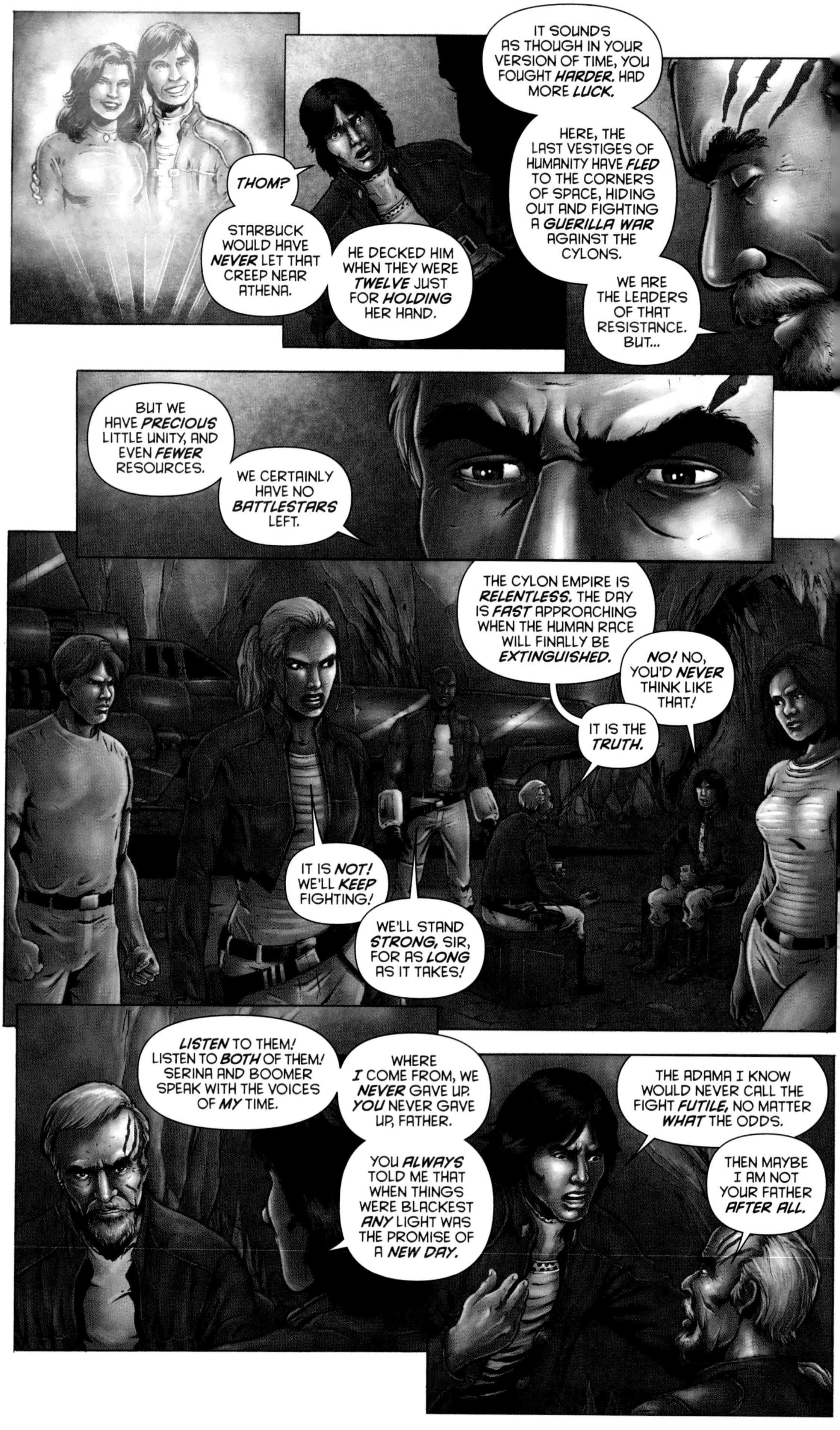
THOM?
STARBUCK WOULD HAVE NEVER LET THAT CREEP NEAR ATHENA.
HE DECKED HIM WHEN THEY WERE TWELVE JUST FOR HOLDING HER HAND.
IT SOUNDS AS THOUGH IN YOUR VERSION OF TIME, YOU FOUGHT HARDER. HAD MORE LUCK.
HERE, THE LAST VESTIGES OF HUMANITY HAVE FLED TO THE CORNERS OF SPACE, HIDING OUT AND FIGHTING A GUERILLA WAR AGAINST THE CYLONS.
WE ARE THE LEADERS OF THAT RESISTANCE. BUT...
BUT WE HAVE PRECIOUS LITTLE UNITY, AND EVEN FEWER RESOURCES.
WE CERTAINLY HAVE NO BATTLESTARS LEFT.
THE CYLON EMPIRE IS RELENTLESS. THE DAY IS FAST APPROACHING WHEN THE HUMAN RACE WILL FINALLY BE EXTINGUISHED.
NO! NO, YOU'D NEVER THINK LIKE THAT!
IT IS THE TRUTH.
IT IS NOT! WE'LL KEEP FIGHTING!
WE'LL STAND STRONG, SIR, FOR AS LONG AS IT TAKES!
LISTEN TO THEM! LISTEN TO BOTH OF THEM! SERINA AND BOOMER SPEAK WITH THE VOICES OF MY TIME.
WHERE I COME FROM, WE NEVER GAVE UP. YOU NEVER GAVE UP, FATHER.
YOU ALWAYS TOLD ME THAT WHEN THINGS WERE BLACKEST ANY LIGHT WAS THE PROMISE OF A NEW DAY.
THE ADAMA I KNOW WOULD NEVER CALL THE FIGHT FUTILE, NO MATTER WHAT THE ODDS.
THEN MAYBE I AM NOT YOUR FATHER AFTER ALL.

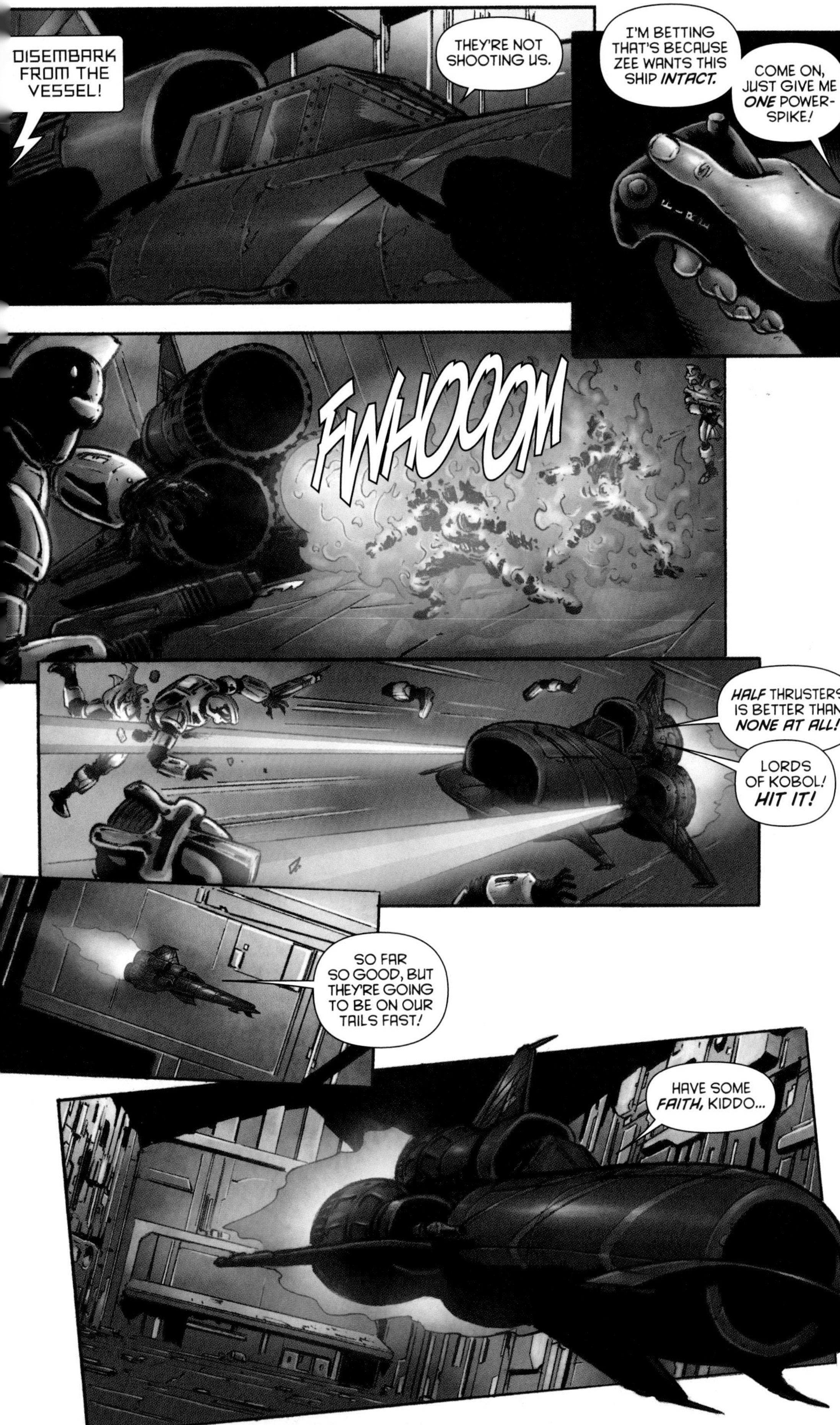
DISEMBARK FROM THE VESSEL!
THEY'RE NOT SHOOTING US.
I'M BETTING THAT'S BECAUSE ZEE WANTS THIS SHIP *INTACT.*
COME ON, JUST GIVE ME *ONE* POWER-SPIKE!
FWHOOOM
HALF THRUSTERS IS BETTER THAN *NONE AT ALL!*
LORDS OF KOBOL! *HIT IT!*
SO FAR SO GOOD, BUT THEY'RE GOING TO BE ON OUR TAILS FAST!
HAVE SOME *FAITH,* KIDDO...

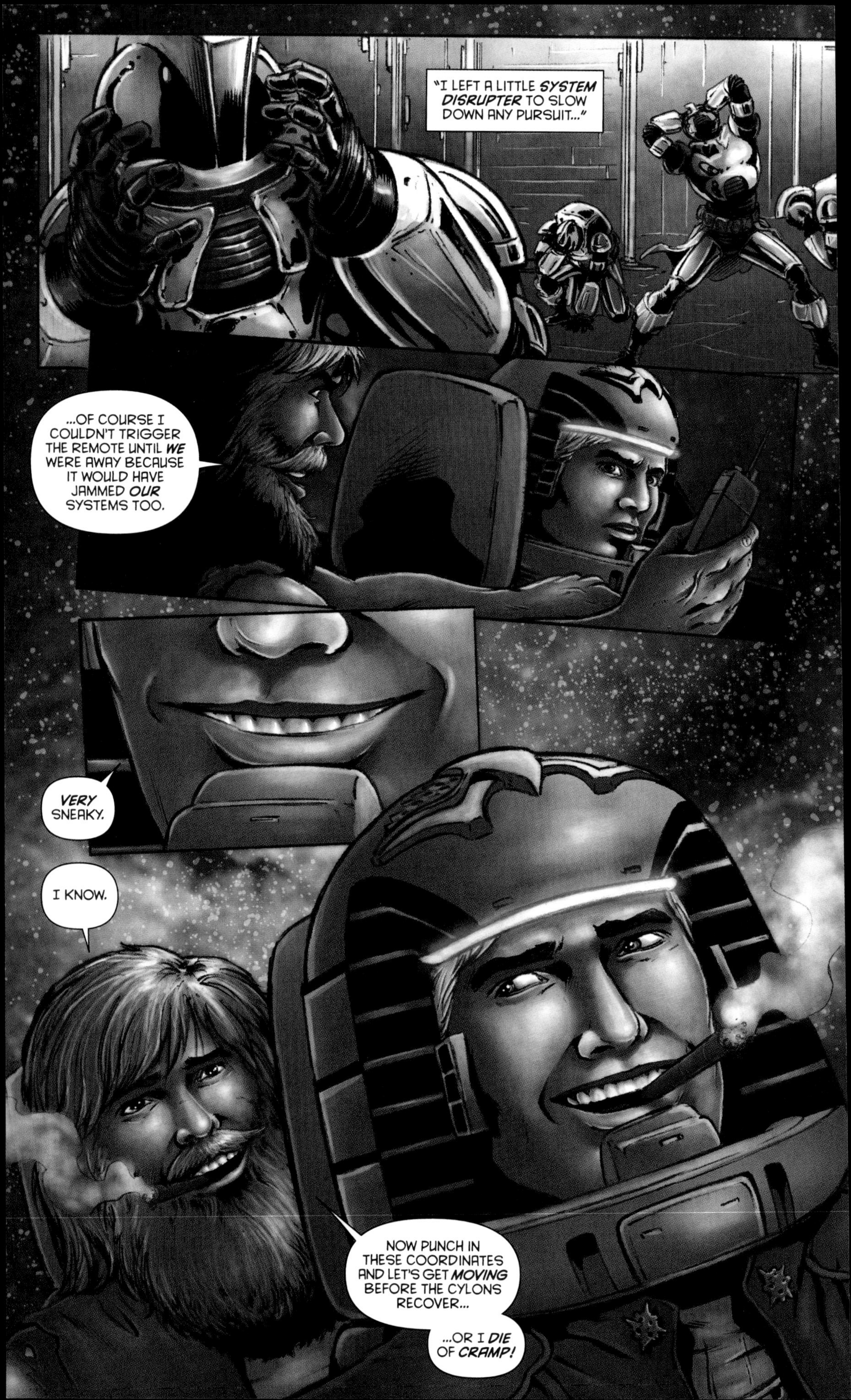
"I LEFT A LITTLE SYSTEM DISRUPTER TO SLOW DOWN ANY PURSUIT..."
...OF COURSE I COULDN'T TRIGGER THE REMOTE UNTIL WE WERE AWAY BECAUSE IT WOULD HAVE JAMMED OUR SYSTEMS TOO.
VERY SNEAKY.
I KNOW.
NOW PUNCH IN THESE COORDINATES AND LET'S GET MOVING BEFORE THE CYLONS RECOVER...
...OR I DIE OF CRAMP!

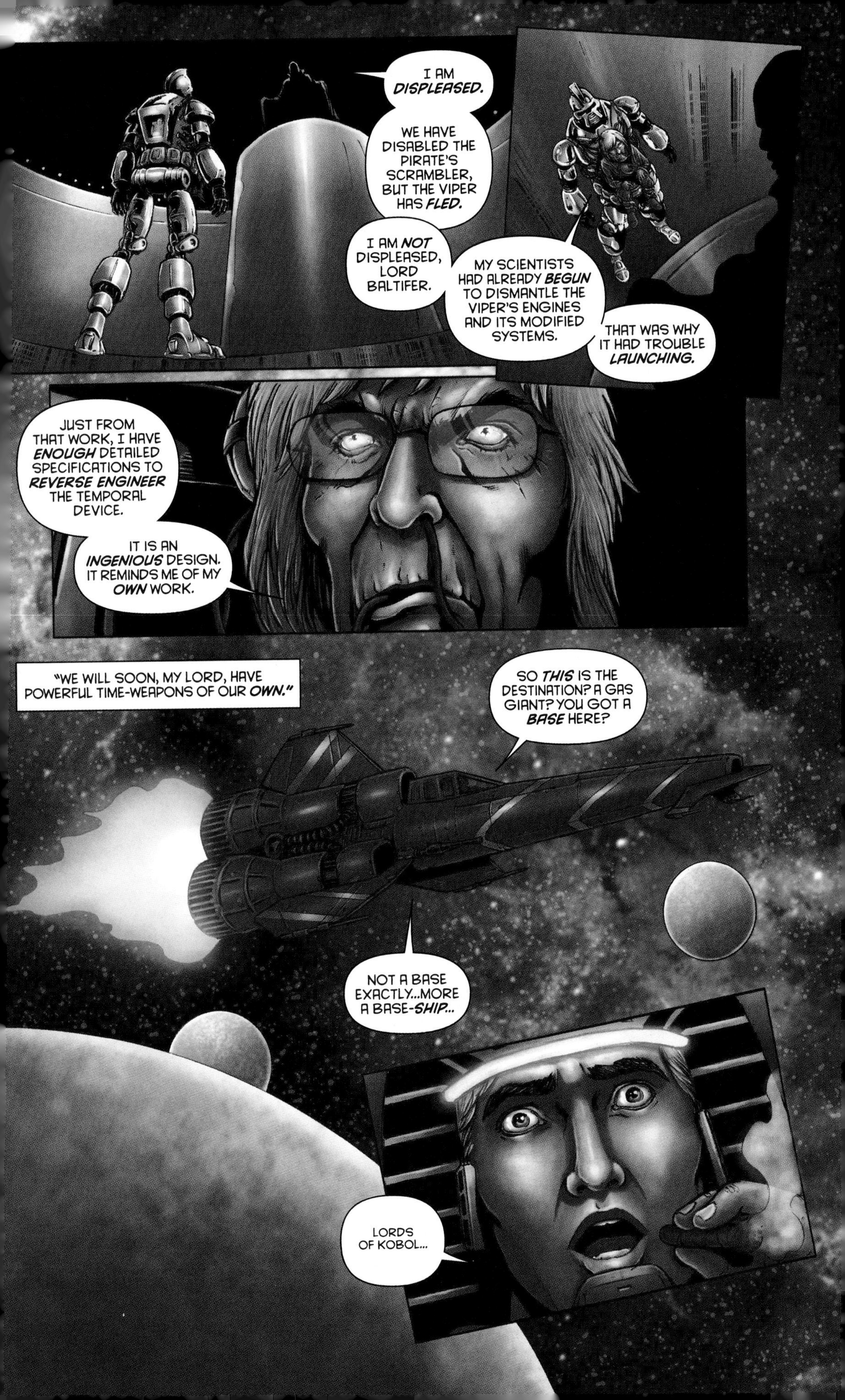
I AM *DISPLEASED.*
WE HAVE DISABLED THE PIRATE'S SCRAMBLER, BUT THE VIPER HAS *FLED.*
I AM *NOT* DISPLEASED, LORD BALTIFER.
MY SCIENTISTS HAD ALREADY *BEGUN* TO DISMANTLE THE VIPER'S ENGINES AND ITS MODIFIED SYSTEMS.
THAT WAS WHY IT HAD TROUBLE *LAUNCHING.*
JUST FROM THAT WORK, I HAVE *ENOUGH* DETAILED SPECIFICATIONS TO *REVERSE ENGINEER* THE TEMPORAL DEVICE.
IT IS AN *INGENIOUS* DESIGN. IT REMINDS ME OF MY *OWN* WORK.
"WE WILL SOON, MY LORD, HAVE POWERFUL TIME-WEAPONS OF OUR *OWN.*"
SO *THIS* IS THE DESTINATION? A GAS GIANT? YOU GOT A *BASE* HERE?
NOT A BASE EXACTLY...MORE A BASE-*SHIP*...
LORDS OF KOBOL...

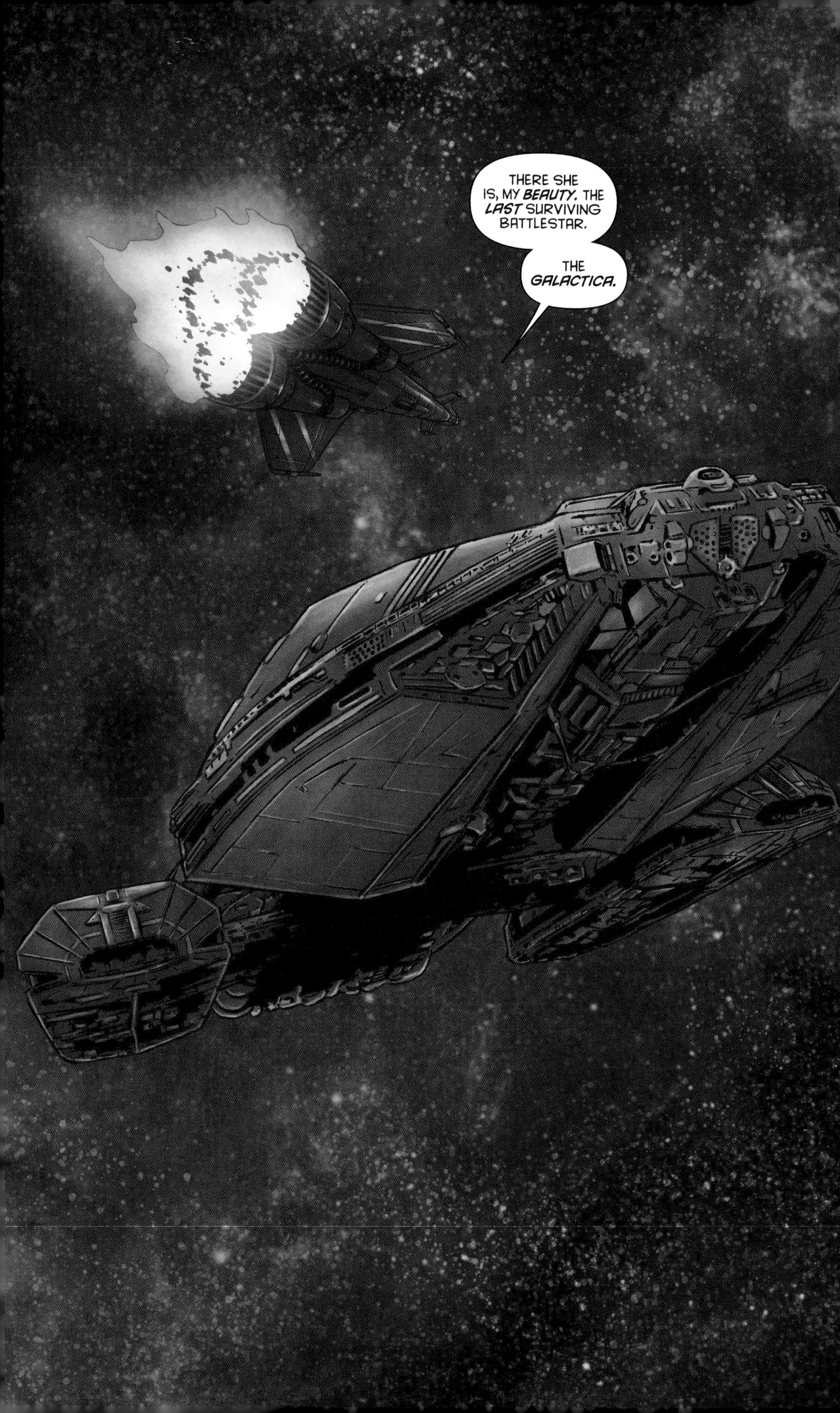
THERE SHE IS, MY *BEAUTY.* THE *LAST* SURVIVING BATTLESTAR.
THE *GALACTICA.*

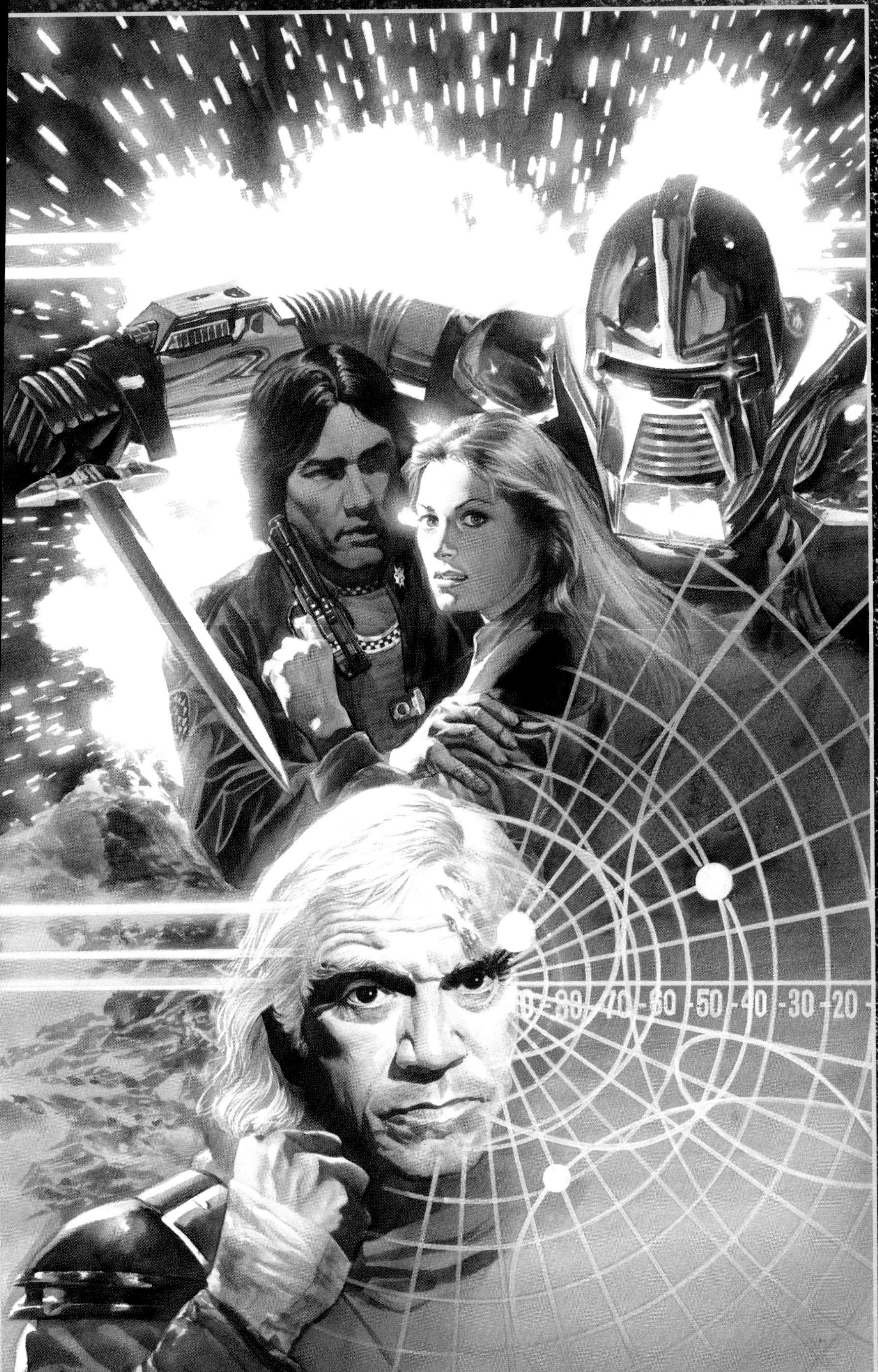
-80 -70 -60 -50 -40 -30 -20

ISSUE 4

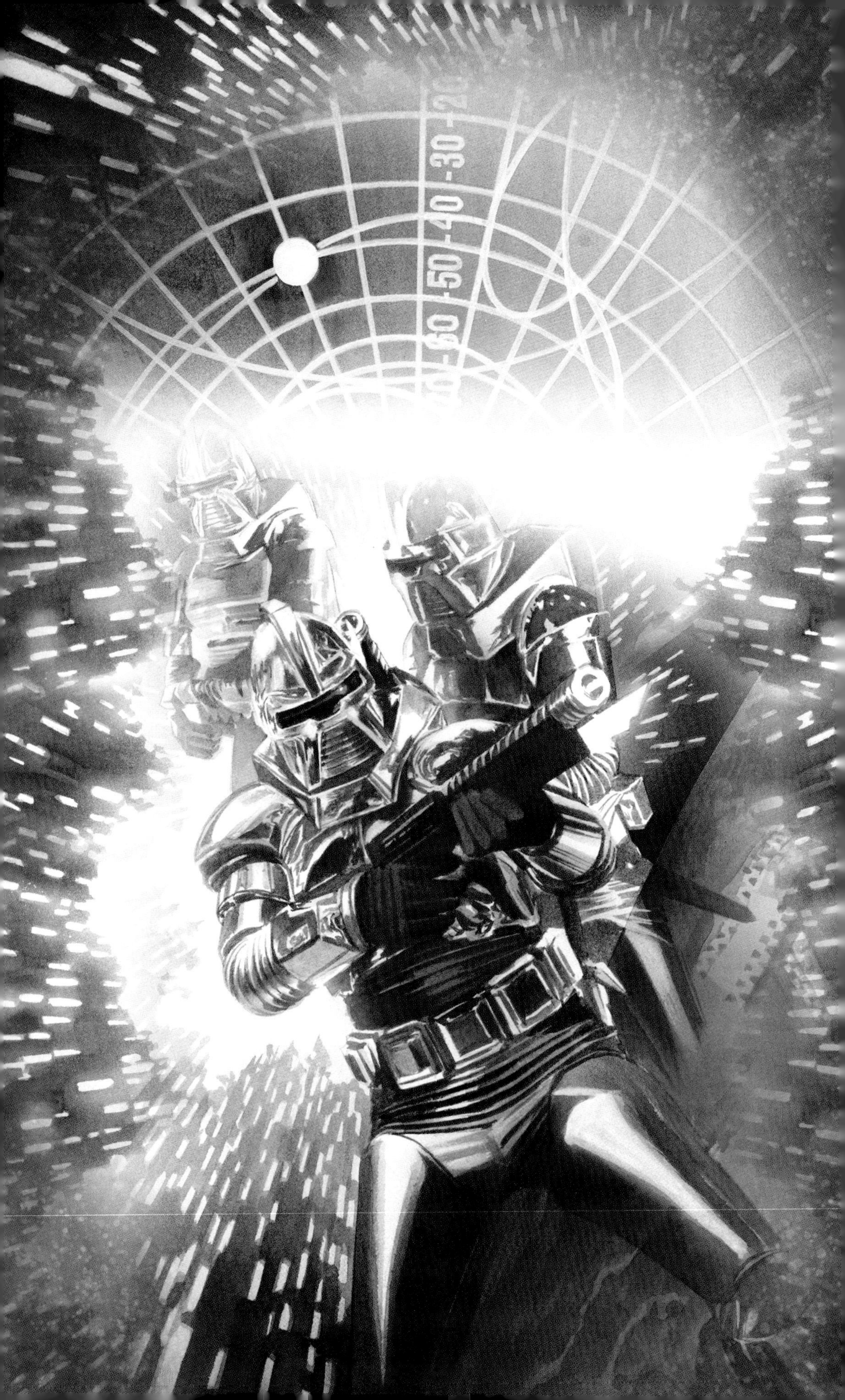

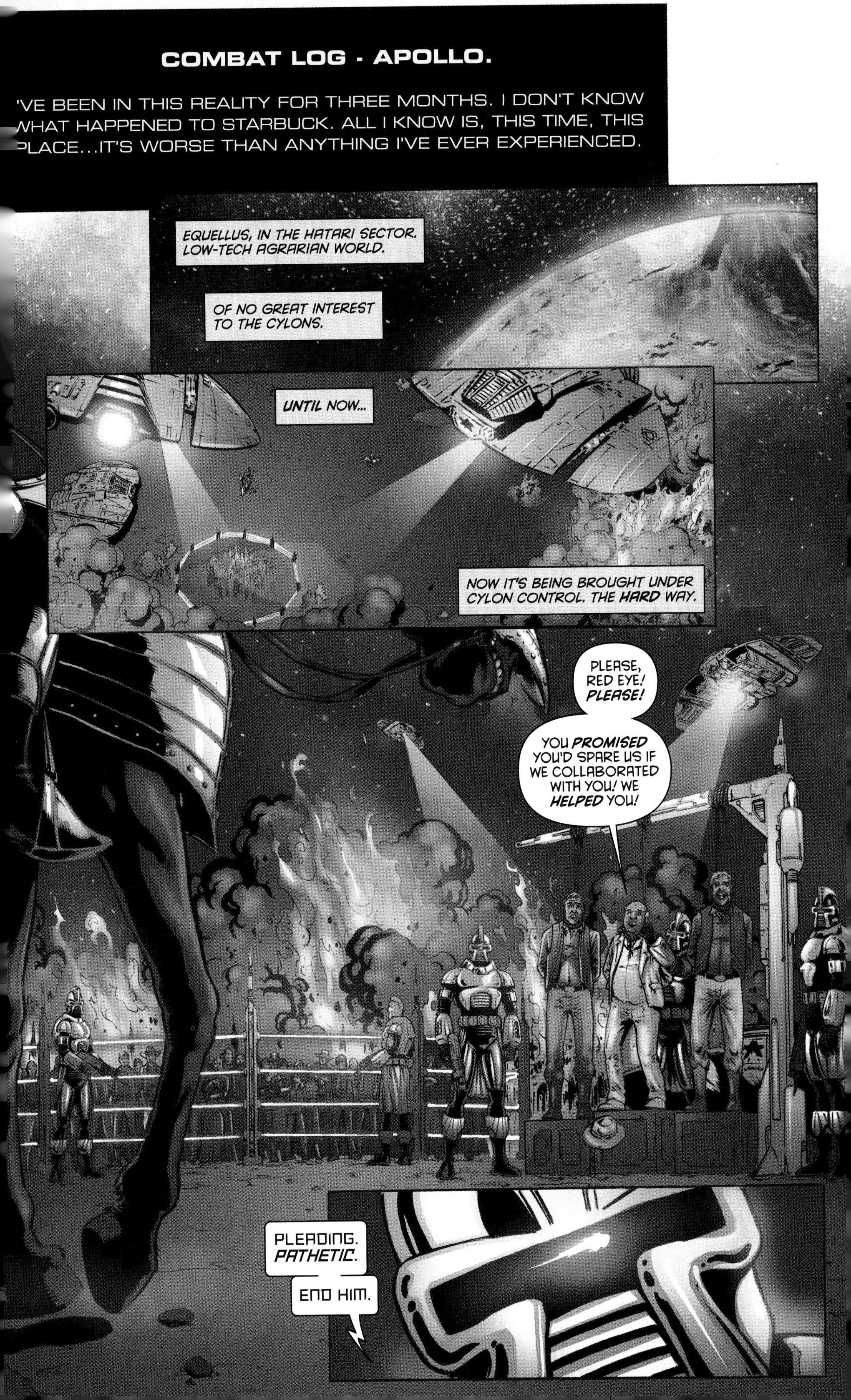
COMBAT LOG - APOLLO.
'VE BEEN IN THIS REALITY FOR THREE MONTHS. I DON'T KNOW WHAT HAPPENED TO STARBUCK. ALL I KNOW IS, THIS TIME, THIS PLACE...IT'S WORSE THAN ANYTHING I'VE EVER EXPERIENCED.
EQUELLUS, IN THE HATARI SECTOR. LOW-TECH AGRARIAN WORLD.
OF NO GREAT INTEREST TO THE CYLONS.
UNTIL NOW...
NOW IT'S BEING BROUGHT UNDER CYLON CONTROL. THE HARD WAY.
PLEASE, RED EYE! PLEASE!
YOU PROMISED YOU'D SPARE US IF WE COLLABORATED WITH YOU! WE HELPED YOU!
PLEADING. PATHETIC.
END HIM.

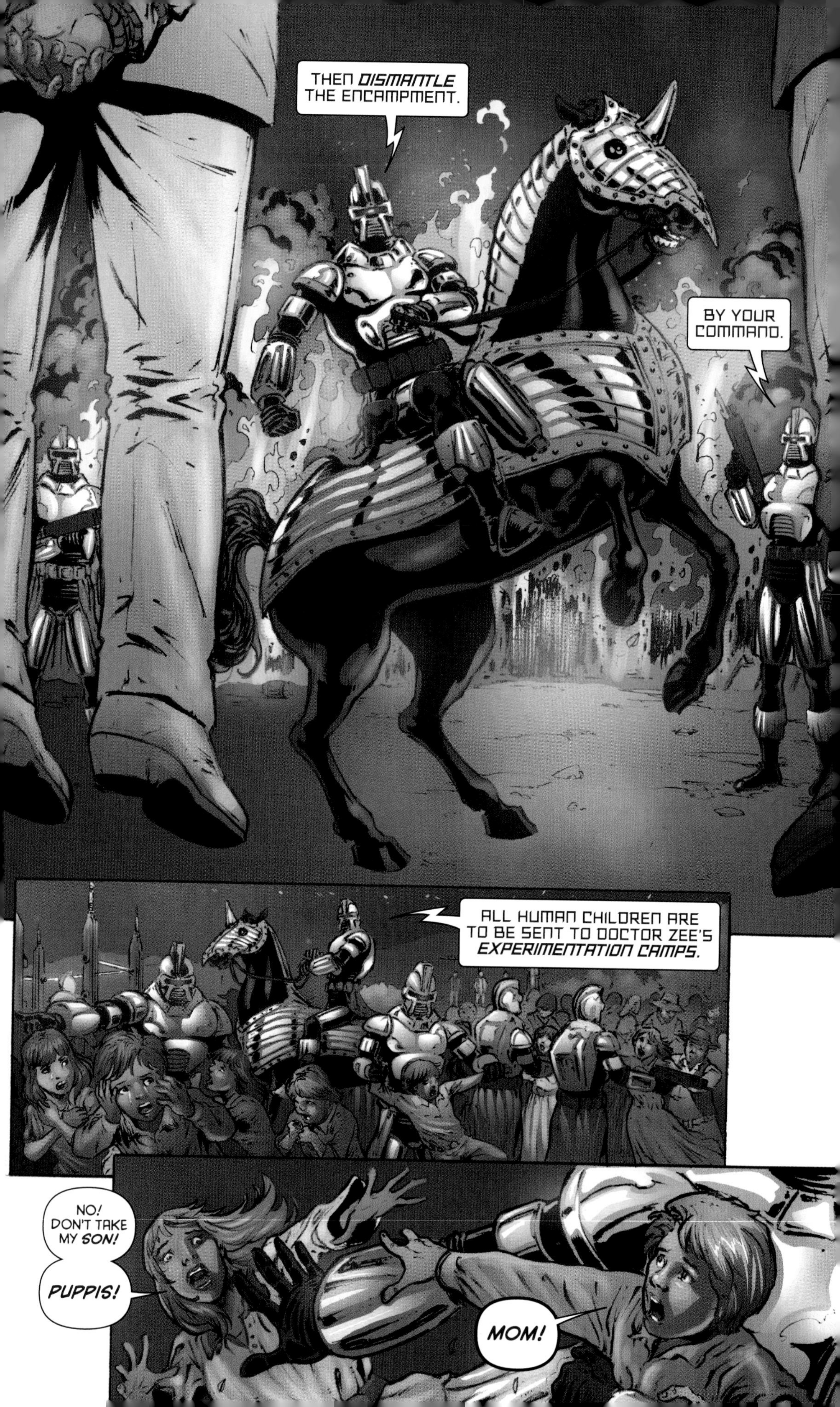
THEN *DISMANTLE* THE ENCAMPMENT.
BY YOUR COMMAND.
ALL HUMAN CHILDREN ARE TO BE SENT TO DOCTOR ZEE'S *EXPERIMENTATION CAMPS.*
NO! DON'T TAKE MY *SON!*
PUPPIS!
MOM!

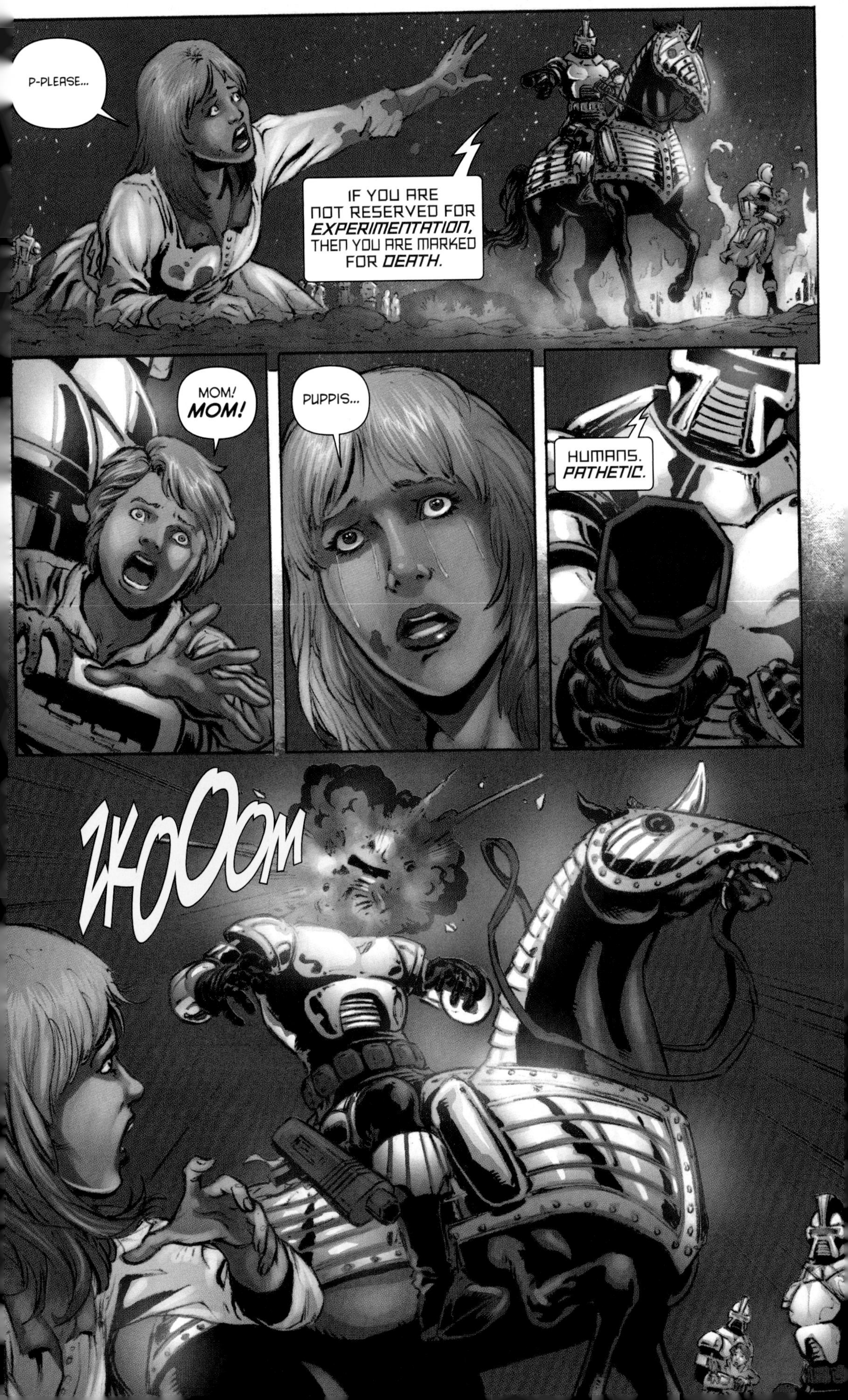
P-PLEASE...
IF YOU ARE NOT RESERVED FOR *EXPERIMENTATION*, THEN YOU ARE MARKED FOR *DEATH*.
MOM! **MOM!**
PUPPIS...
HUMANS. *PATHETIC*.
ZKOOOOM

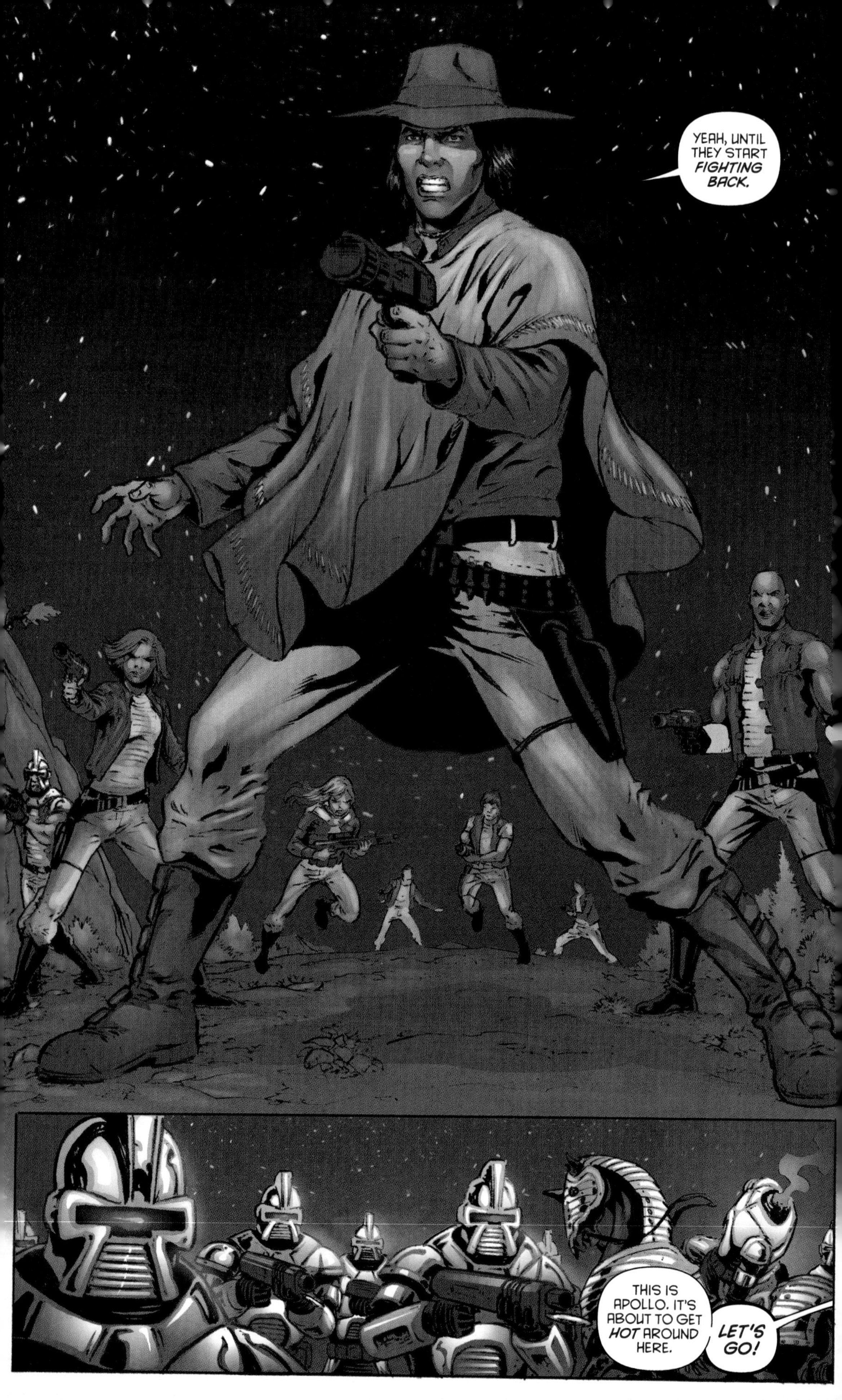
YEAH, UNTIL THEY START *FIGHTING BACK.*
THIS IS APOLLO. IT'S ABOUT TO GET *HOT* AROUND HERE.
LET'S GO!

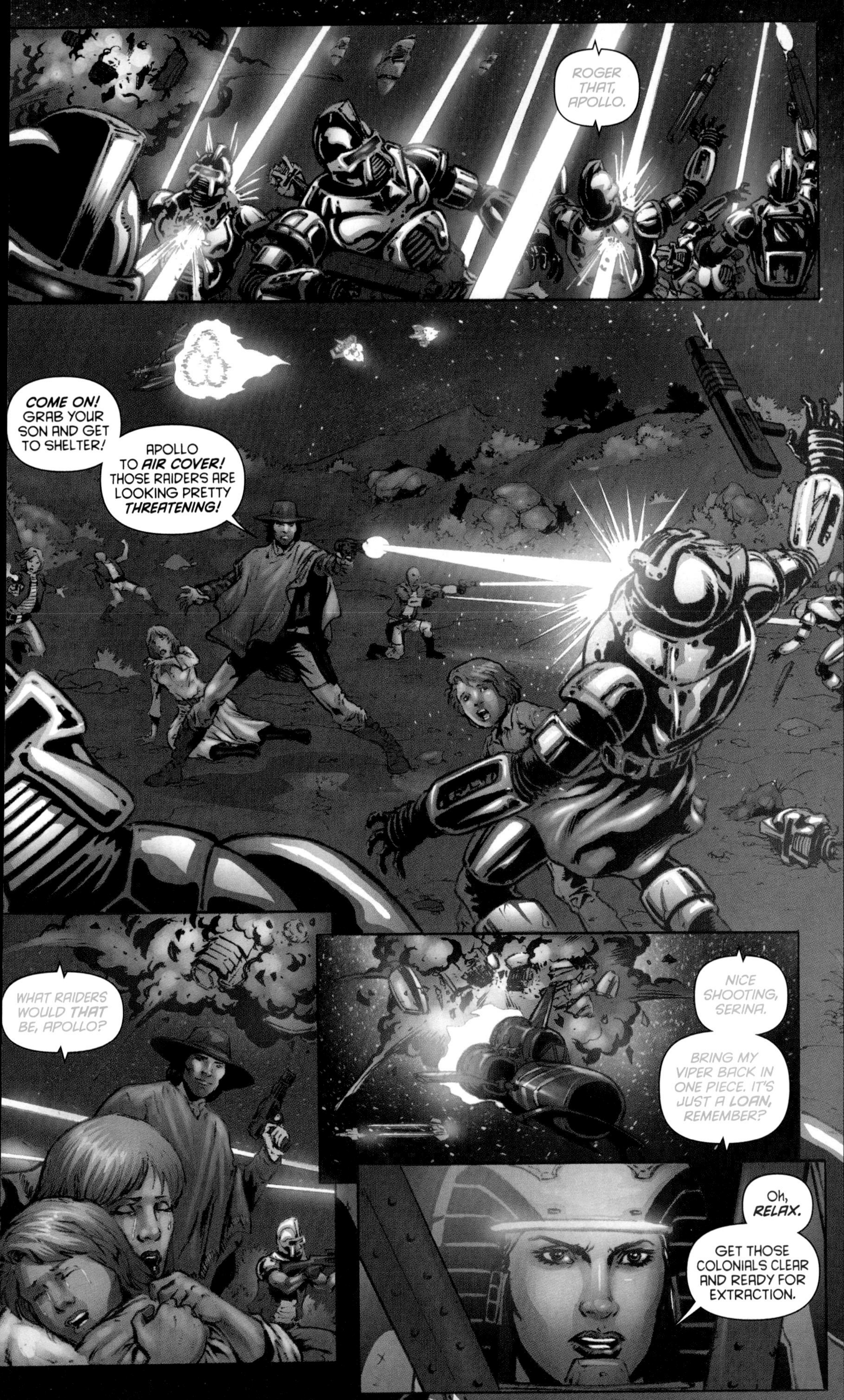
ROGER THAT, APOLLO.
COME ON! GRAB YOUR SON AND GET TO SHELTER!
APOLLO TO AIR COVER! THOSE RAIDERS ARE LOOKING PRETTY THREATENING!
WHAT RAIDERS WOULD THAT BE, APOLLO?
NICE SHOOTING, SERINA.
BRING MY VIPER BACK IN ONE PIECE. IT'S JUST A LOAN, REMEMBER?
Oh, RELAX.
GET THOSE COLONIALS CLEAR AND READY FOR EXTRACTION.

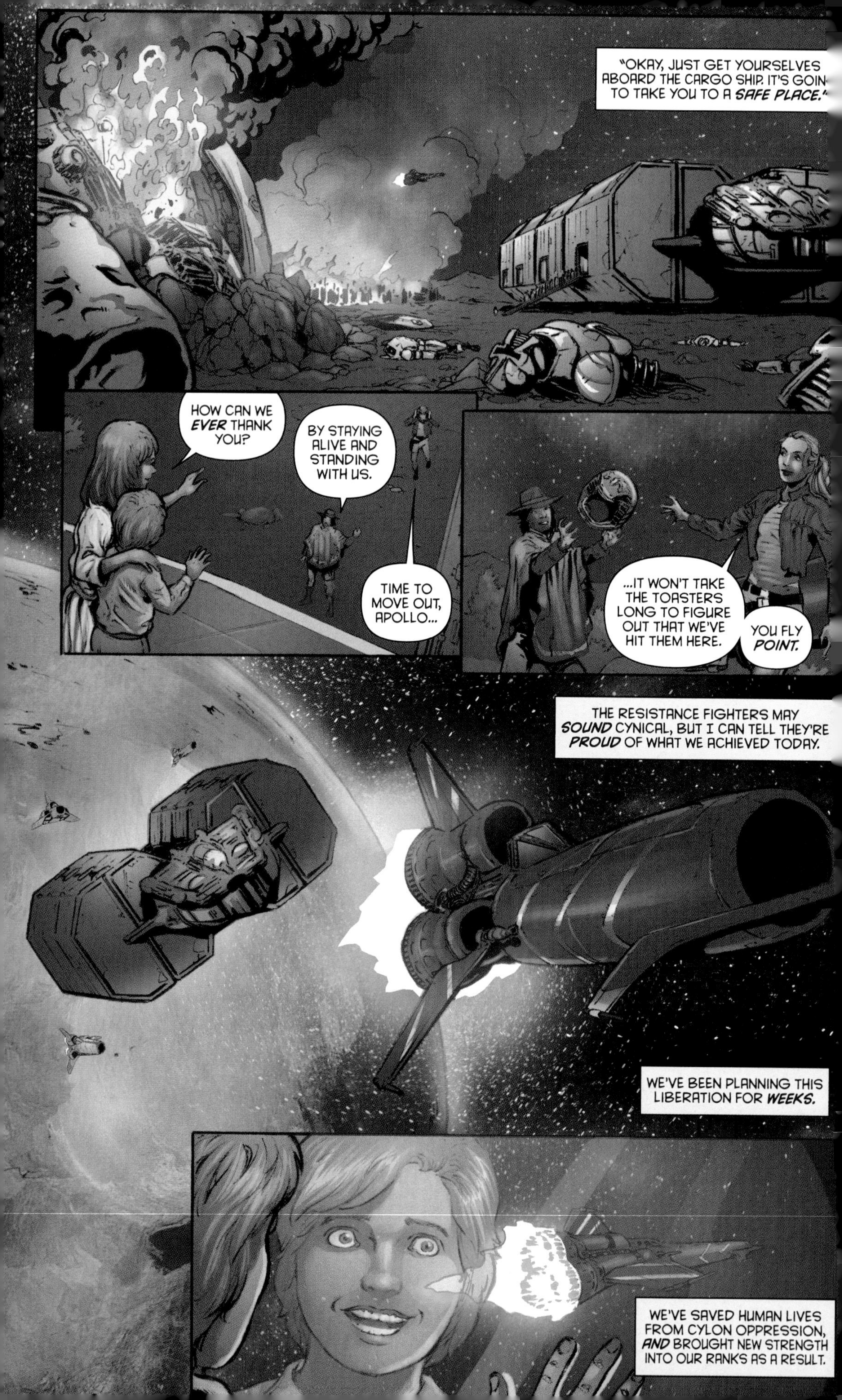
"OKAY, JUST GET YOURSELVES ABOARD THE CARGO SHIP. IT'S GOIN TO TAKE YOU TO A *SAFE PLACE.*"
HOW CAN WE *EVER* THANK YOU?
BY STAYING ALIVE AND STANDING WITH US.
TIME TO MOVE OUT, APOLLO...
...IT WON'T TAKE THE TOASTERS LONG TO FIGURE OUT THAT WE'VE HIT THEM HERE.
YOU FLY *POINT.*
THE RESISTANCE FIGHTERS MAY *SOUND* CYNICAL, BUT I CAN TELL THEY'RE *PROUD* OF WHAT WE ACHIEVED TODAY.
WE'VE BEEN PLANNING THIS LIBERATION FOR *WEEKS.*
WE'VE SAVED HUMAN LIVES FROM CYLON OPPRESSION, *AND* BROUGHT NEW STRENGTH INTO OUR RANKS AS A RESULT.

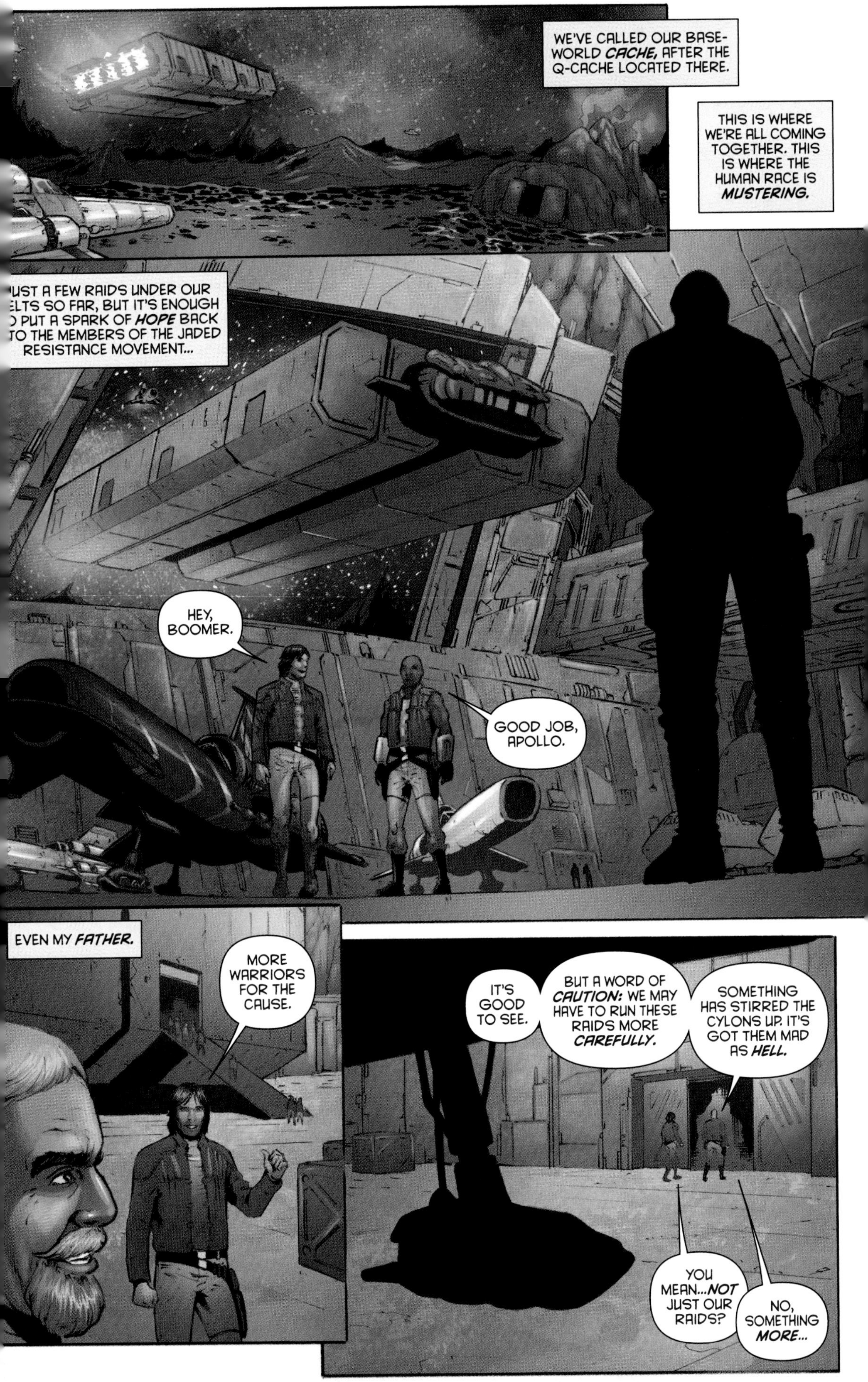

WE'VE CALLED OUR BASE-WORLD CACHE, AFTER THE Q-CACHE LOCATED THERE.
THIS IS WHERE WE'RE ALL COMING TOGETHER. THIS IS WHERE THE HUMAN RACE IS MUSTERING.
UST A FEW RAIDS UNDER OUR ELTS SO FAR, BUT IT'S ENOUGH O PUT A SPARK OF HOPE BACK TO THE MEMBERS OF THE JADED RESISTANCE MOVEMENT...
HEY, BOOMER.
GOOD JOB, APOLLO.
EVEN MY FATHER.
MORE WARRIORS FOR THE CAUSE.
IT'S GOOD TO SEE.
BUT A WORD OF CAUTION: WE MAY HAVE TO RUN THESE RAIDS MORE CAREFULLY.
SOMETHING HAS STIRRED THE CYLONS UP. IT'S GOT THEM MAD AS HELL.
YOU MEAN...NOT JUST OUR RAIDS?
NO, SOMETHING MORE...

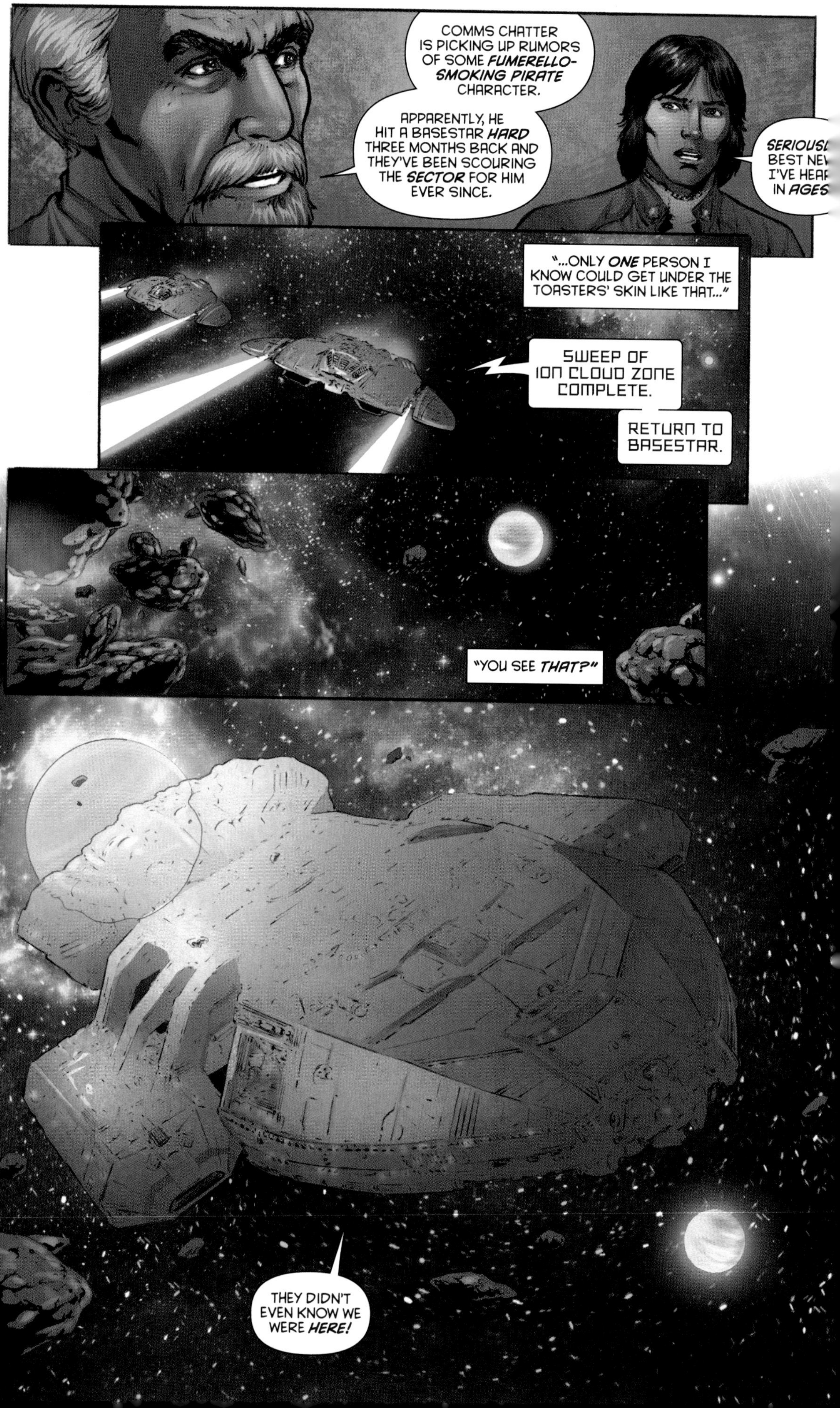
COMMS CHATTER IS PICKING UP RUMORS OF SOME *FUMERELLO-SMOKING PIRATE* CHARACTER.
APPARENTLY, HE HIT A BASESTAR *HARD* THREE MONTHS BACK AND THEY'VE BEEN SCOURING THE *SECTOR* FOR HIM EVER SINCE.
"...ONLY *ONE* PERSON I KNOW COULD GET UNDER THE TOASTERS' SKIN LIKE THAT..."
SWEEP OF ION CLOUD ZONE COMPLETE.
RETURN TO BASESTAR.
"YOU SEE *THAT?*"
THEY DIDN'T EVEN KNOW WE WERE *HERE!*

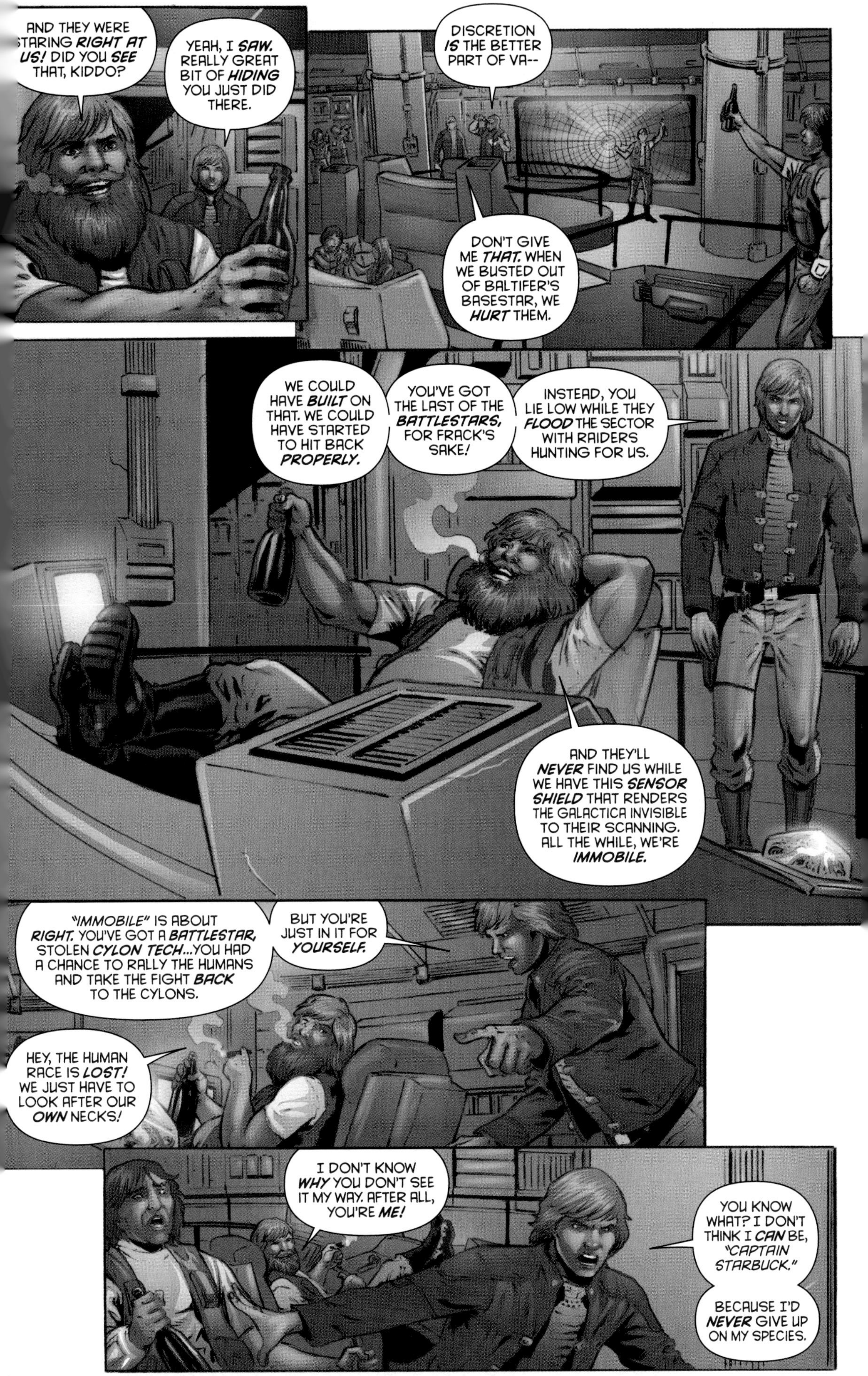
AND THEY WERE STARING RIGHT AT US! DID YOU SEE THAT, KIDDO?
YEAH, I SAW. REALLY GREAT BIT OF HIDING YOU JUST DID THERE.
DISCRETION IS THE BETTER PART OF VA--
DON'T GIVE ME THAT. WHEN WE BUSTED OUT OF BALTIFER'S BASESTAR, WE HURT THEM.
WE COULD HAVE BUILT ON THAT. WE COULD HAVE STARTED TO HIT BACK PROPERLY.
YOU'VE GOT THE LAST OF THE BATTLESTARS, FOR FRACK'S SAKE!
INSTEAD, YOU LIE LOW WHILE THEY FLOOD THE SECTOR WITH RAIDERS HUNTING FOR US.
AND THEY'LL NEVER FIND US WHILE WE HAVE THIS SENSOR SHIELD THAT RENDERS THE GALACTICA INVISIBLE TO THEIR SCANNING. ALL THE WHILE, WE'RE IMMOBILE.
"IMMOBILE" IS ABOUT RIGHT. YOU'VE GOT A BATTLESTAR, STOLEN CYLON TECH...YOU HAD A CHANCE TO RALLY THE HUMANS AND TAKE THE FIGHT BACK TO THE CYLONS.
BUT YOU'RE JUST IN IT FOR YOURSELF.
HEY, THE HUMAN RACE IS LOST! WE JUST HAVE TO LOOK AFTER OUR OWN NECKS!
I DON'T KNOW WHY YOU DON'T SEE IT MY WAY. AFTER ALL, YOU'RE ME!
YOU KNOW WHAT? I DON'T THINK I CAN BE, "CAPTAIN STARBUCK."
BECAUSE I'D NEVER GIVE UP ON MY SPECIES.

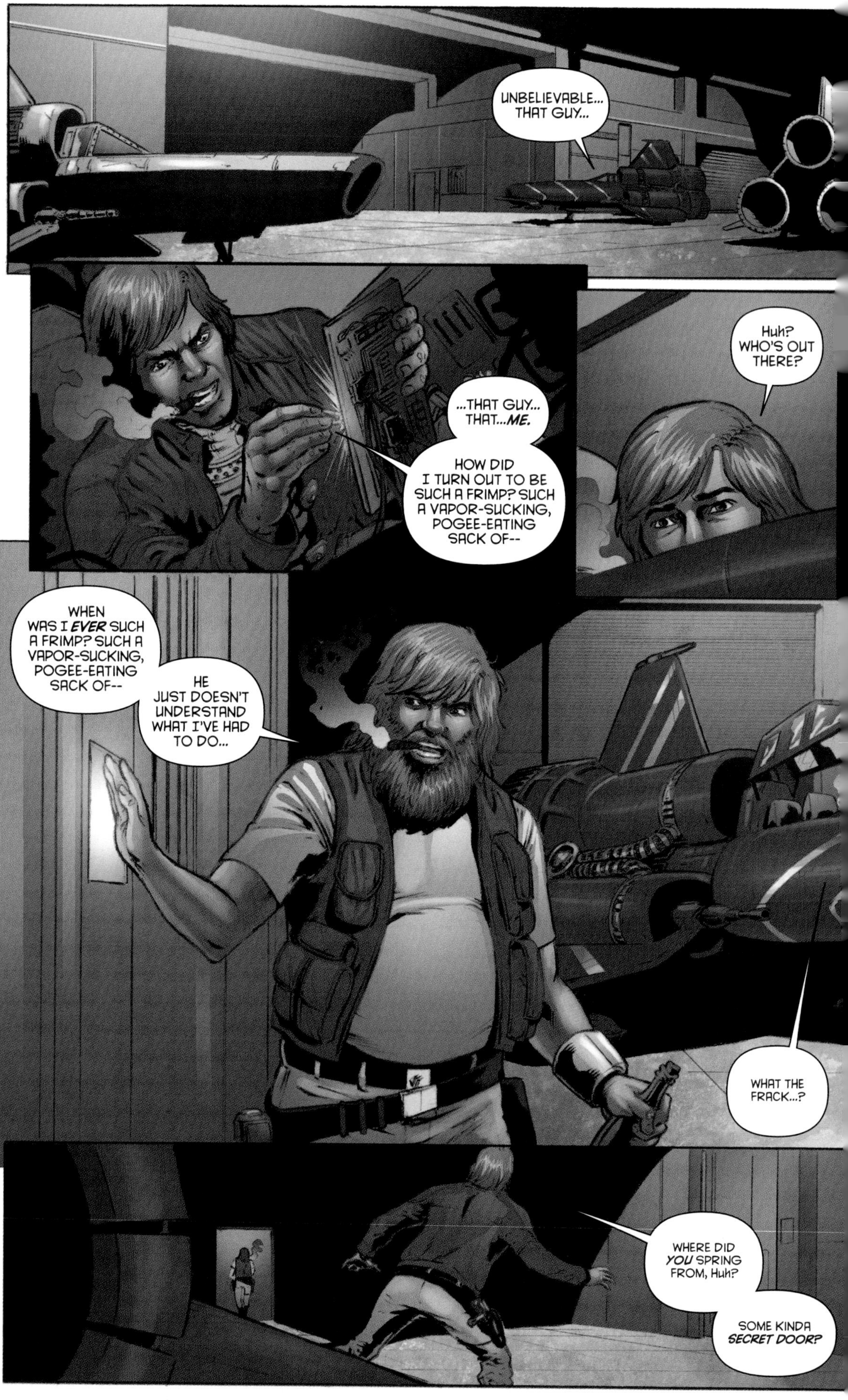
UNBELIEVABLE... THAT GUY...
...THAT GUY... THAT...*ME.*
HOW DID I TURN OUT TO BE SUCH A FRIMP? SUCH A VAPOR-SUCKING, POGEE-EATING SACK OF--
Huh? WHO'S OUT THERE?
WHEN WAS I *EVER* SUCH A FRIMP? SUCH A VAPOR-SUCKING, POGEE-EATING SACK OF--
HE JUST DOESN'T UNDERSTAND WHAT I'VE HAD TO DO...
WHAT THE FRACK...?
WHERE DID *YOU* SPRING FROM, Huh?
SOME KINDA *SECRET DOOR?*

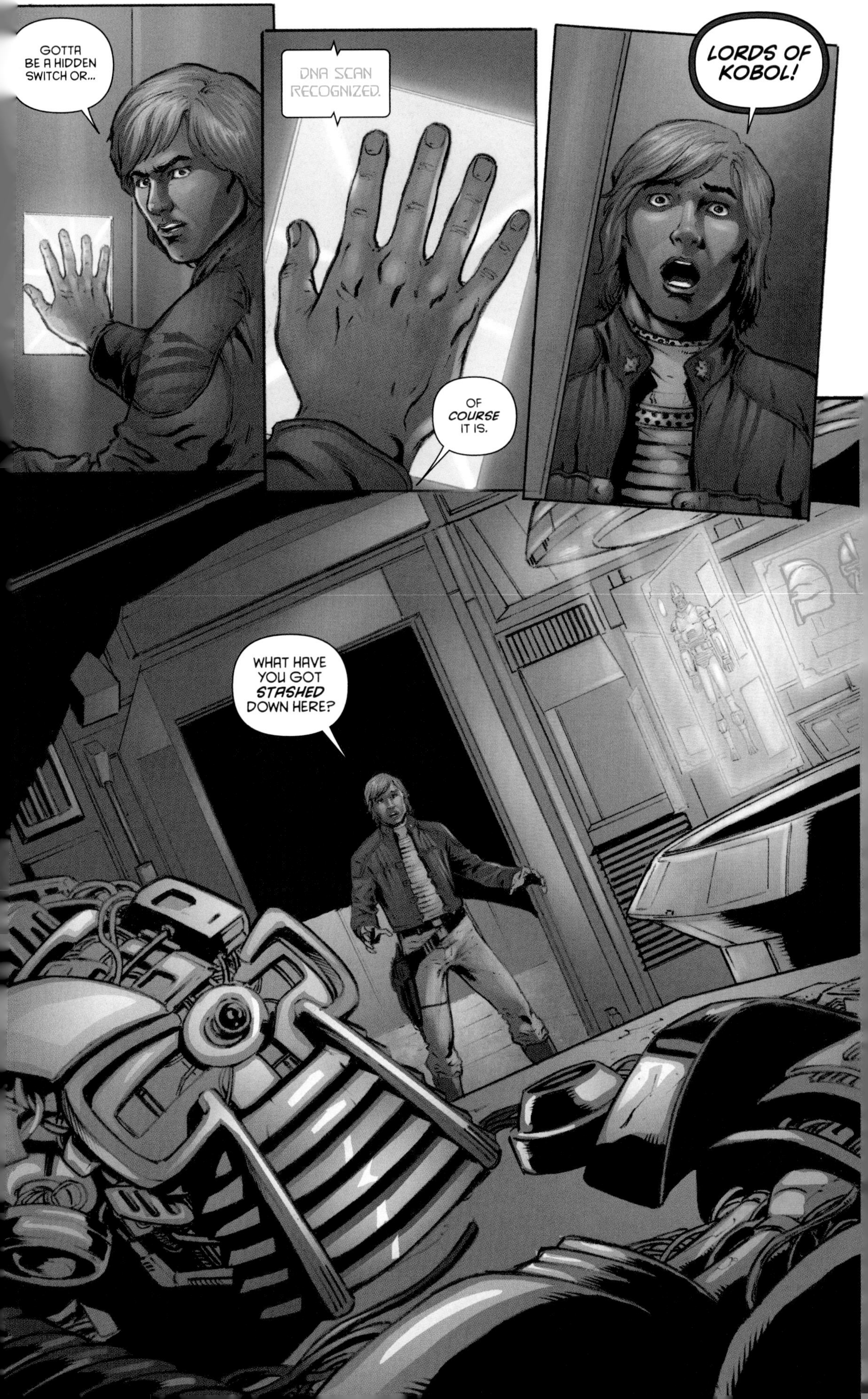
GOTTA BE A HIDDEN SWITCH OR...
DNA SCAN RECOGNIZED.
OF *COURSE* IT IS.
LORDS OF KOBOL!
WHAT HAVE YOU GOT *STASHED* DOWN HERE?

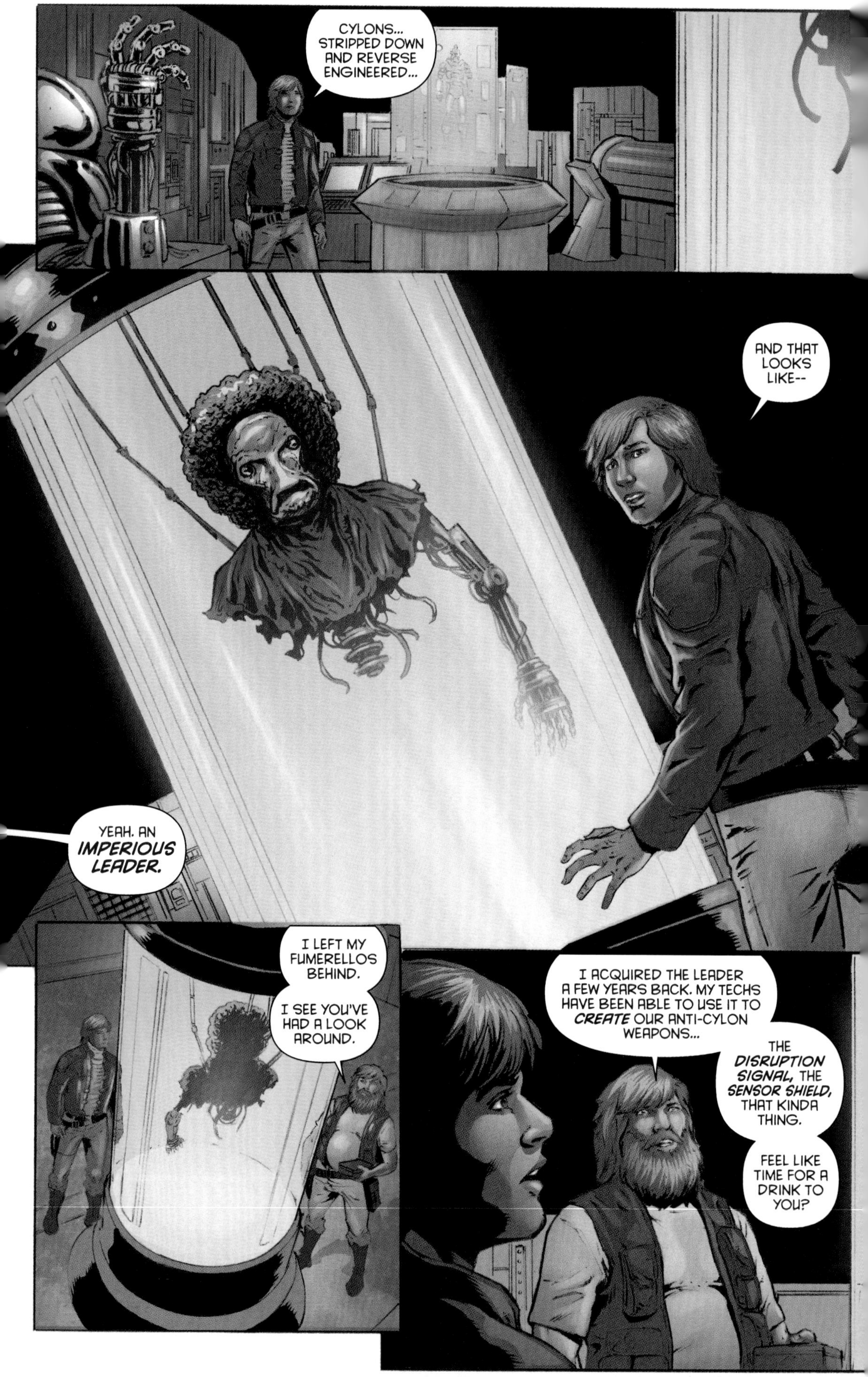
CYLONS... STRIPPED DOWN AND REVERSE ENGINEERED...
AND THAT LOOKS LIKE--
YEAH. AN *IMPERIOUS LEADER.*
I LEFT MY FUMERELLOS BEHIND.
I SEE YOU'VE HAD A LOOK AROUND.
I ACQUIRED THE LEADER A FEW YEARS BACK. MY TECHS HAVE BEEN ABLE TO USE IT TO *CREATE* OUR ANTI-CYLON WEAPONS...
THE *DISRUPTION SIGNAL,* THE *SENSOR SHIELD,* THAT KINDA THING.
FEEL LIKE TIME FOR A DRINK TO YOU?

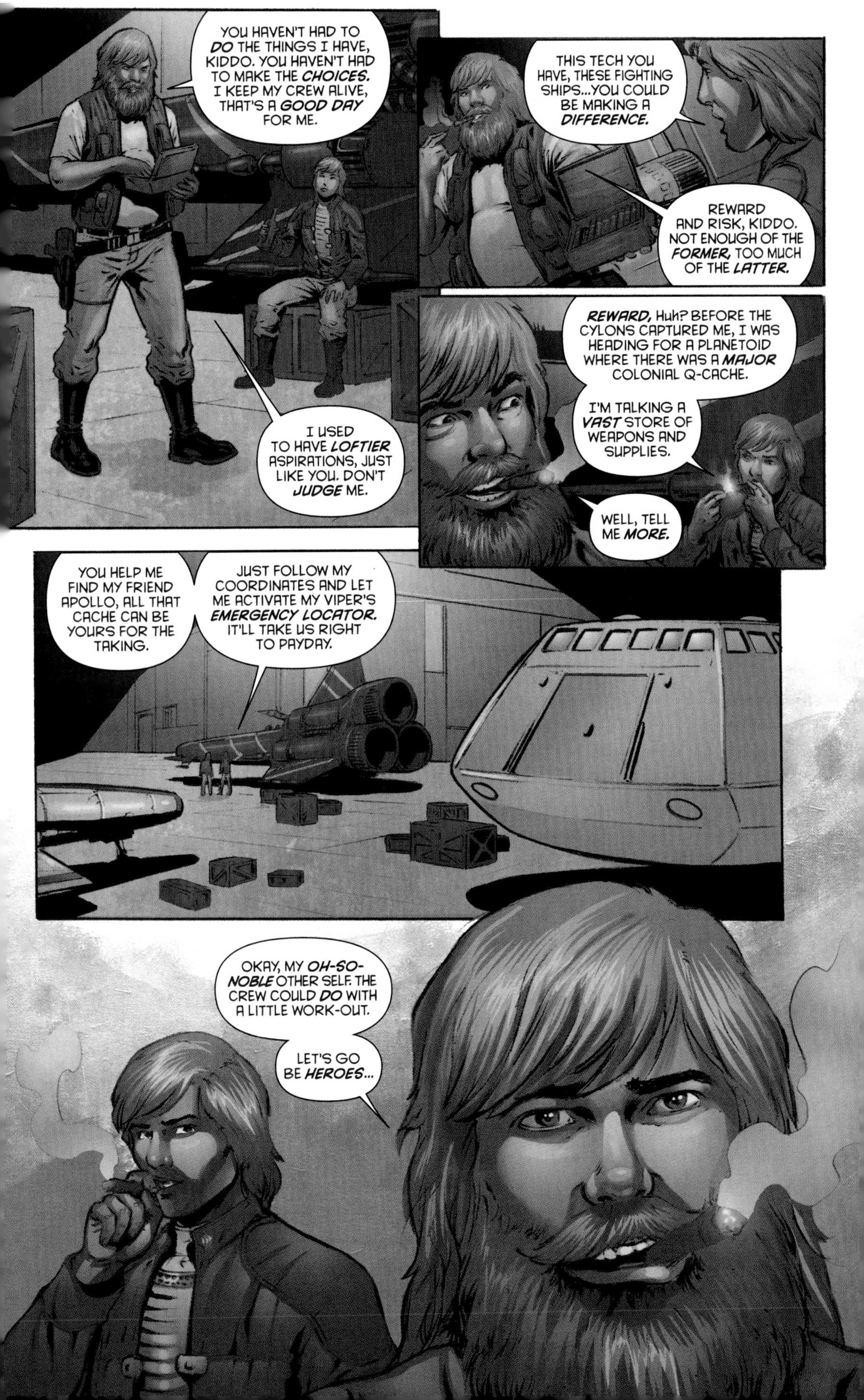
YOU HAVEN'T HAD TO DO THE THINGS I HAVE, KIDDO. YOU HAVEN'T HAD TO MAKE THE CHOICES. I KEEP MY CREW ALIVE, THAT'S A GOOD DAY FOR ME.
I USED TO HAVE LOFTIER ASPIRATIONS, JUST LIKE YOU. DON'T JUDGE ME.
THIS TECH YOU HAVE, THESE FIGHTING SHIPS...YOU COULD BE MAKING A DIFFERENCE.
REWARD AND RISK, KIDDO. NOT ENOUGH OF THE FORMER, TOO MUCH OF THE LATTER.
REWARD, Huh? BEFORE THE CYLONS CAPTURED ME, I WAS HEADING FOR A PLANETOID WHERE THERE WAS A MAJOR COLONIAL Q-CACHE.
I'M TALKING A VAST STORE OF WEAPONS AND SUPPLIES.
WELL, TELL ME MORE.
YOU HELP ME FIND MY FRIEND APOLLO, ALL THAT CACHE CAN BE YOURS FOR THE TAKING.
JUST FOLLOW MY COORDINATES AND LET ME ACTIVATE MY VIPER'S EMERGENCY LOCATOR. IT'LL TAKE US RIGHT TO PAYDAY.
OKAY, MY OH-SO-NOBLE OTHER SELF. THE CREW COULD DO WITH A LITTLE WORK-OUT.
LET'S GO BE HEROES...

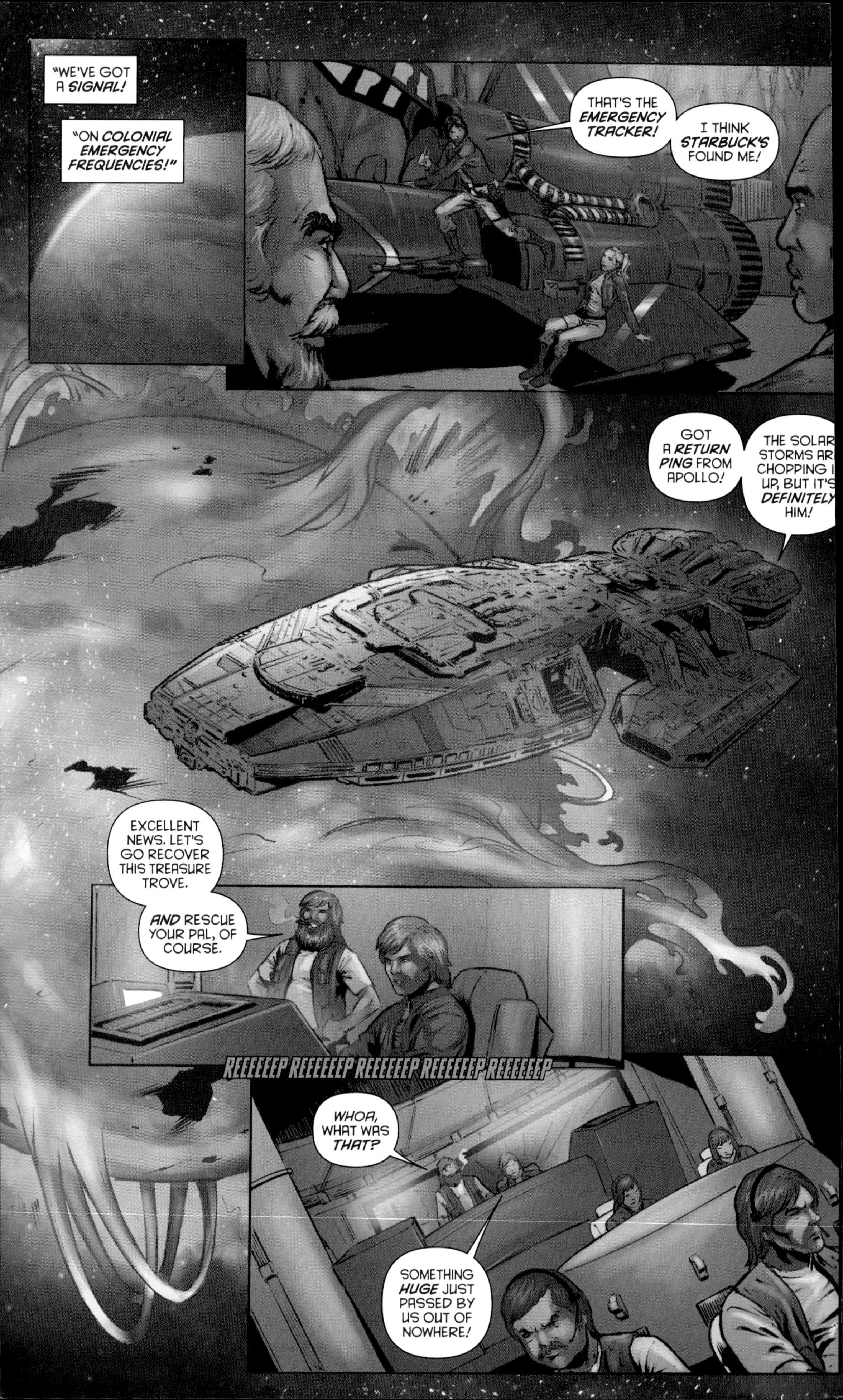

"WE'VE GOT A SIGNAL!"
"ON COLONIAL EMERGENCY FREQUENCIES!"
THAT'S THE EMERGENCY TRACKER!
I THINK STARBUCK'S FOUND ME!
GOT A RETURN PING FROM APOLLO!
THE SOLAR STORMS AR CHOPPING I UP, BUT IT'S DEFINITELY HIM!
EXCELLENT NEWS. LET'S GO RECOVER THIS TREASURE TROVE.
AND RESCUE YOUR PAL, OF COURSE.
REEEEEEP REEEEEEP REEEEEEP REEEEEEP REEEEEEP
WHOA, WHAT WAS THAT?
SOMETHING HUGE JUST PASSED BY US OUT OF NOWHERE!

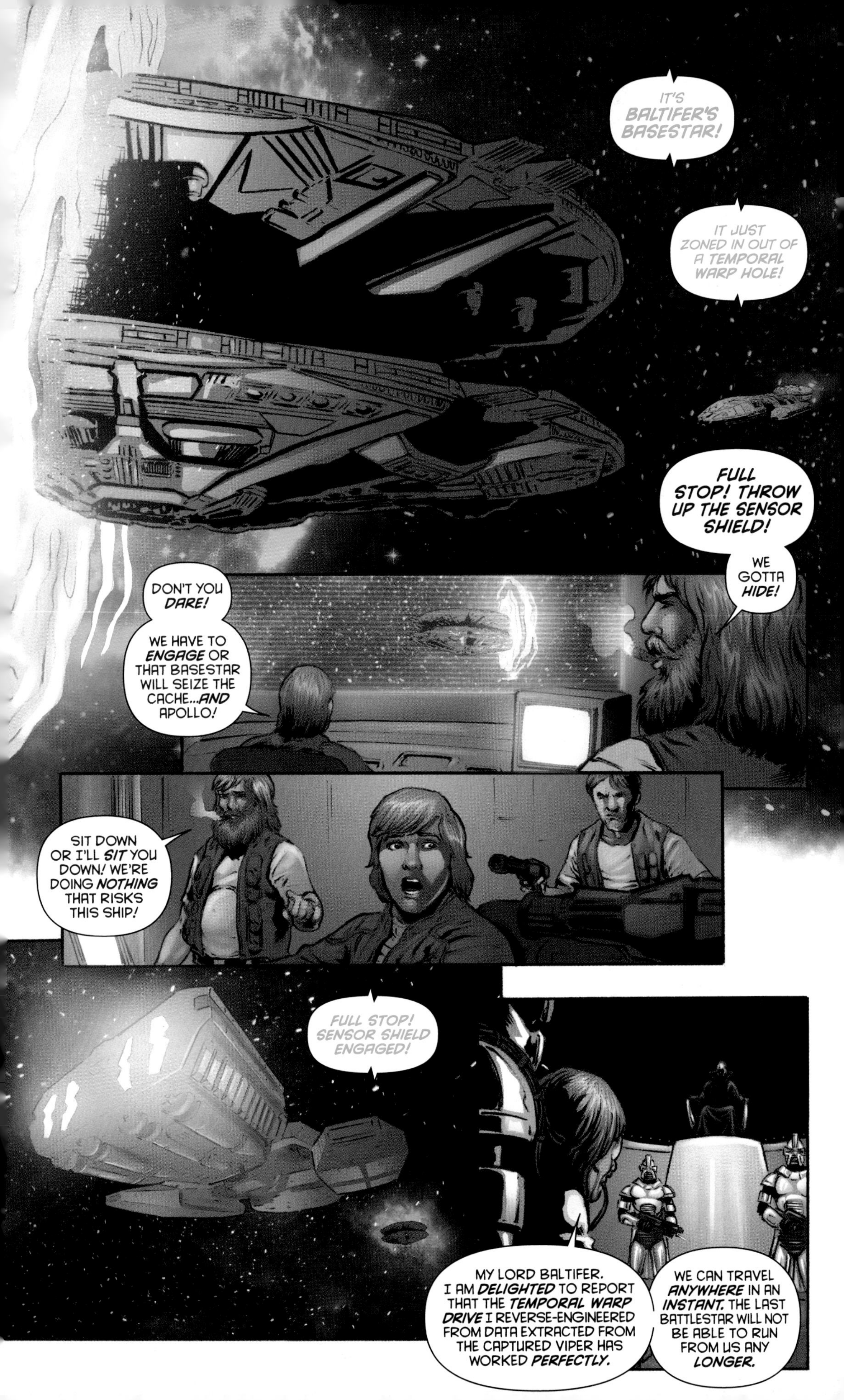
IT'S BALTIFER'S BASESTAR!
IT JUST ZONED IN OUT OF A TEMPORAL WARP HOLE!
FULL STOP! THROW UP THE SENSOR SHIELD!
WE GOTTA HIDE!
DON'T YOU DARE!
WE HAVE TO ENGAGE OR THAT BASESTAR WILL SEIZE THE CACHE...AND APOLLO!
SIT DOWN OR I'LL SIT YOU DOWN! WE'RE DOING NOTHING THAT RISKS THIS SHIP!
FULL STOP! SENSOR SHIELD ENGAGED!
MY LORD BALTIFER. I AM DELIGHTED TO REPORT THAT THE TEMPORAL WARP DRIVE I REVERSE-ENGINEERED FROM DATA EXTRACTED FROM THE CAPTURED VIPER HAS WORKED PERFECTLY.
WE CAN TRAVEL ANYWHERE IN AN INSTANT. THE LAST BATTLESTAR WILL NOT BE ABLE TO RUN FROM US ANY LONGER.

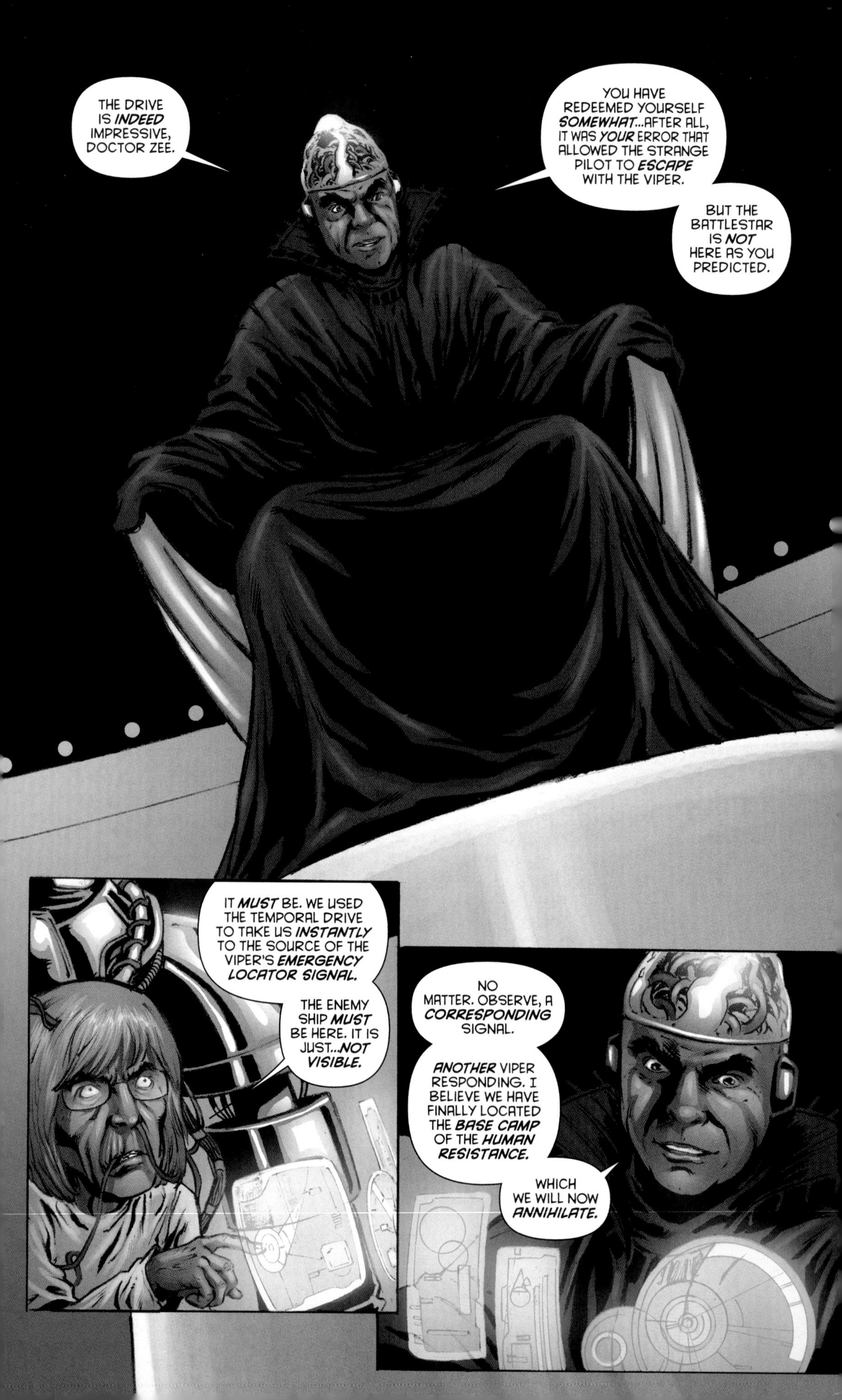
THE DRIVE IS *INDEED* IMPRESSIVE, DOCTOR ZEE.
YOU HAVE REDEEMED YOURSELF *SOMEWHAT*...AFTER ALL, IT WAS *YOUR* ERROR THAT ALLOWED THE STRANGE PILOT TO *ESCAPE* WITH THE VIPER.
BUT THE BATTLESTAR IS *NOT* HERE AS YOU PREDICTED.
IT *MUST* BE. WE USED THE TEMPORAL DRIVE TO TAKE US *INSTANTLY* TO THE SOURCE OF THE VIPER'S *EMERGENCY LOCATOR SIGNAL.*
THE ENEMY SHIP *MUST* BE HERE. IT IS JUST...*NOT VISIBLE.*
NO MATTER. OBSERVE, A *CORRESPONDING* SIGNAL.
ANOTHER VIPER RESPONDING. I BELIEVE WE HAVE FINALLY LOCATED THE *BASE CAMP* OF THE *HUMAN RESISTANCE.*
WHICH WE WILL NOW *ANNIHILATE.*

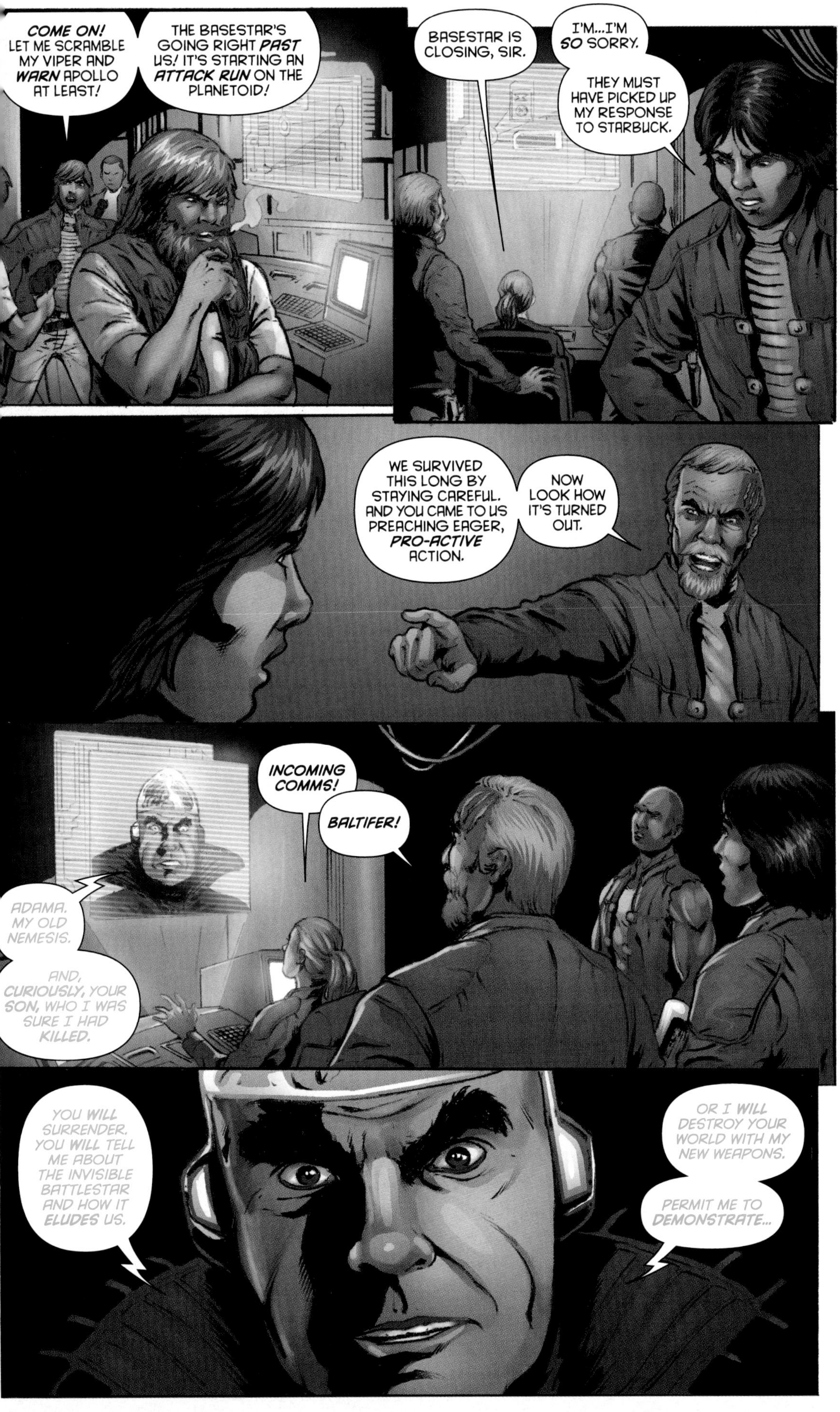
COME ON! LET ME SCRAMBLE MY VIPER AND WARN APOLLO AT LEAST!
THE BASESTAR'S GOING RIGHT PAST US! IT'S STARTING AN ATTACK RUN ON THE PLANETOID!
BASESTAR IS CLOSING, SIR.
I'M...I'M SO SORRY.
THEY MUST HAVE PICKED UP MY RESPONSE TO STARBUCK.
WE SURVIVED THIS LONG BY STAYING CAREFUL. AND YOU CAME TO US PREACHING EAGER, PRO-ACTIVE ACTION.
NOW LOOK HOW IT'S TURNED OUT.
INCOMING COMMS!
BALTIFER!
ADAMA. MY OLD NEMESIS.
AND, CURIOUSLY, YOUR SON, WHO I WAS SURE I HAD KILLED.
YOU WILL SURRENDER. YOU WILL TELL ME ABOUT THE INVISIBLE BATTLESTAR AND HOW IT ELUDES US.
OR I WILL DESTROY YOUR WORLD WITH MY NEW WEAPONS.
PERMIT ME TO DEMONSTRATE...

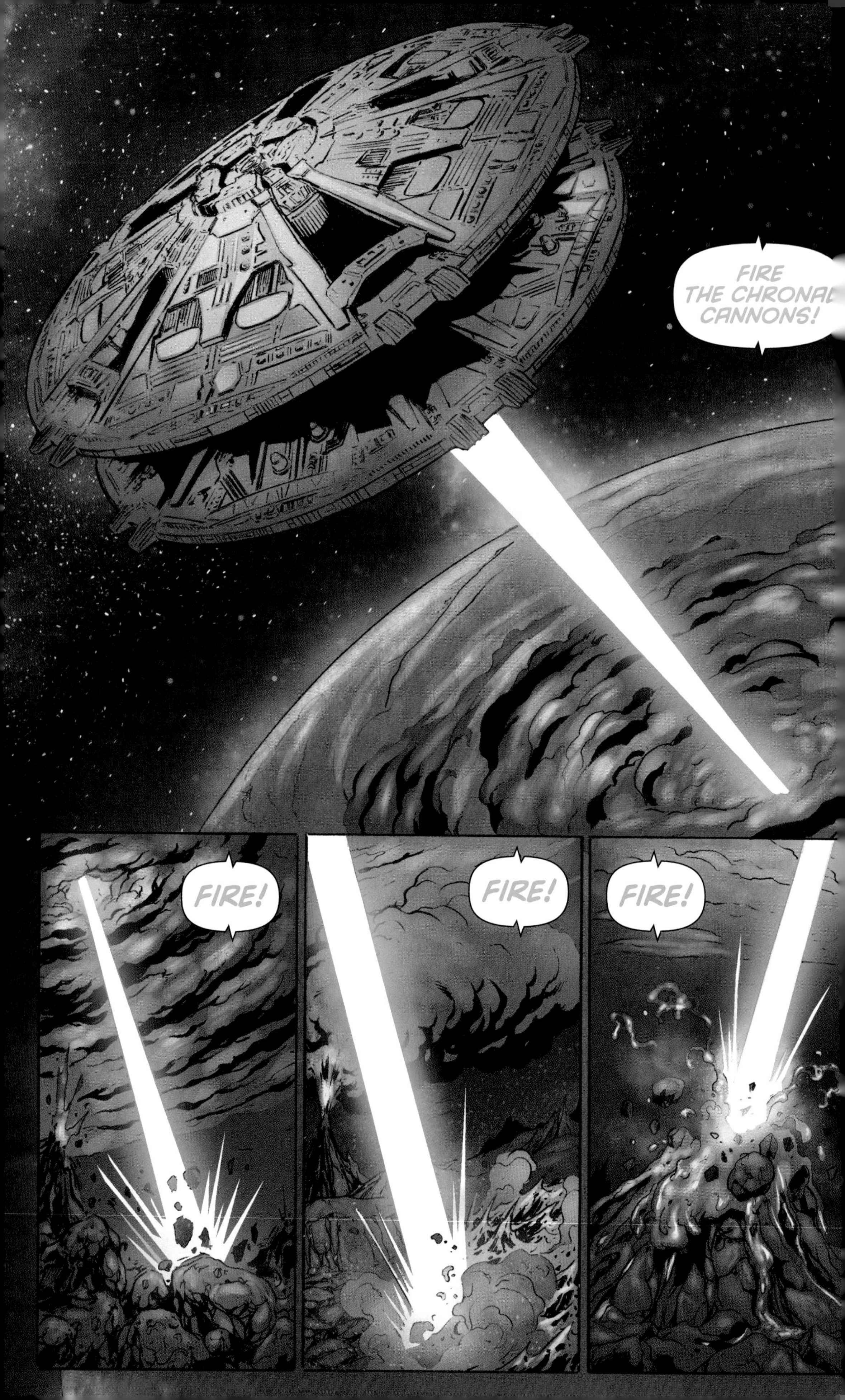
FIRE THE CHRONAL CANNONS!
FIRE!
FIRE!
FIRE!

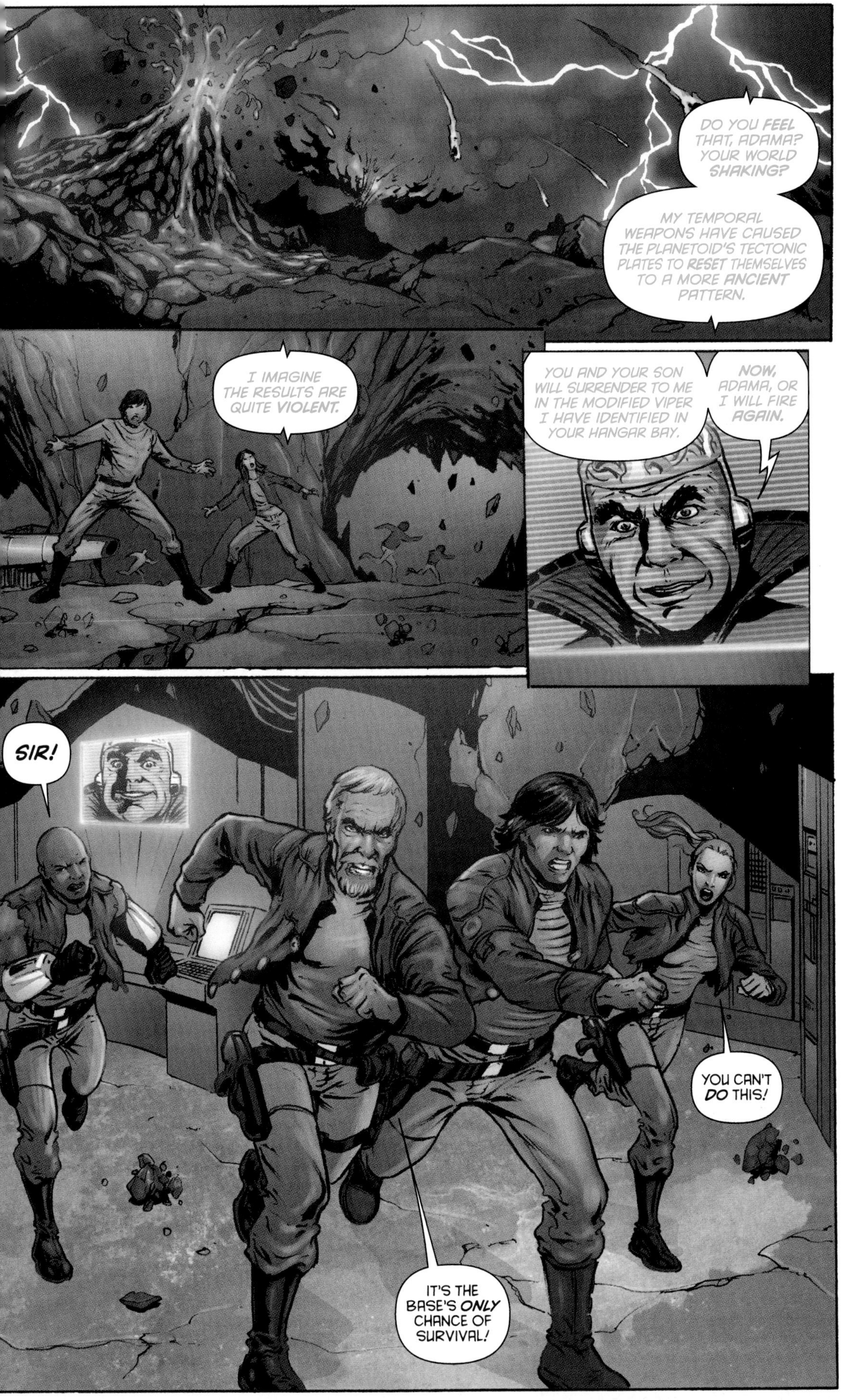
DO YOU FEEL THAT, ADAMA? YOUR WORLD SHAKING?
MY TEMPORAL WEAPONS HAVE CAUSED THE PLANETOID'S TECTONIC PLATES TO RESET THEMSELVES TO A MORE ANCIENT PATTERN.
I IMAGINE THE RESULTS ARE QUITE VIOLENT.
YOU AND YOUR SON WILL SURRENDER TO ME IN THE MODIFIED VIPER I HAVE IDENTIFIED IN YOUR HANGAR BAY.
NOW, ADAMA, OR I WILL FIRE AGAIN.
SIR!
YOU CAN'T DO THIS!
IT'S THE BASE'S ONLY CHANCE OF SURVIVAL!

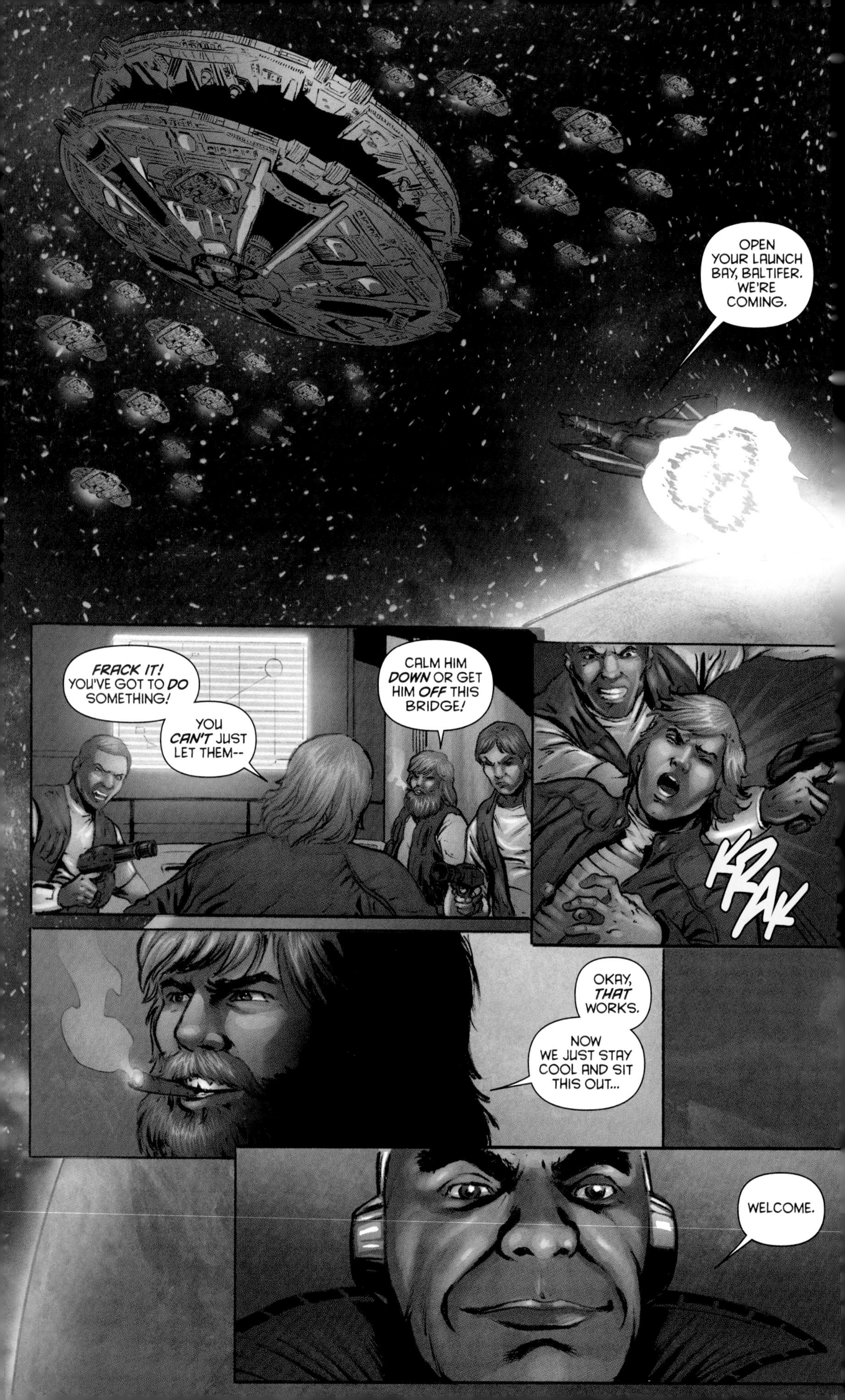
OPEN YOUR LAUNCH BAY, BALTIFER. WE'RE COMING.
FRACK IT! YOU'VE GOT TO DO SOMETHING!
YOU CAN'T JUST LET THEM--
CALM HIM DOWN OR GET HIM OFF THIS BRIDGE!
KRAK
OKAY, THAT WORKS.
NOW WE JUST STAY COOL AND SIT THIS OUT...
WELCOME.

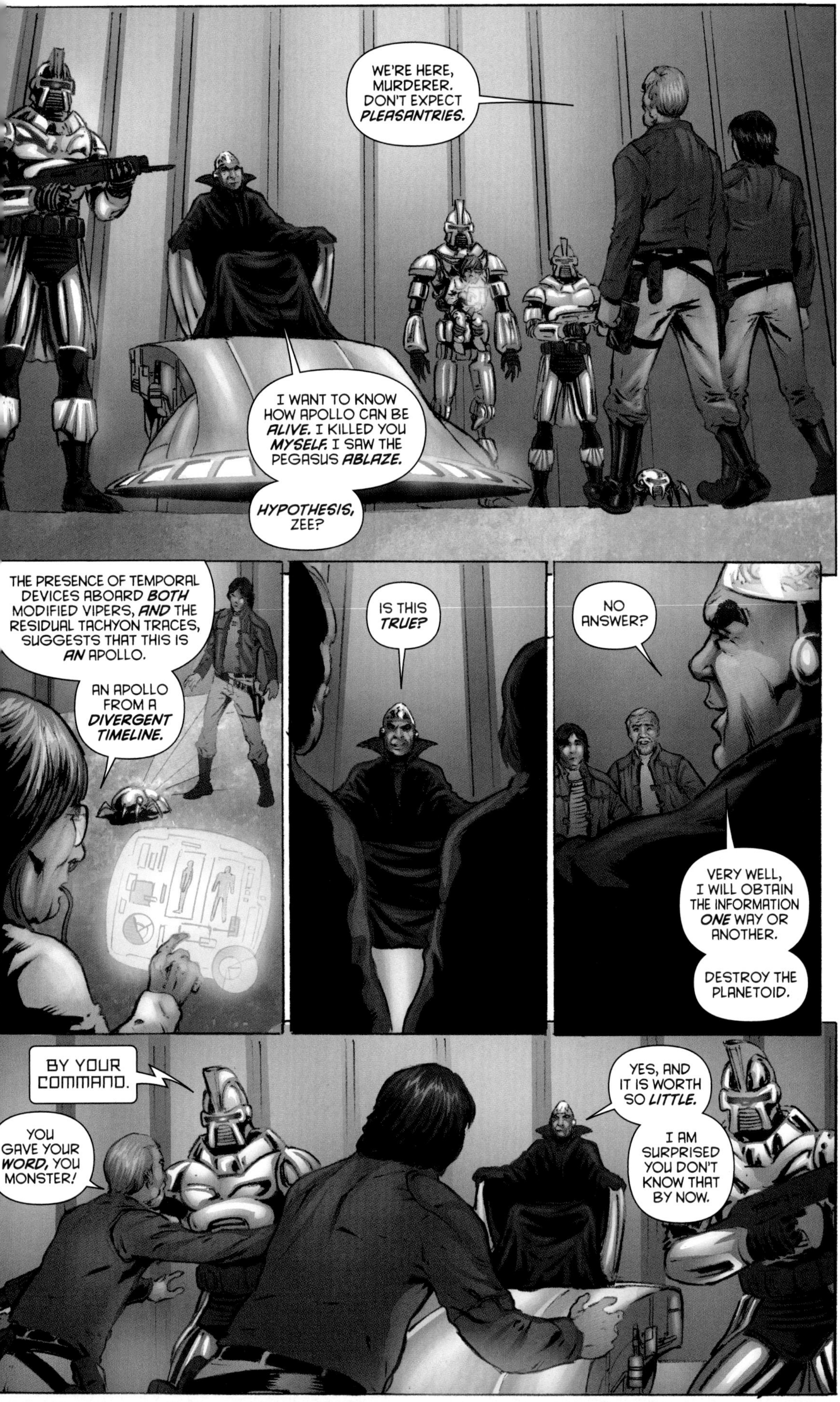
WE'RE HERE, MURDERER. DON'T EXPECT PLEASANTRIES.
I WANT TO KNOW HOW APOLLO CAN BE ALIVE. I KILLED YOU MYSELF. I SAW THE PEGASUS ABLAZE.
HYPOTHESIS, ZEE?
THE PRESENCE OF TEMPORAL DEVICES ABOARD BOTH MODIFIED VIPERS, AND THE RESIDUAL TACHYON TRACES, SUGGESTS THAT THIS IS AN APOLLO.
AN APOLLO FROM A DIVERGENT TIMELINE.
IS THIS TRUE?
NO ANSWER?
VERY WELL, I WILL OBTAIN THE INFORMATION ONE WAY OR ANOTHER.
DESTROY THE PLANETOID.
BY YOUR COMMAND.
YOU GAVE YOUR WORD, YOU MONSTER!
YES, AND IT IS WORTH SO LITTLE.
I AM SURPRISED YOU DON'T KNOW THAT BY NOW.

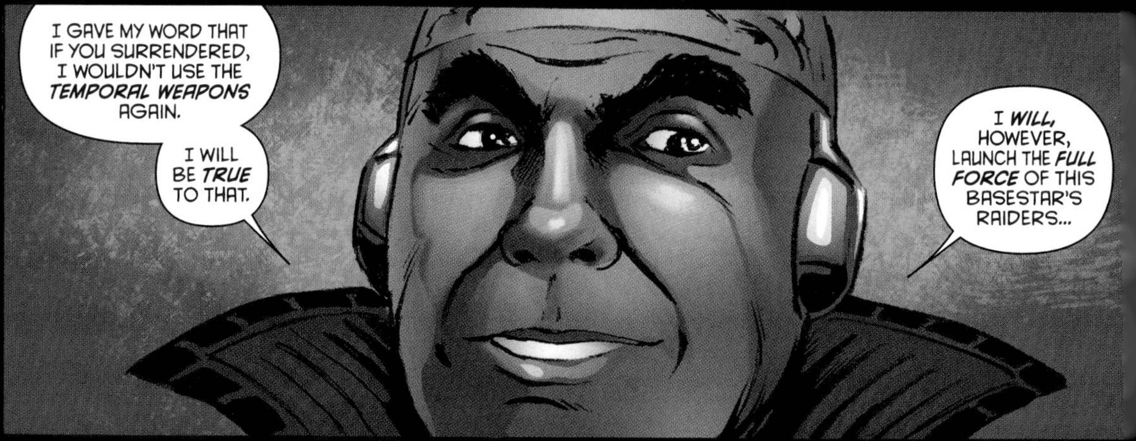
I GAVE MY WORD THAT IF YOU SURRENDERED, I WOULDN'T USE THE *TEMPORAL WEAPONS* AGAIN.
I WILL BE *TRUE* TO THAT.
I *WILL*, HOWEVER, LAUNCH THE *FULL FORCE* OF THIS BASESTAR'S RAIDERS...

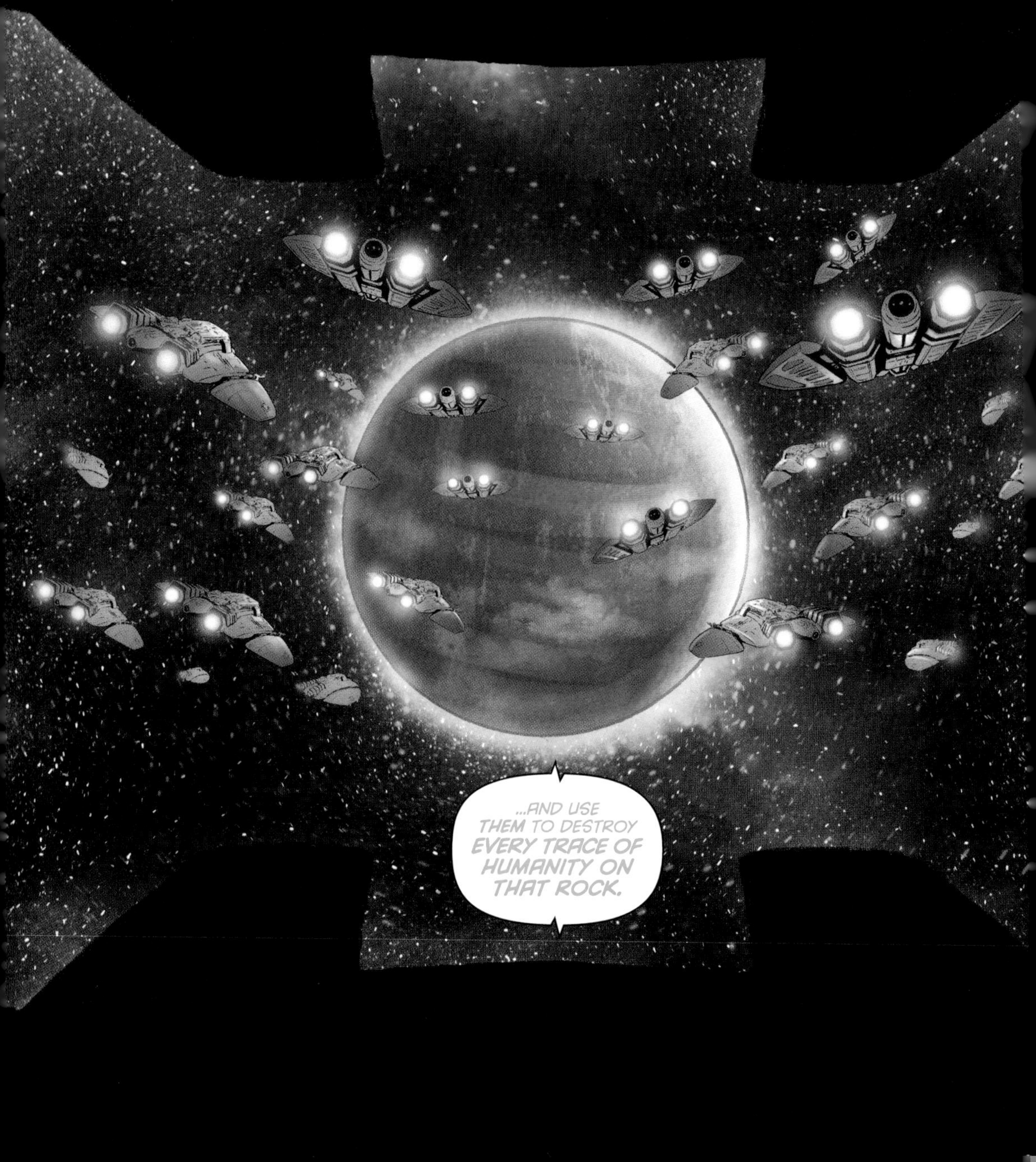
...AND USE THEM TO DESTROY *EVERY TRACE OF HUMANITY ON THAT ROCK.*

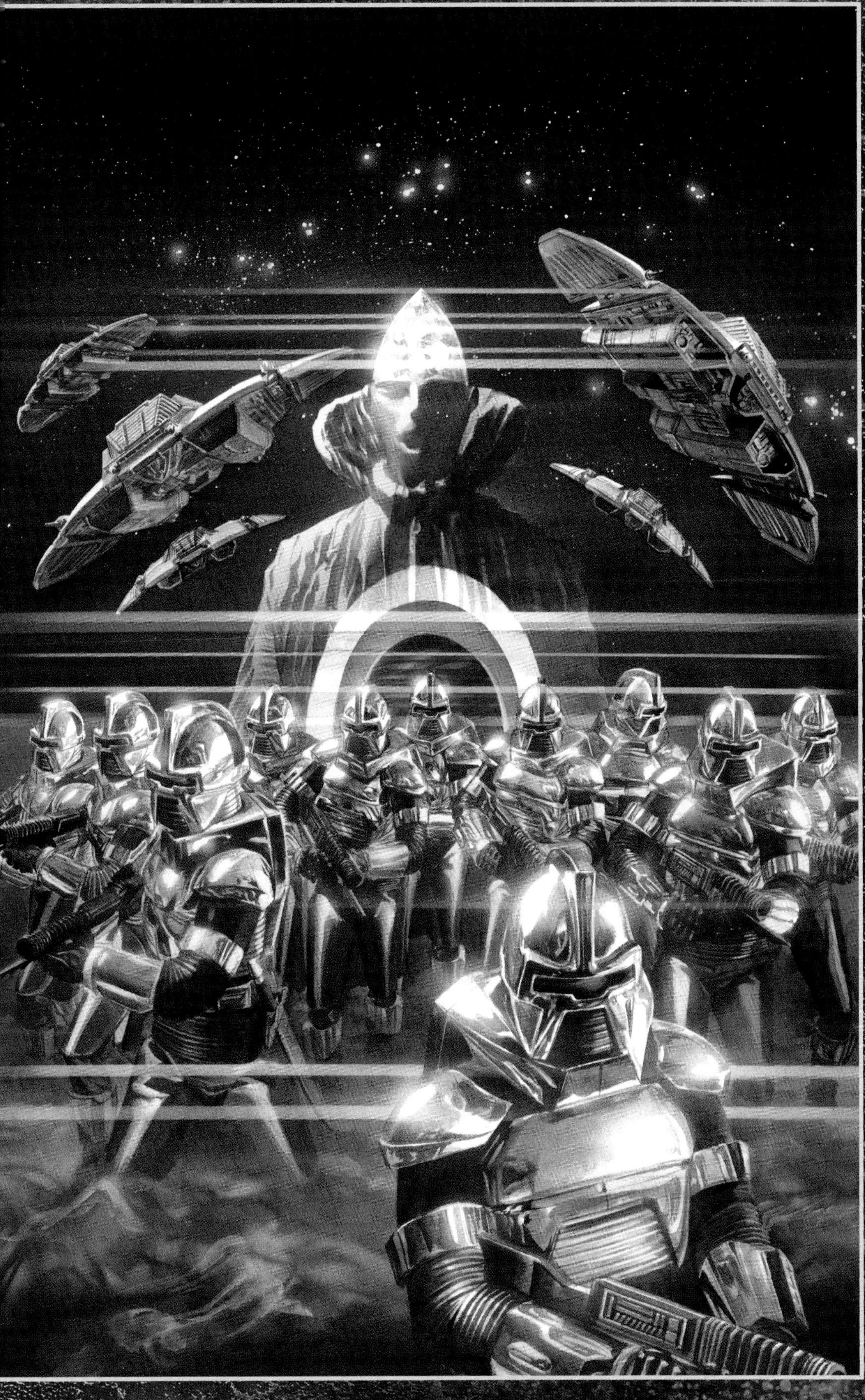

ISSUE 5

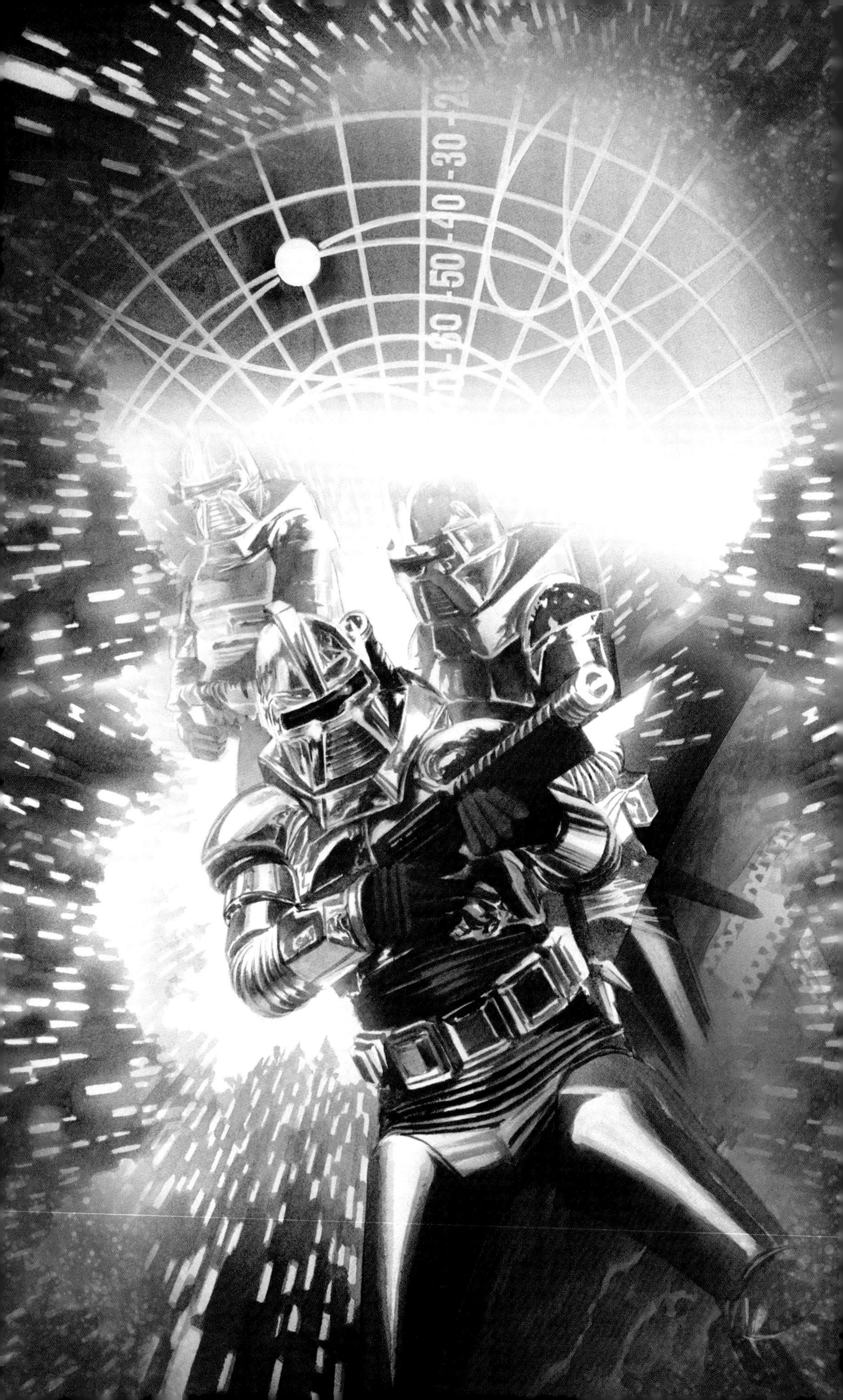

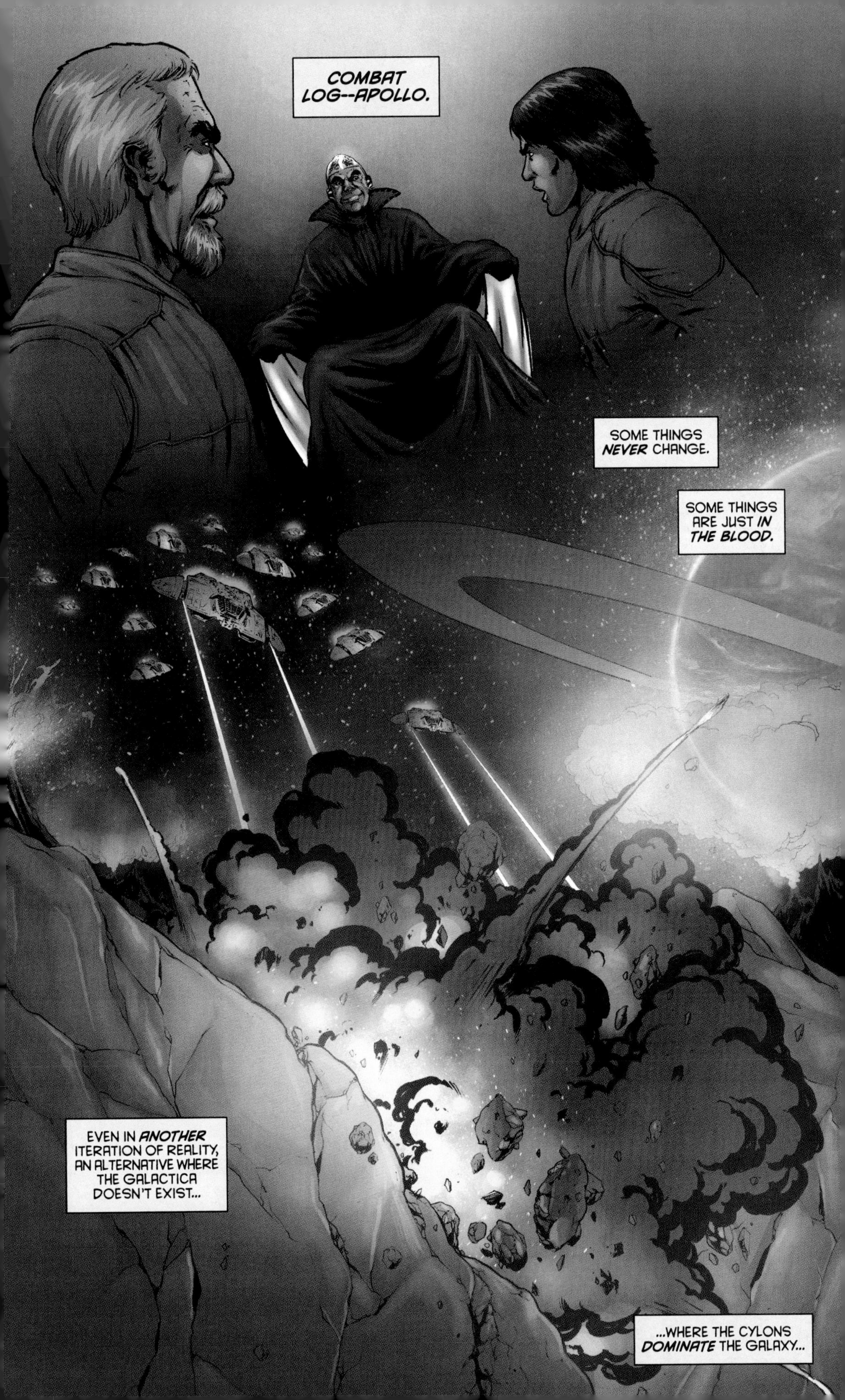
COMBAT LOG--APOLLO.
SOME THINGS NEVER CHANGE.
SOME THINGS ARE JUST IN THE BLOOD.
EVEN IN ANOTHER ITERATION OF REALITY, AN ALTERNATIVE WHERE THE GALACTICA DOESN'T EXIST...
...WHERE THE CYLONS DOMINATE THE GALAXY...

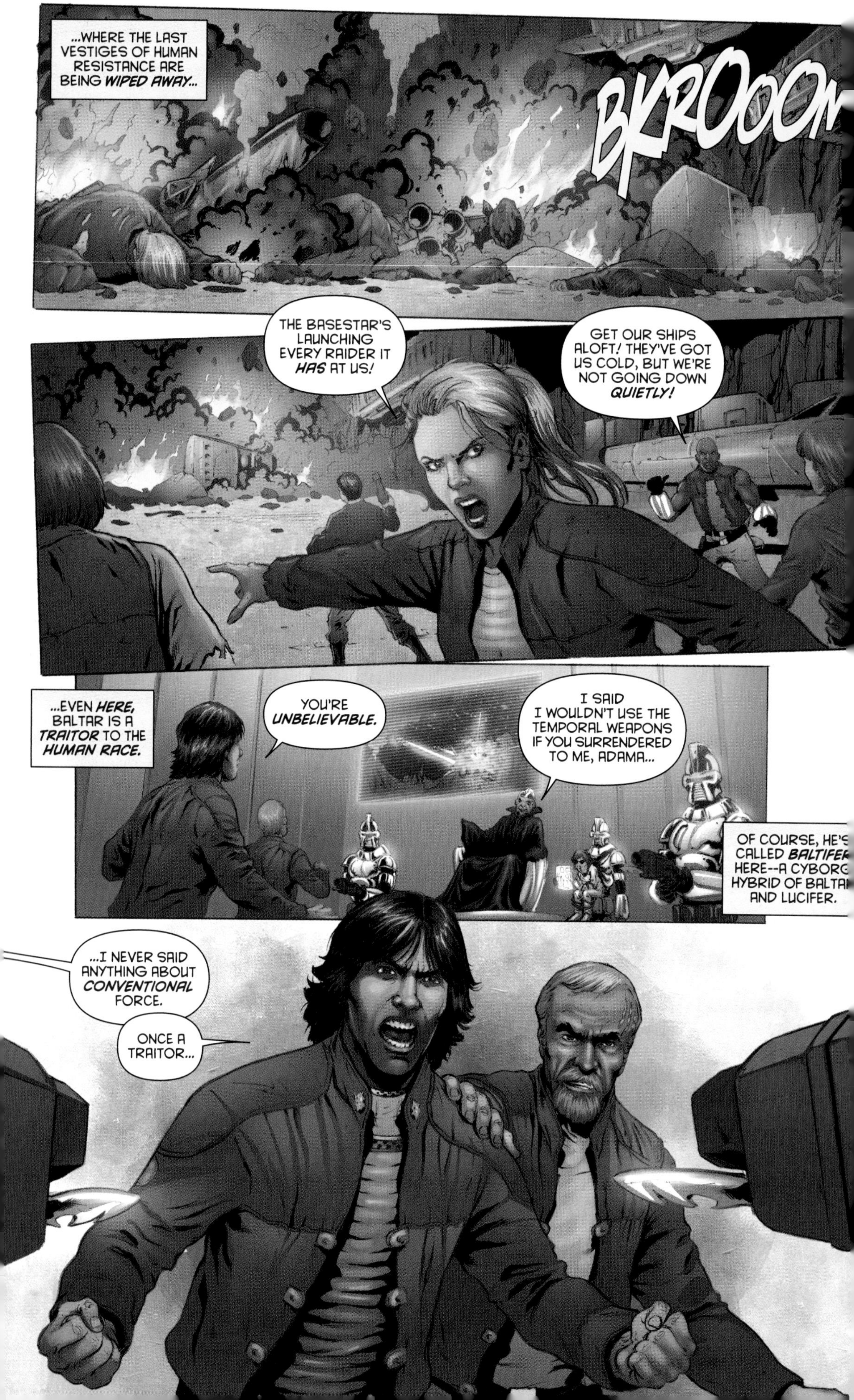
...WHERE THE LAST VESTIGES OF HUMAN RESISTANCE ARE BEING WIPED AWAY...
BKROOOM
THE BASESTAR'S LAUNCHING EVERY RAIDER IT HAS AT US!
GET OUR SHIPS ALOFT! THEY'VE GOT US COLD, BUT WE'RE NOT GOING DOWN QUIETLY!
...EVEN HERE, BALTAR IS A TRAITOR TO THE HUMAN RACE.
YOU'RE UNBELIEVABLE.
I SAID I WOULDN'T USE THE TEMPORAL WEAPONS IF YOU SURRENDERED TO ME, ADAMA...
OF COURSE, HE'S CALLED BALTIFER HERE--A CYBORG HYBRID OF BALTAR AND LUCIFER.
...I NEVER SAID ANYTHING ABOUT CONVENTIONAL FORCE.
ONCE A TRAITOR...

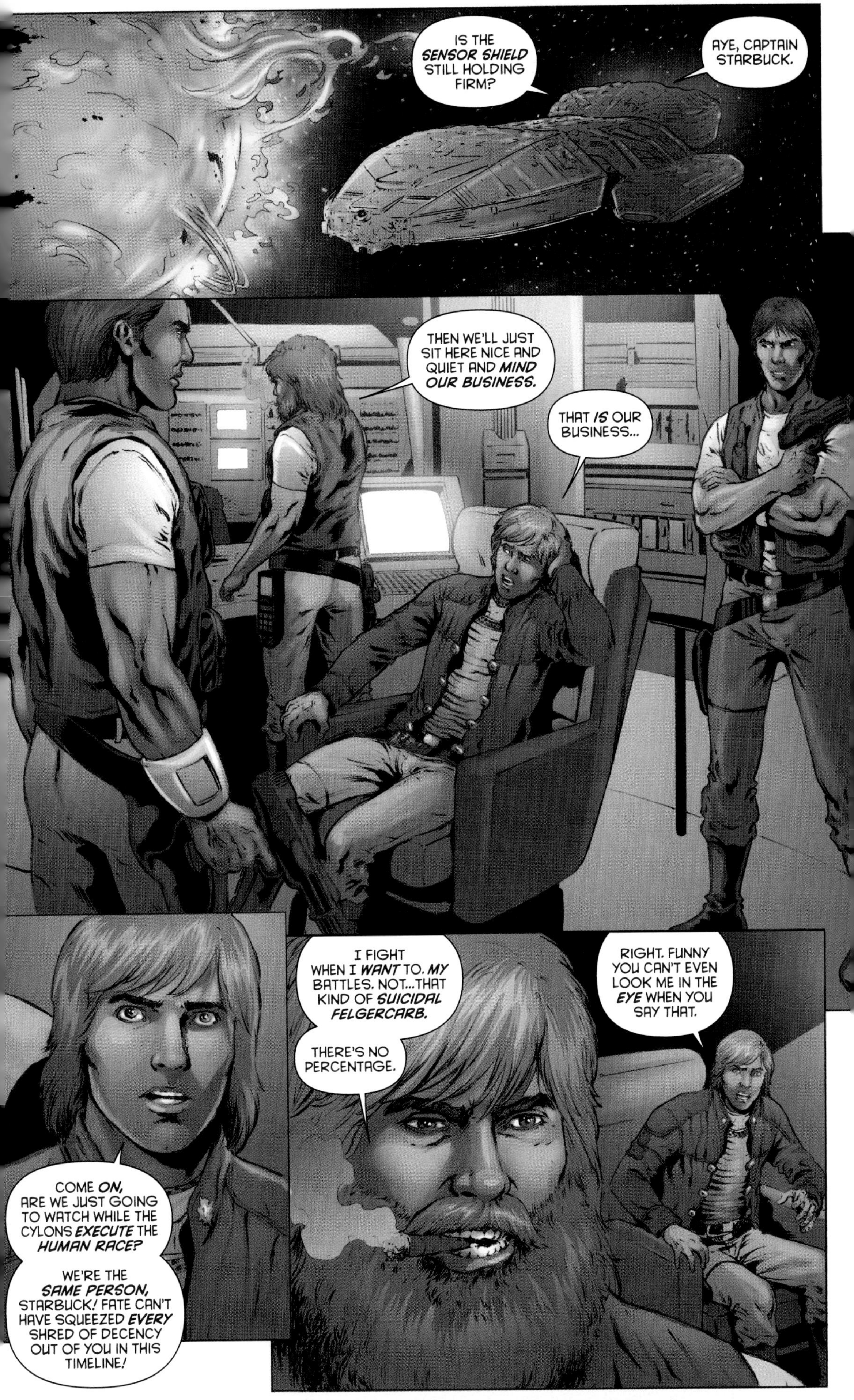
IS THE SENSOR SHIELD STILL HOLDING FIRM?
AYE, CAPTAIN STARBUCK.
THEN WE'LL JUST SIT HERE NICE AND QUIET AND MIND OUR BUSINESS.
THAT IS OUR BUSINESS...
COME ON, ARE WE JUST GOING TO WATCH WHILE THE CYLONS EXECUTE THE HUMAN RACE?
WE'RE THE SAME PERSON, STARBUCK! FATE CAN'T HAVE SQUEEZED EVERY SHRED OF DECENCY OUT OF YOU IN THIS TIMELINE!
I FIGHT WHEN I WANT TO. MY BATTLES. NOT...THAT KIND OF SUICIDAL FELGERCARB.
THERE'S NO PERCENTAGE.
RIGHT. FUNNY YOU CAN'T EVEN LOOK ME IN THE EYE WHEN YOU SAY THAT.

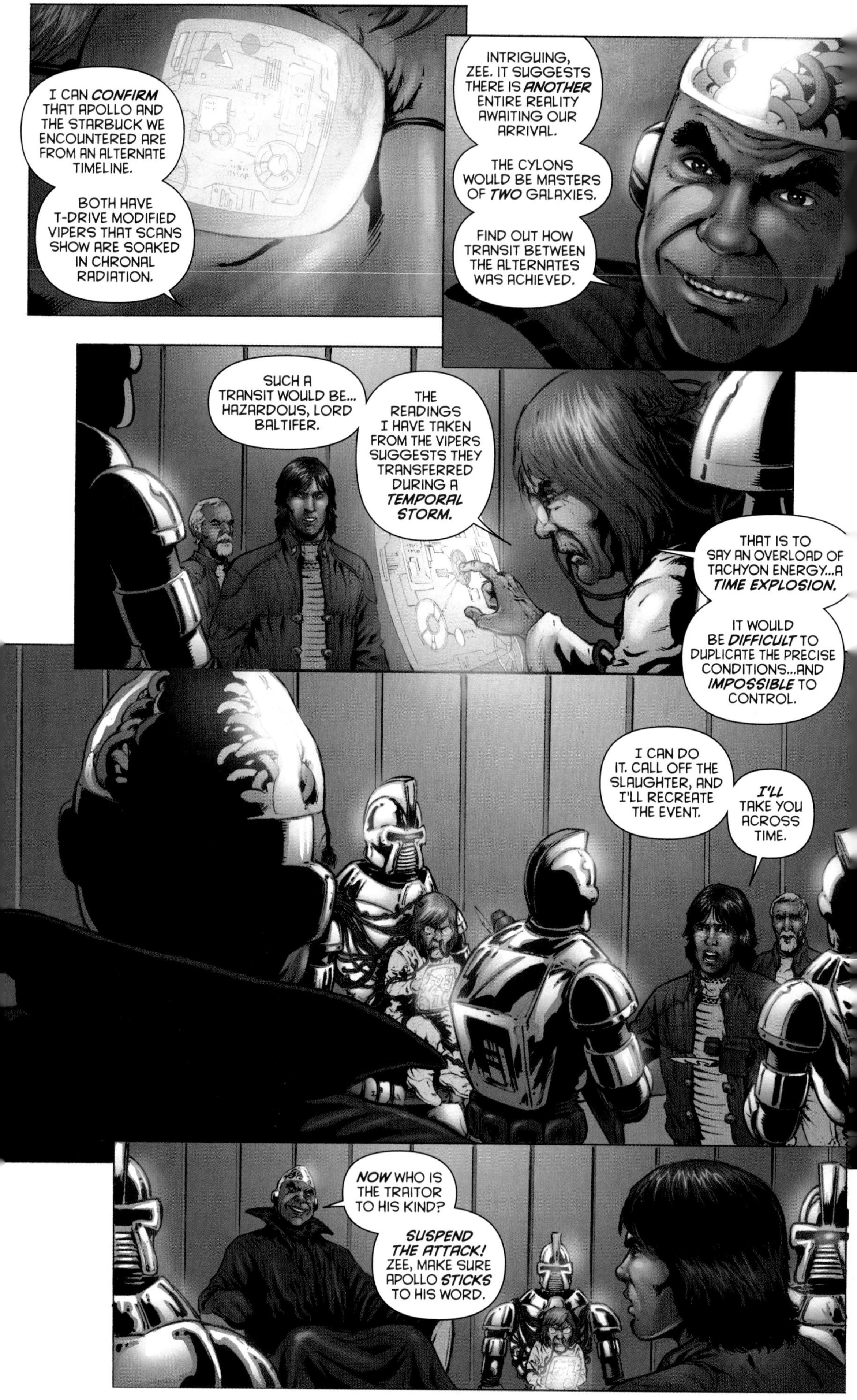
I CAN *CONFIRM* THAT APOLLO AND THE STARBUCK WE ENCOUNTERED ARE FROM AN ALTERNATE TIMELINE.
BOTH HAVE T-DRIVE MODIFIED VIPERS THAT SCANS SHOW ARE SOAKED IN CHRONAL RADIATION.
INTRIGUING, ZEE. IT SUGGESTS THERE IS *ANOTHER* ENTIRE REALITY AWAITING OUR ARRIVAL.
THE CYLONS WOULD BE MASTERS OF *TWO* GALAXIES.
FIND OUT HOW TRANSIT BETWEEN THE ALTERNATES WAS ACHIEVED.
SUCH A TRANSIT WOULD BE... HAZARDOUS, LORD BALTIFER.
THE READINGS I HAVE TAKEN FROM THE VIPERS SUGGESTS THEY TRANSFERRED DURING A *TEMPORAL STORM.*
THAT IS TO SAY AN OVERLOAD OF TACHYON ENERGY...A *TIME EXPLOSION.*
IT WOULD BE *DIFFICULT* TO DUPLICATE THE PRECISE CONDITIONS...AND *IMPOSSIBLE* TO CONTROL.
I CAN DO IT. CALL OFF THE SLAUGHTER, AND I'LL RECREATE THE EVENT.
I'LL TAKE YOU ACROSS TIME.
NOW WHO IS THE TRAITOR TO HIS KIND?
SUSPEND THE ATTACK! ZEE, MAKE SURE APOLLO *STICKS* TO HIS WORD.

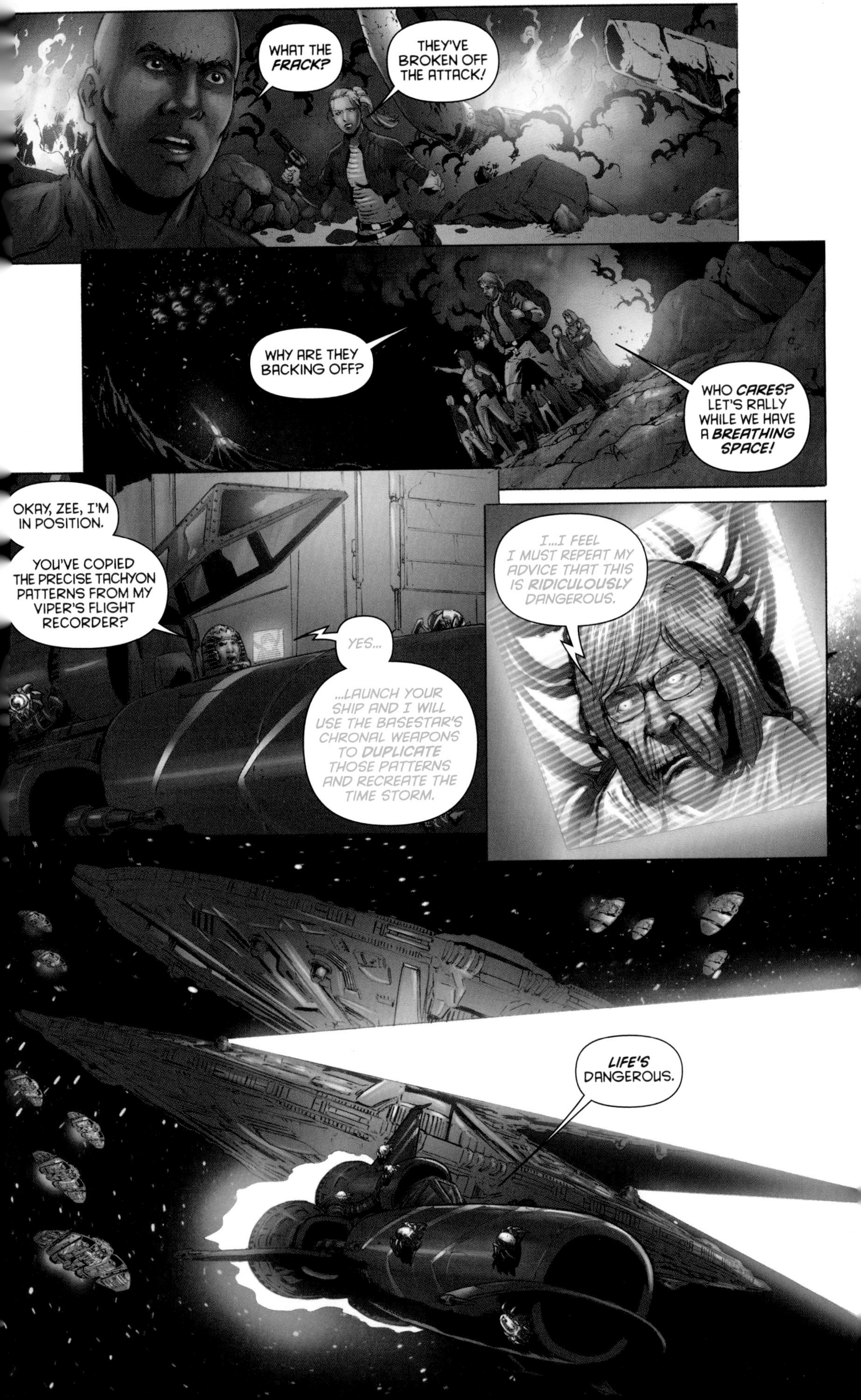
WHAT THE FRACK?
THEY'VE BROKEN OFF THE ATTACK!
WHY ARE THEY BACKING OFF?
WHO CARES? LET'S RALLY WHILE WE HAVE A BREATHING SPACE!
OKAY, ZEE, I'M IN POSITION.
YOU'VE COPIED THE PRECISE TACHYON PATTERNS FROM MY VIPER'S FLIGHT RECORDER?
YES...
...LAUNCH YOUR SHIP AND I WILL USE THE BASESTAR'S CHRONAL WEAPONS TO DUPLICATE THOSE PATTERNS AND RECREATE THE TIME STORM.
I...I FEEL I MUST REPEAT MY ADVICE THAT THIS IS RIDICULOUSLY DANGEROUS.
LIFE'S DANGEROUS.

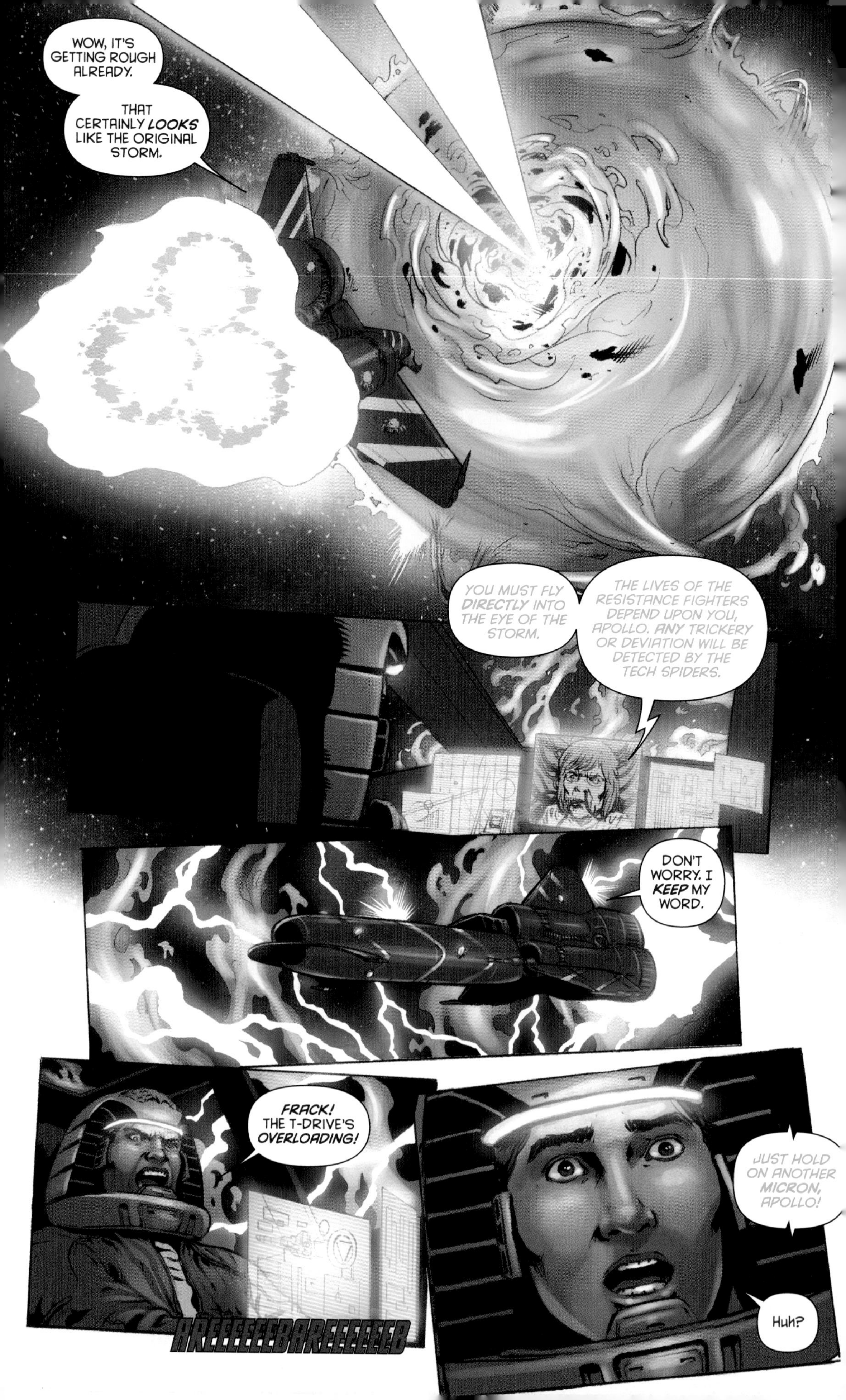
WOW, IT'S GETTING ROUGH ALREADY.
THAT CERTAINLY LOOKS LIKE THE ORIGINAL STORM.
YOU MUST FLY DIRECTLY INTO THE EYE OF THE STORM.
THE LIVES OF THE RESISTANCE FIGHTERS DEPEND UPON YOU, APOLLO. ANY TRICKERY OR DEVIATION WILL BE DETECTED BY THE TECH SPIDERS.
DON'T WORRY. I KEEP MY WORD.
FRACK! THE T-DRIVE'S OVERLOADING!
AREEEEEEBAREEEEEEEB
JUST HOLD ON ANOTHER MICRON, APOLLO!
Huh?

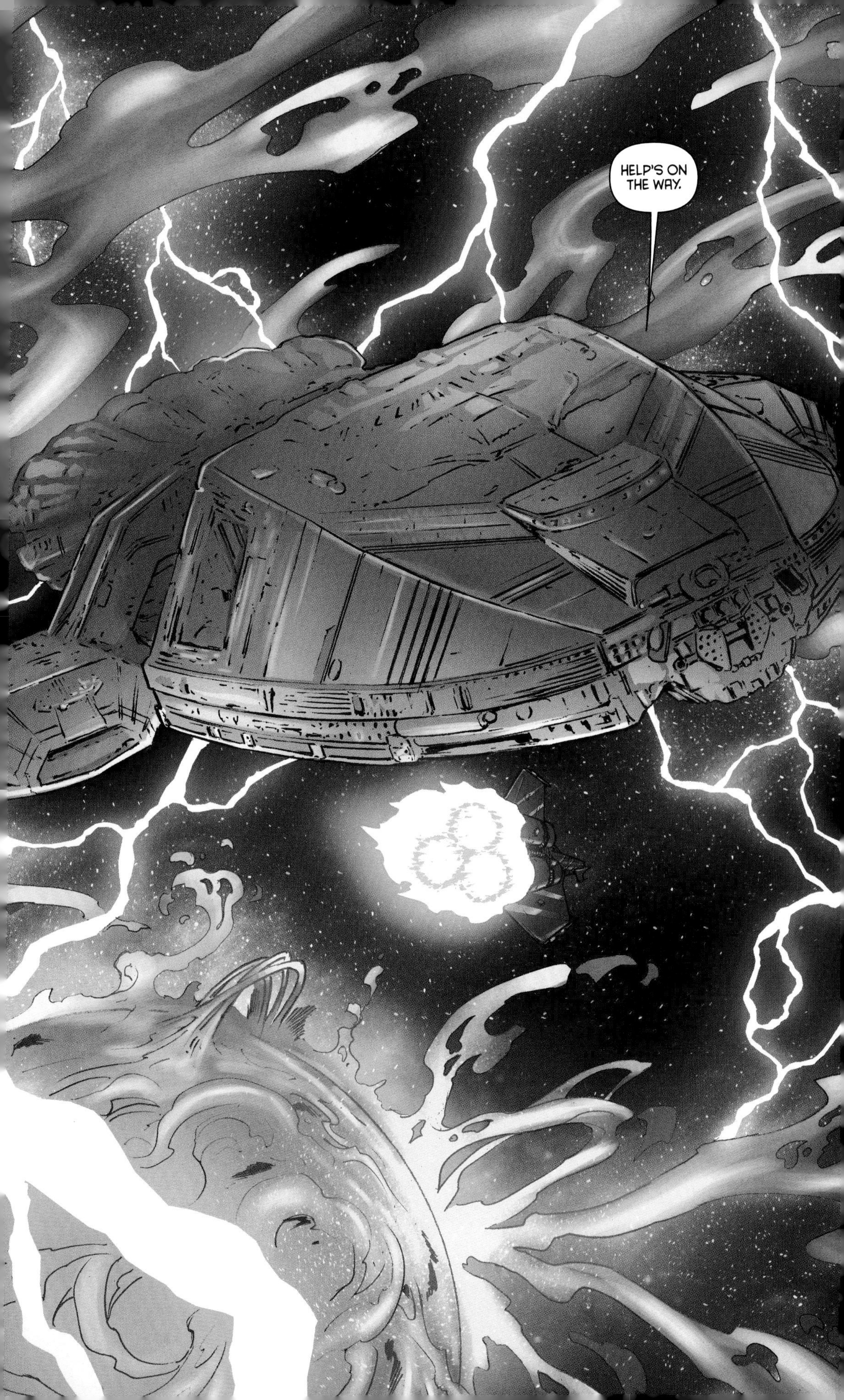
HELP'S ON THE WAY.

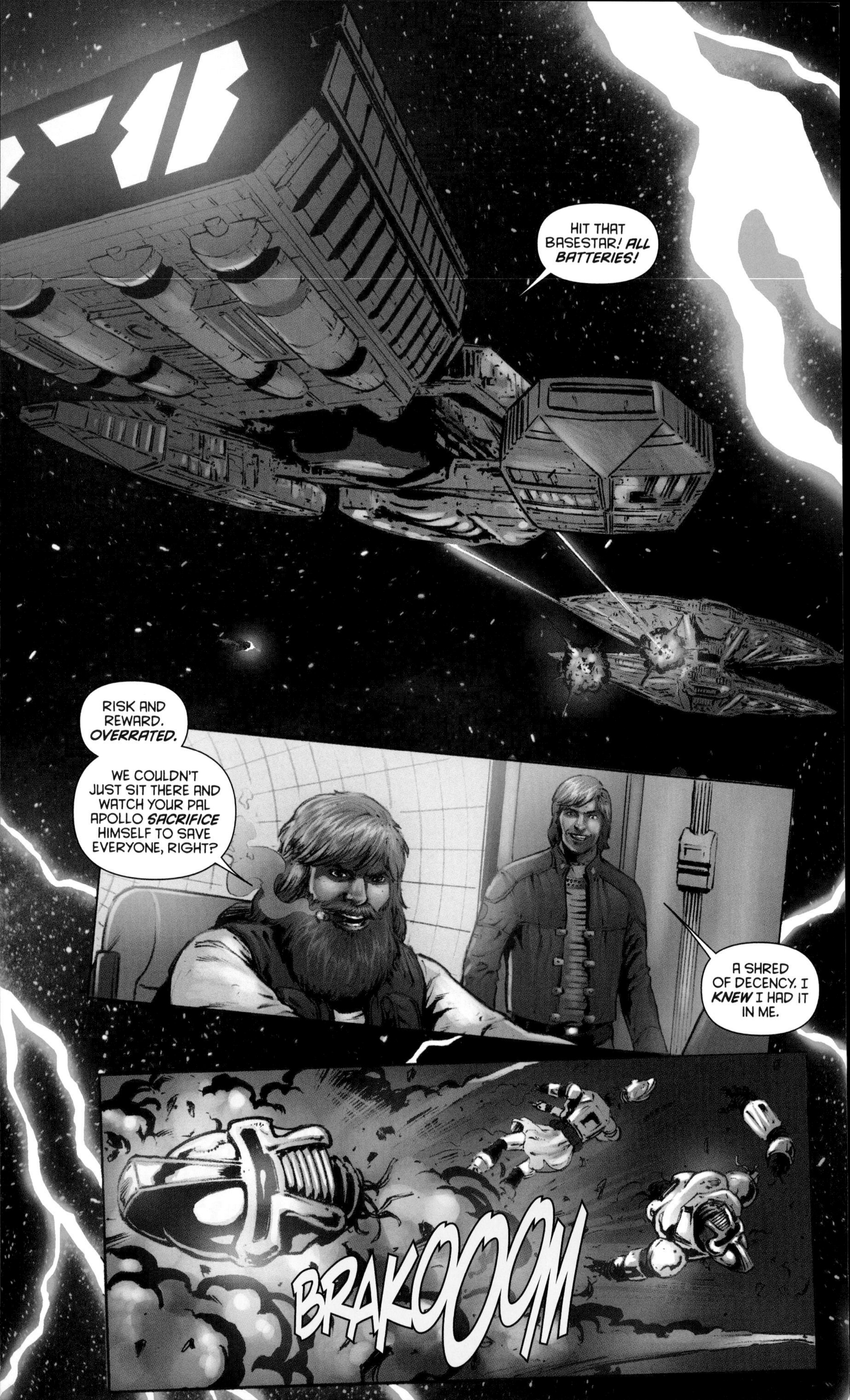
HIT THAT BASESTAR! ALL BATTERIES!
RISK AND REWARD. OVERRATED.
WE COULDN'T JUST SIT THERE AND WATCH YOUR PAL APOLLO SACRIFICE HIMSELF TO SAVE EVERYONE, RIGHT?
A SHRED OF DECENCY. I KNEW I HAD IT IN ME.
BRAKOOOM

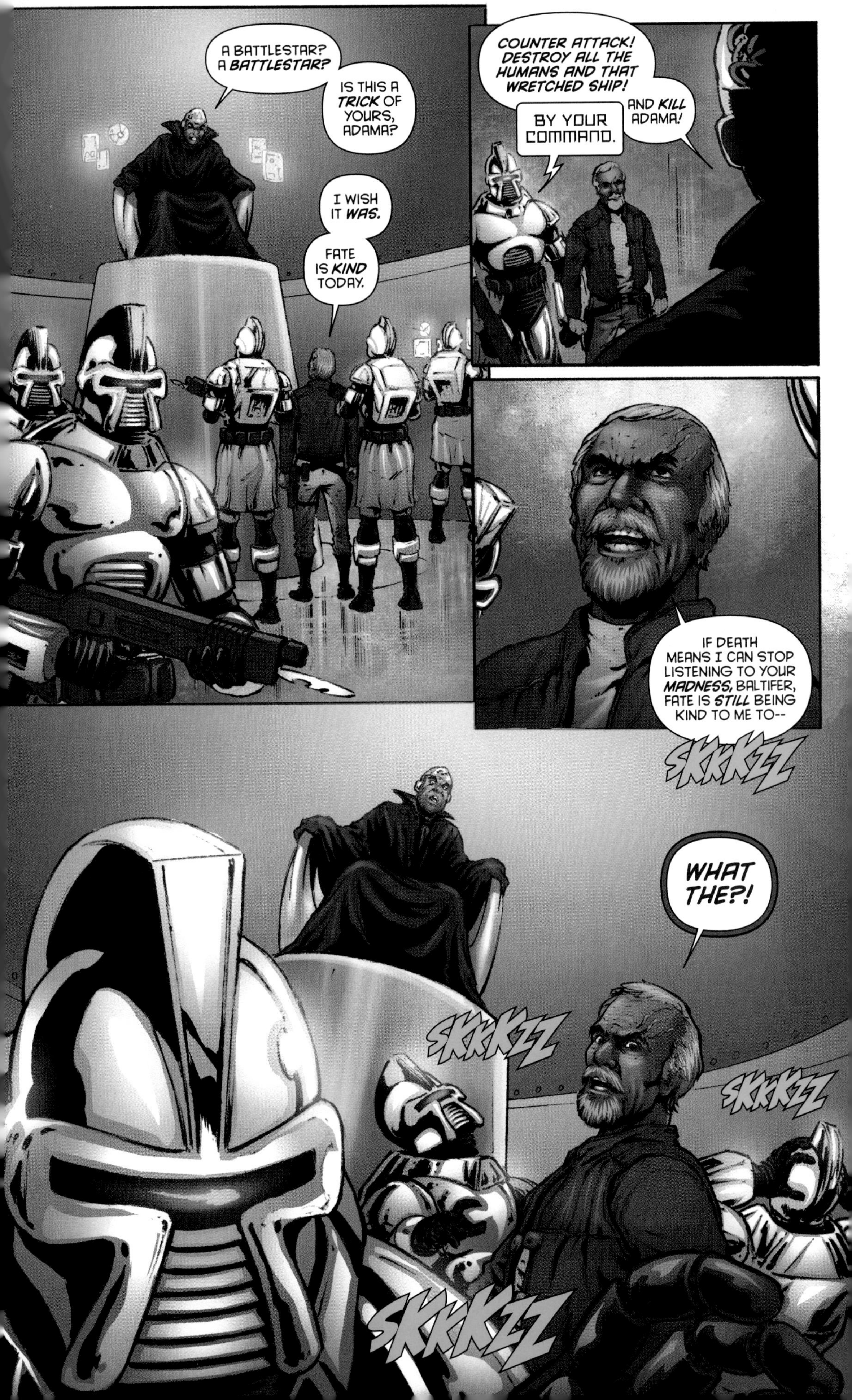
A BATTLESTAR? A BATTLESTAR?
IS THIS A TRICK OF YOURS, ADAMA?
I WISH IT WAS.
FATE IS KIND TODAY.
COUNTER ATTACK! DESTROY ALL THE HUMANS AND THAT WRETCHED SHIP!
AND KILL ADAMA!
BY YOUR COMMAND.
IF DEATH MEANS I CAN STOP LISTENING TO YOUR MADNESS, BALTIFER, FATE IS STILL BEING KIND TO ME TO--
SKKKZZ
WHAT THE?!
SKKKZZ
SKKKZZ
SKKKZZ

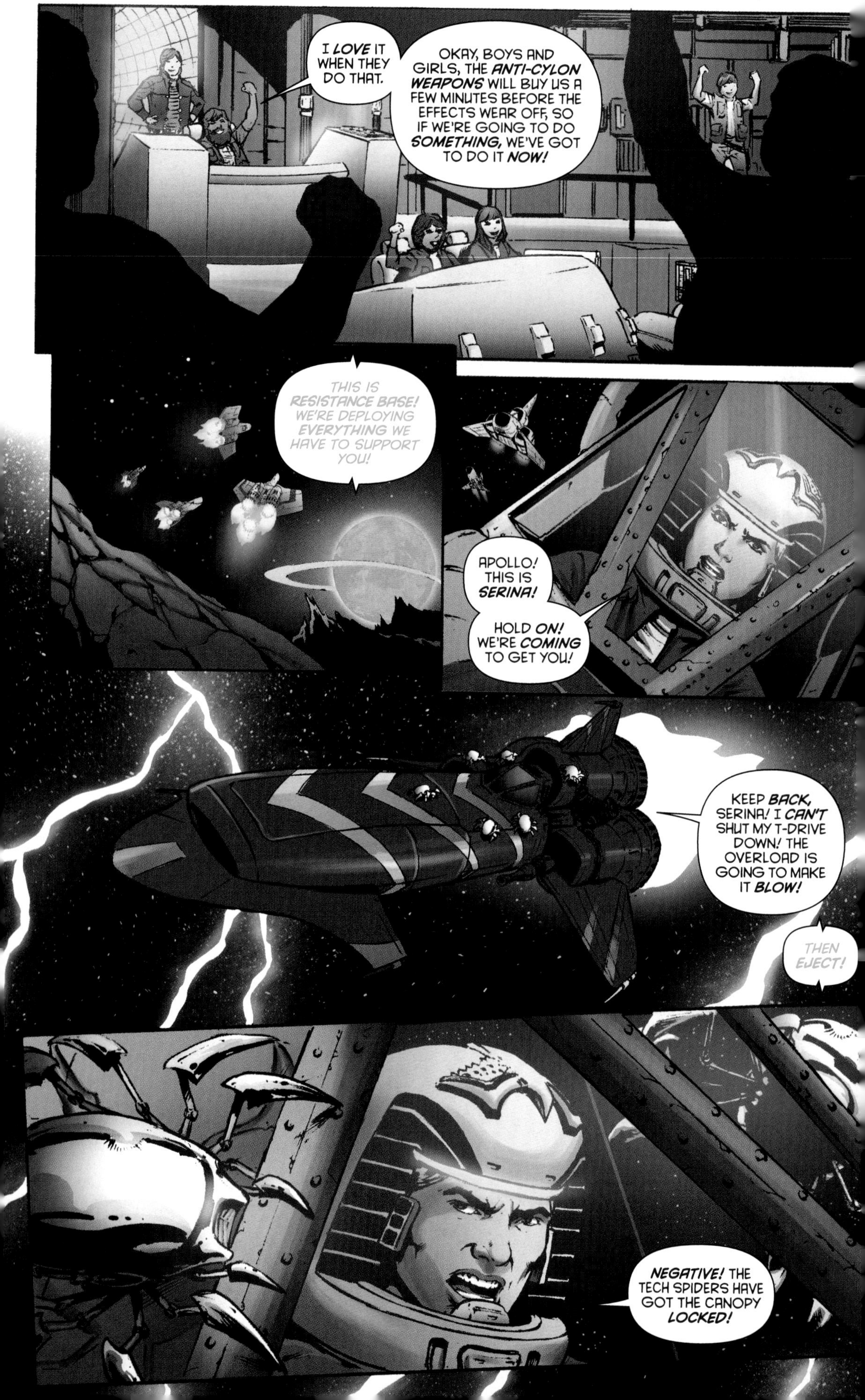
I LOVE IT WHEN THEY DO THAT.
OKAY, BOYS AND GIRLS, THE ANTI-CYLON WEAPONS WILL BUY US A FEW MINUTES BEFORE THE EFFECTS WEAR OFF, SO IF WE'RE GOING TO DO SOMETHING, WE'VE GOT TO DO IT NOW!
THIS IS RESISTANCE BASE! WE'RE DEPLOYING EVERYTHING WE HAVE TO SUPPORT YOU!
APOLLO! THIS IS SERINA!
HOLD ON! WE'RE COMING TO GET YOU!
KEEP BACK, SERINA! I CAN'T SHUT MY T-DRIVE DOWN! THE OVERLOAD IS GOING TO MAKE IT BLOW!
THEN EJECT!
NEGATIVE! THE TECH SPIDERS HAVE GOT THE CANOPY LOCKED!

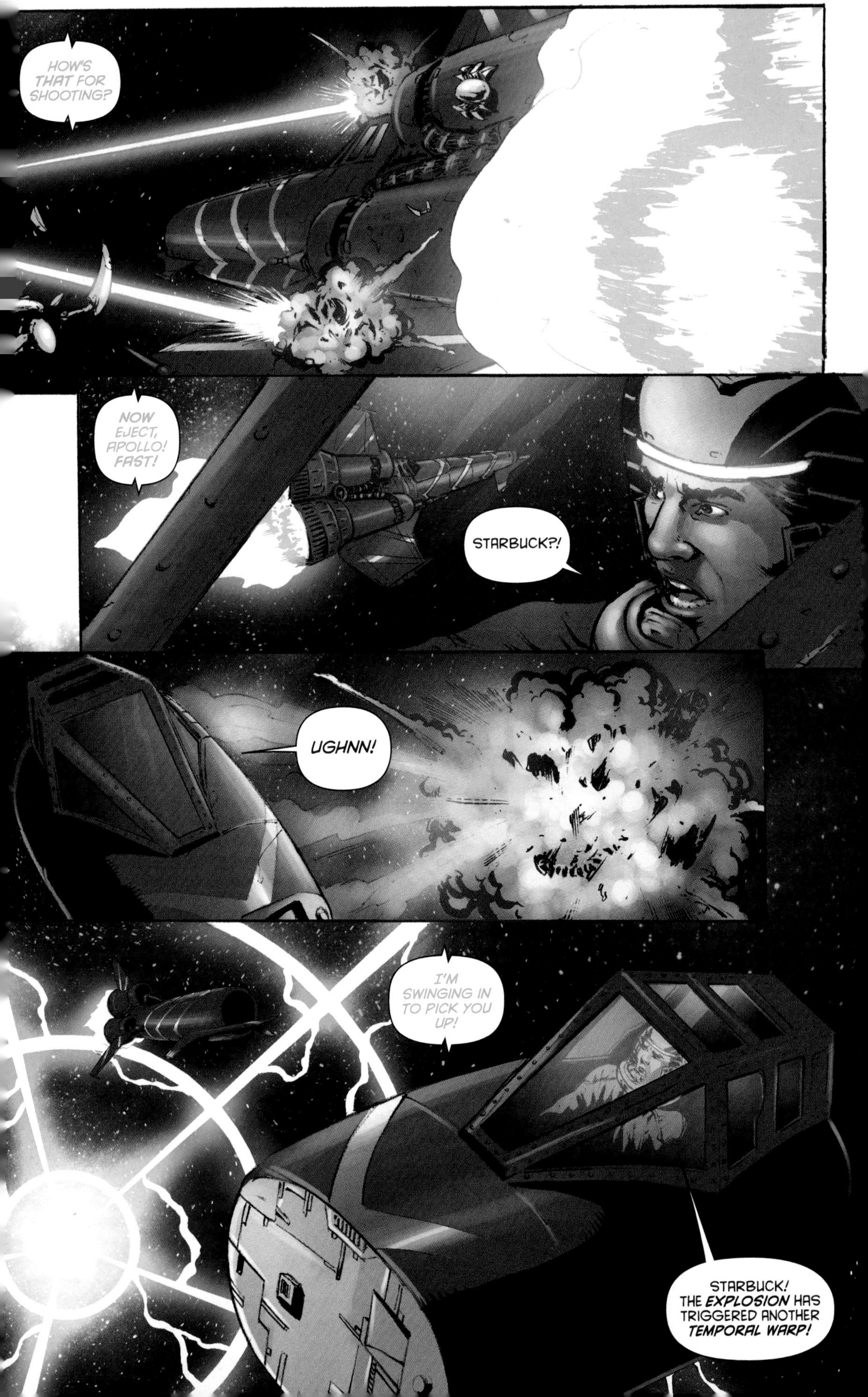
HOW'S THAT FOR SHOOTING?
NOW EJECT, APOLLO! FAST!
STARBUCK?!
UGHNN!
I'M SWINGING IN TO PICK YOU UP!
STARBUCK! THE EXPLOSION HAS TRIGGERED ANOTHER TEMPORAL WARP!

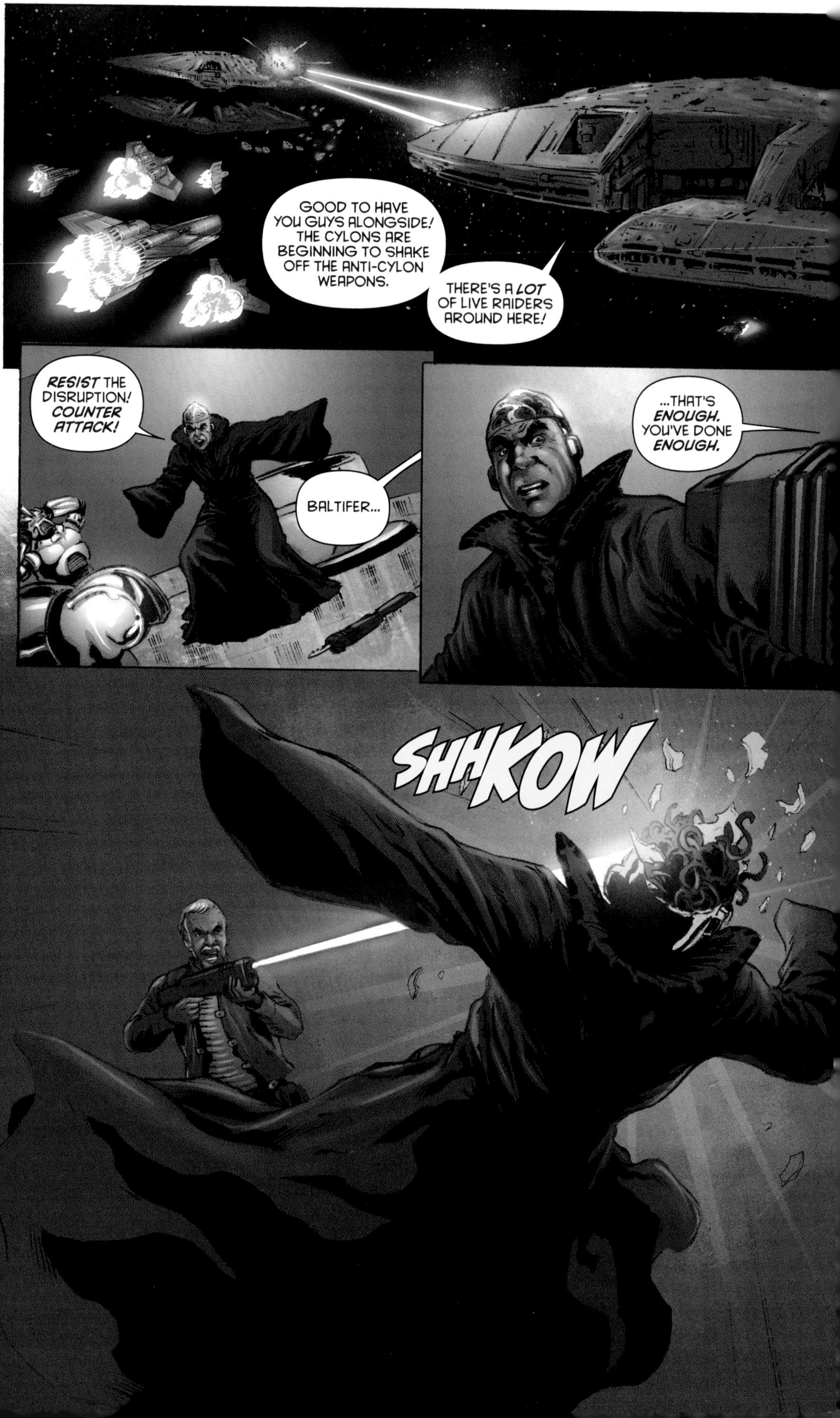
GOOD TO HAVE YOU GUYS ALONGSIDE! THE CYLONS ARE BEGINNING TO SHAKE OFF THE ANTI-CYLON WEAPONS.
THERE'S A *LOT* OF LIVE RAIDERS AROUND HERE!
RESIST THE DISRUPTION! *COUNTER ATTACK!*
BALTIFER...
...THAT'S *ENOUGH.* YOU'VE DONE *ENOUGH.*
SHHKOW

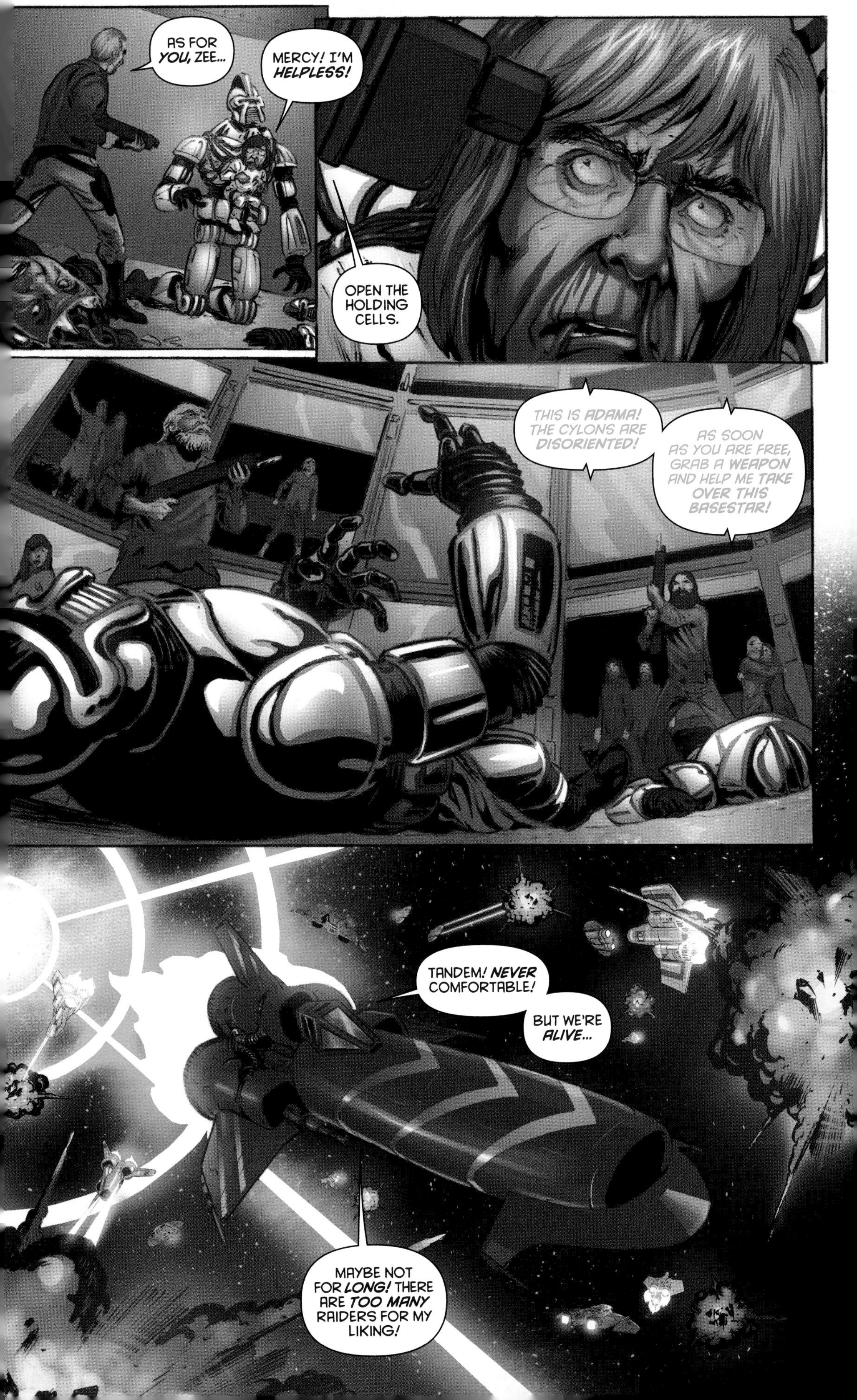
AS FOR *YOU,* ZEE...
MERCY! I'M *HELPLESS!*
OPEN THE HOLDING CELLS.
THIS IS *ADAMA!* THE CYLONS ARE *DISORIENTED!*
AS SOON AS YOU ARE FREE, GRAB A *WEAPON* AND HELP ME *TAKE OVER THIS BASESTAR!*
TANDEM! *NEVER* COMFORTABLE!
BUT WE'RE *ALIVE...*
MAYBE NOT FOR *LONG!* THERE ARE *TOO MANY* RAIDERS FOR MY LIKING!

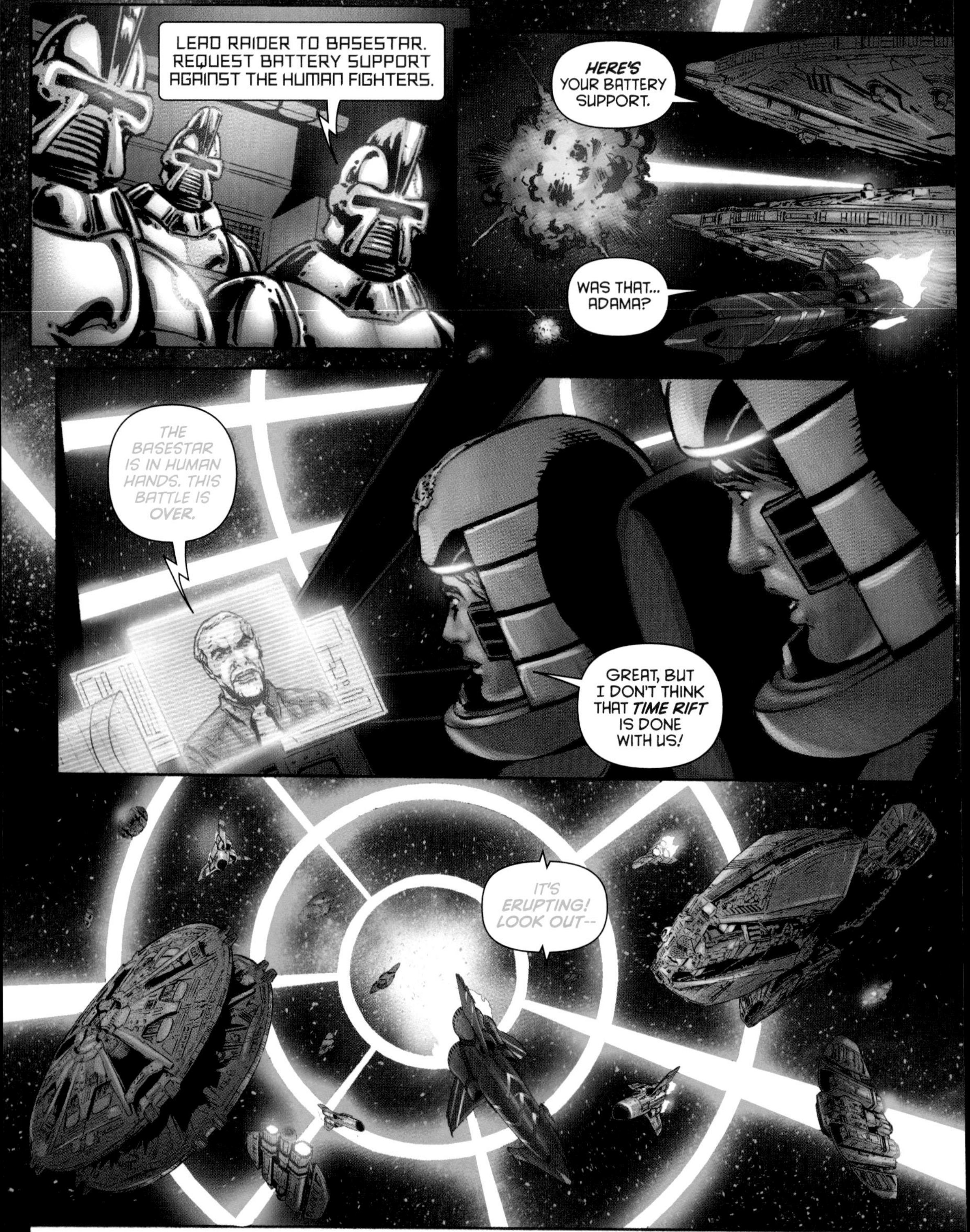
LEAD RAIDER TO BASESTAR. REQUEST BATTERY SUPPORT AGAINST THE HUMAN FIGHTERS.
HERE'S YOUR BATTERY SUPPORT.
WAS THAT... ADAMA?
THE BASESTAR IS IN HUMAN HANDS. THIS BATTLE IS *OVER.*
GREAT, BUT I DON'T THINK THAT *TIME RIFT* IS DONE WITH US!
IT'S ERUPTING! LOOK OUT--

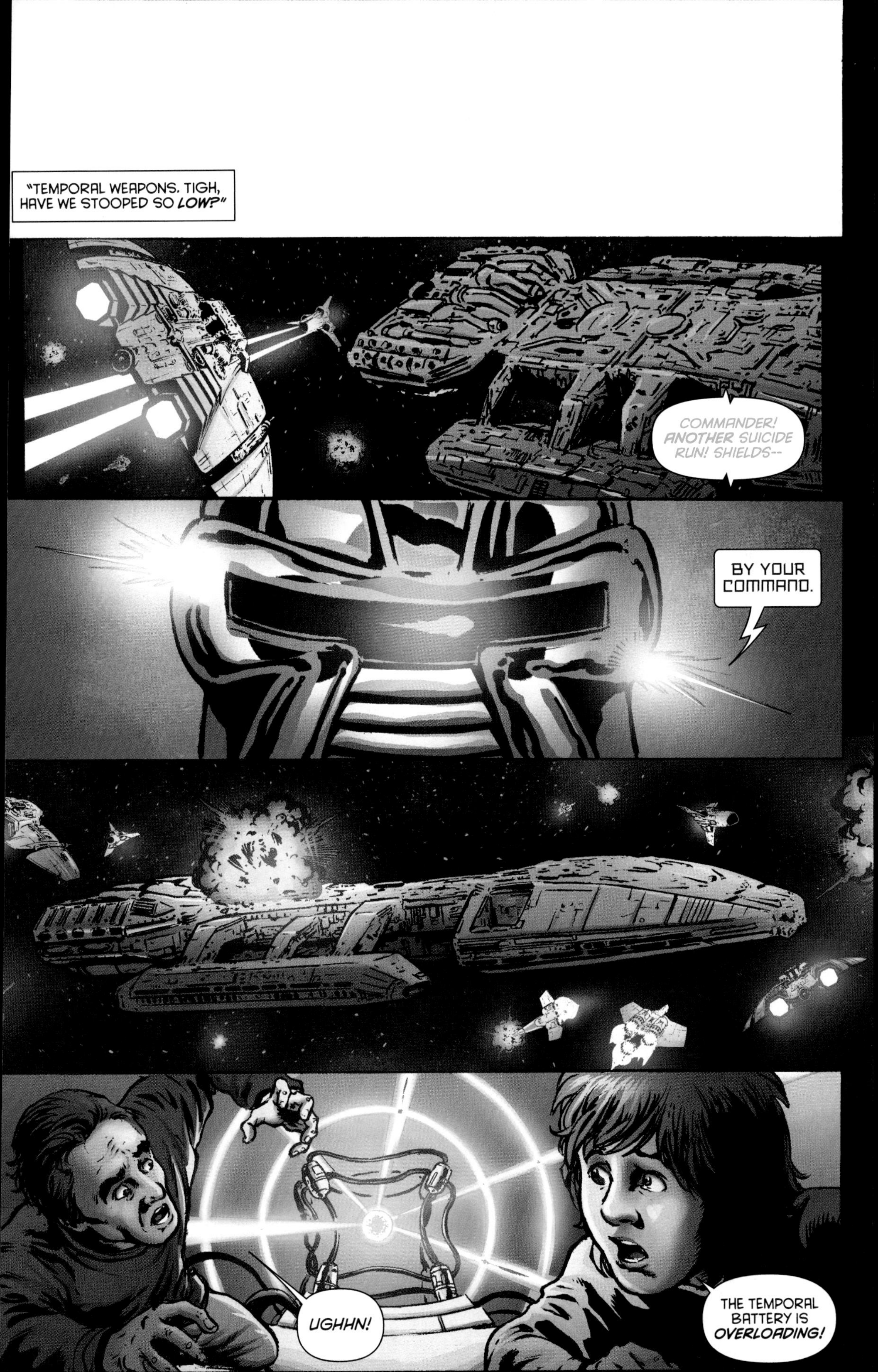
"TEMPORAL WEAPONS. TIGH, HAVE WE STOOPED SO LOW?"
COMMANDER! ANOTHER SUICIDE RUN! SHIELDS--
BY YOUR COMMAND.
UGHHN!
THE TEMPORAL BATTERY IS OVERLOADING!

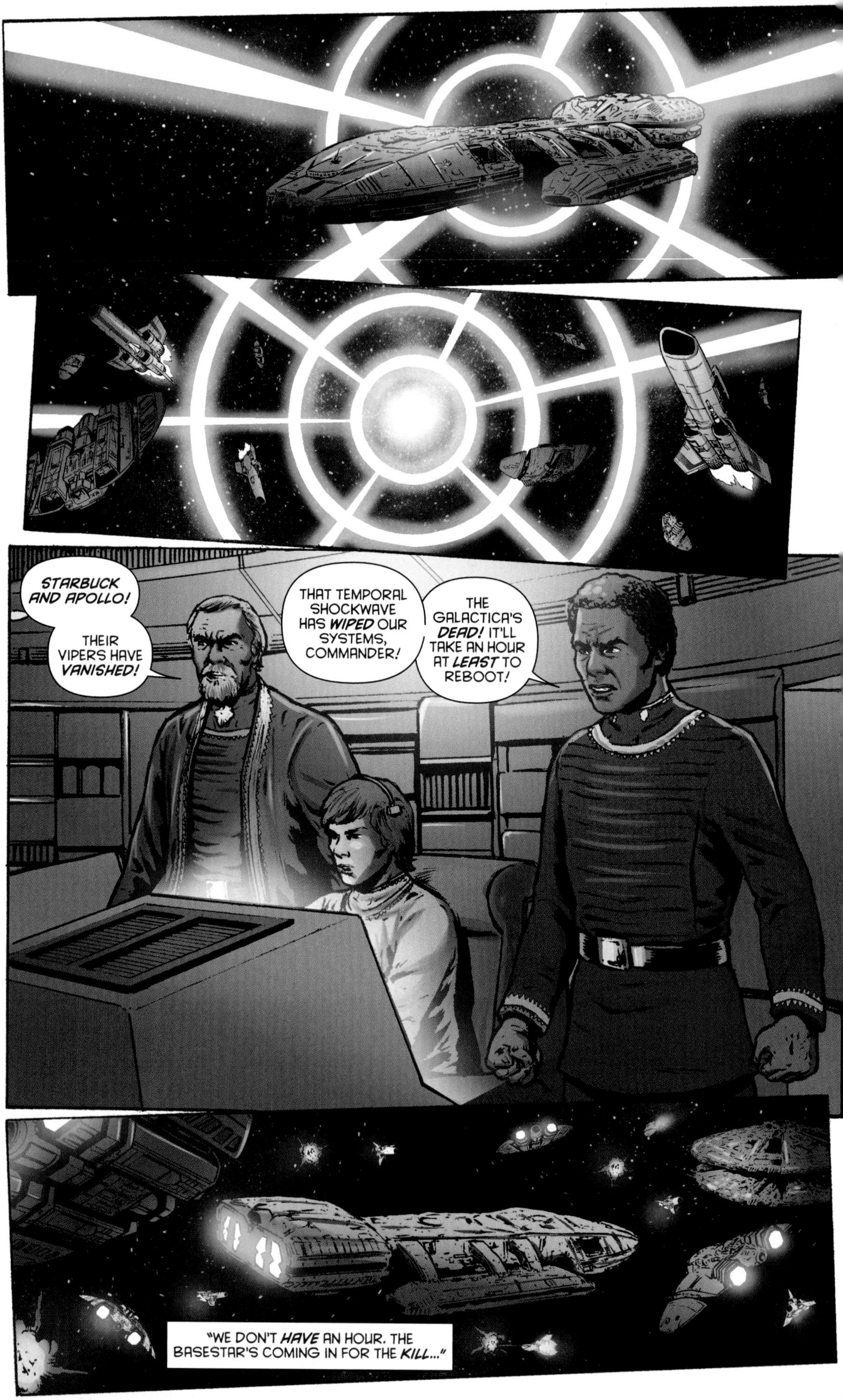
STARBUCK AND APOLLO!
THEIR VIPERS HAVE VANISHED!
THAT TEMPORAL SHOCKWAVE HAS WIPED OUR SYSTEMS, COMMANDER!
THE GALACTICA'S DEAD! IT'LL TAKE AN HOUR AT LEAST TO REBOOT!
"WE DON'T HAVE AN HOUR. THE BASESTAR'S COMING IN FOR THE KILL..."

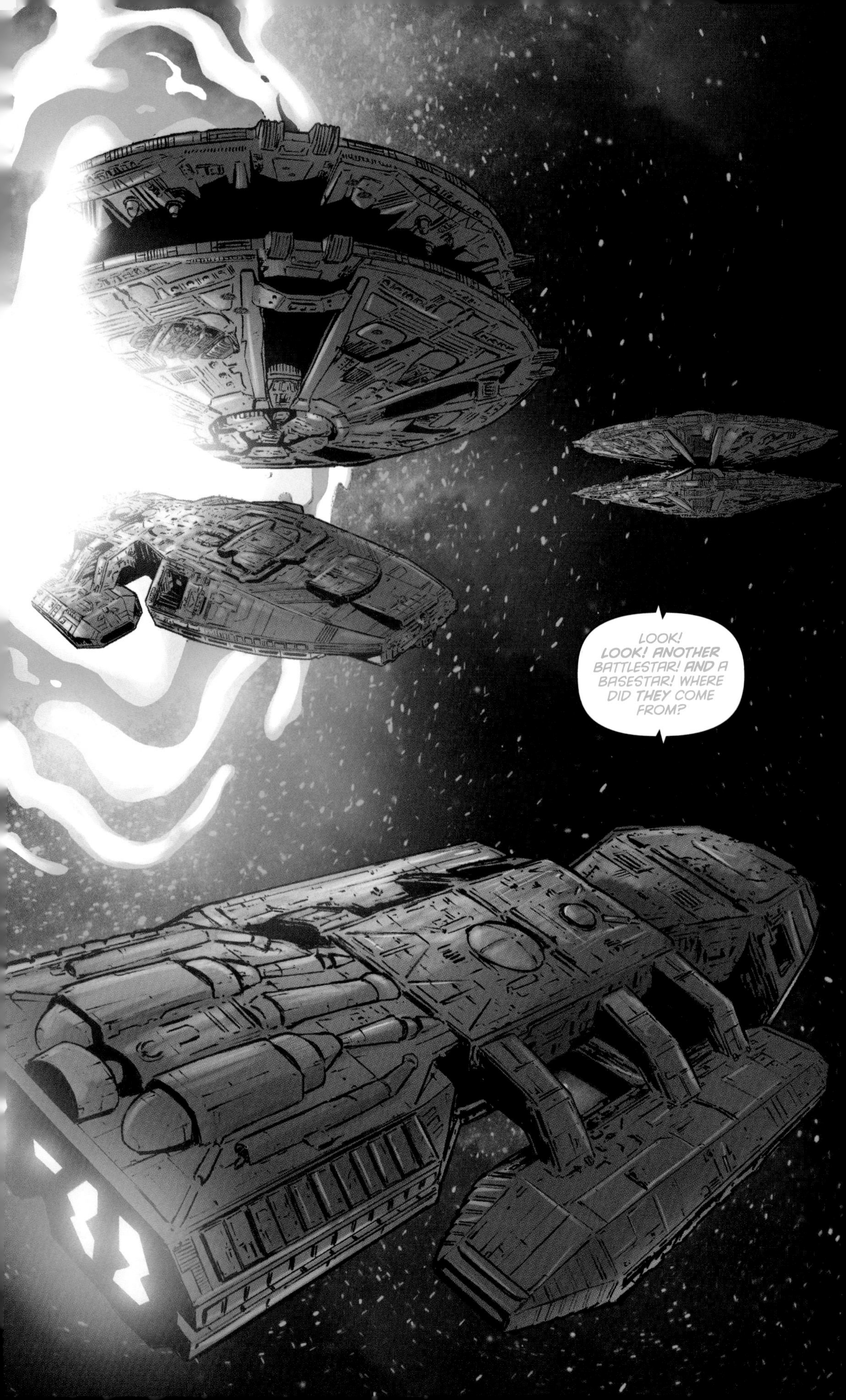
LOOK! LOOK! ANOTHER BATTLESTAR! AND A BASESTAR! WHERE DID THEY COME FROM?

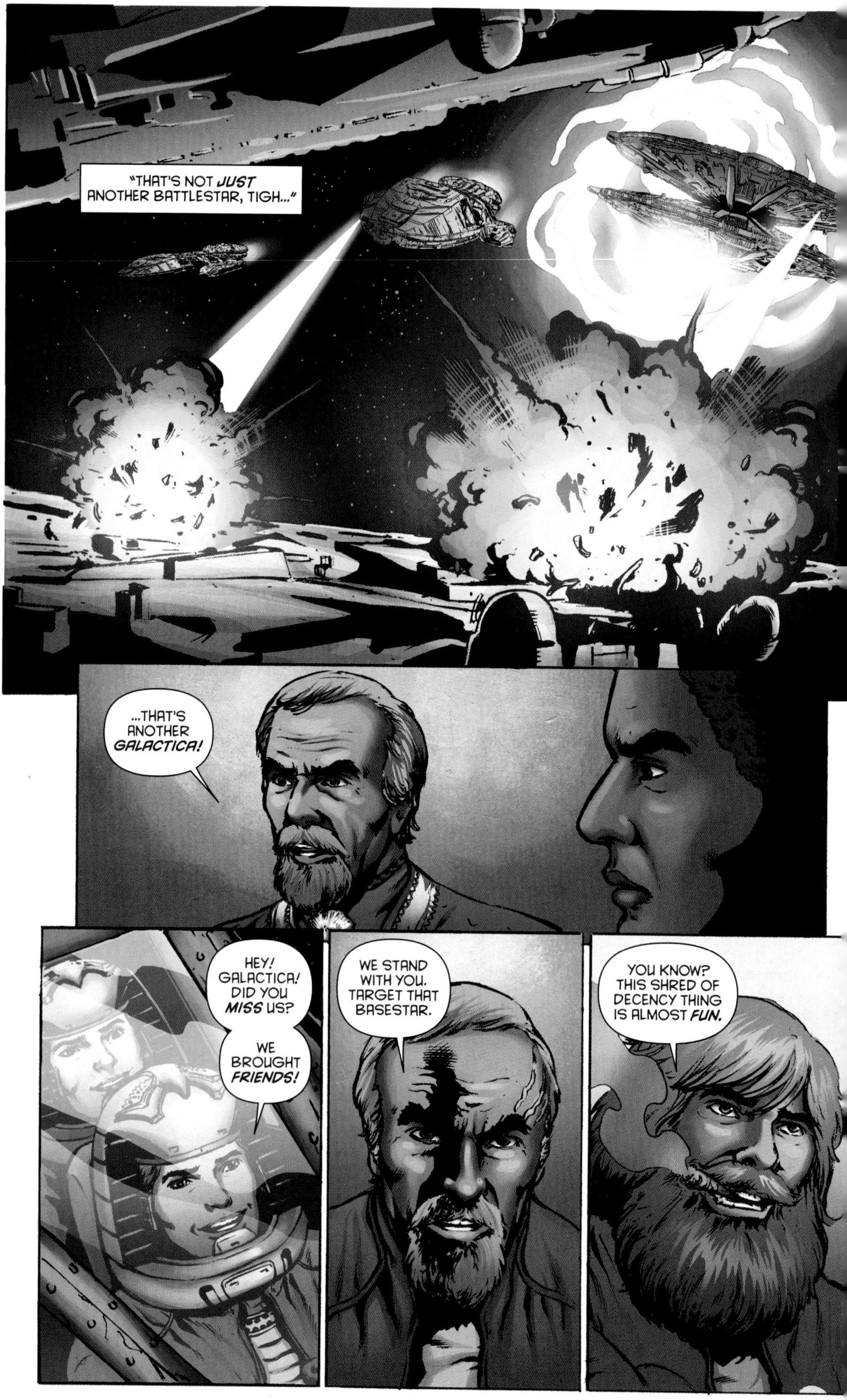
"THAT'S NOT JUST ANOTHER BATTLESTAR, TIGH..."
...THAT'S ANOTHER GALACTICA!
HEY! GALACTICA! DID YOU MISS US?
WE BROUGHT FRIENDS!
WE STAND WITH YOU. TARGET THAT BASESTAR.
YOU KNOW? THIS SHRED OF DECENCY THING IS ALMOST FUN.

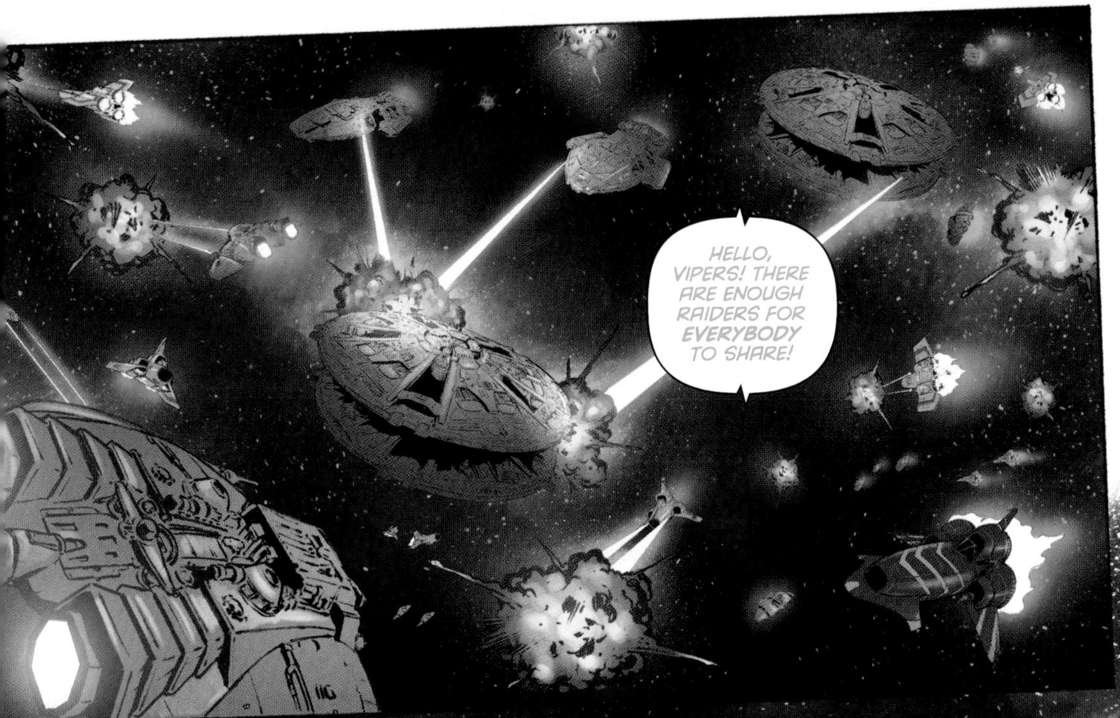
HELLO, VIPERS! THERE ARE ENOUGH RAIDERS FOR EVERYBODY TO SHARE!

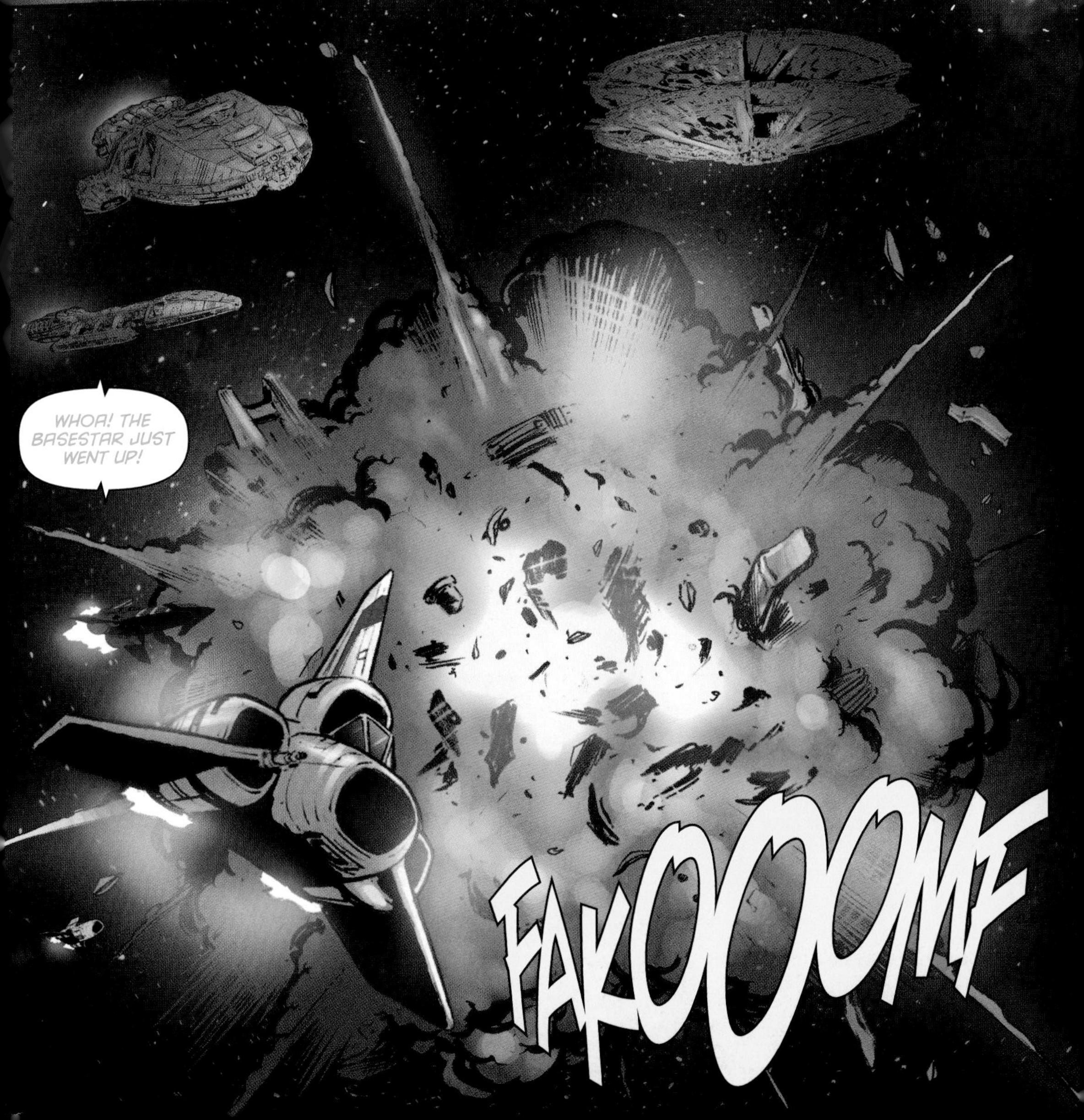
WHOA! THE BASESTAR JUST WENT UP!
FAKOOOMF

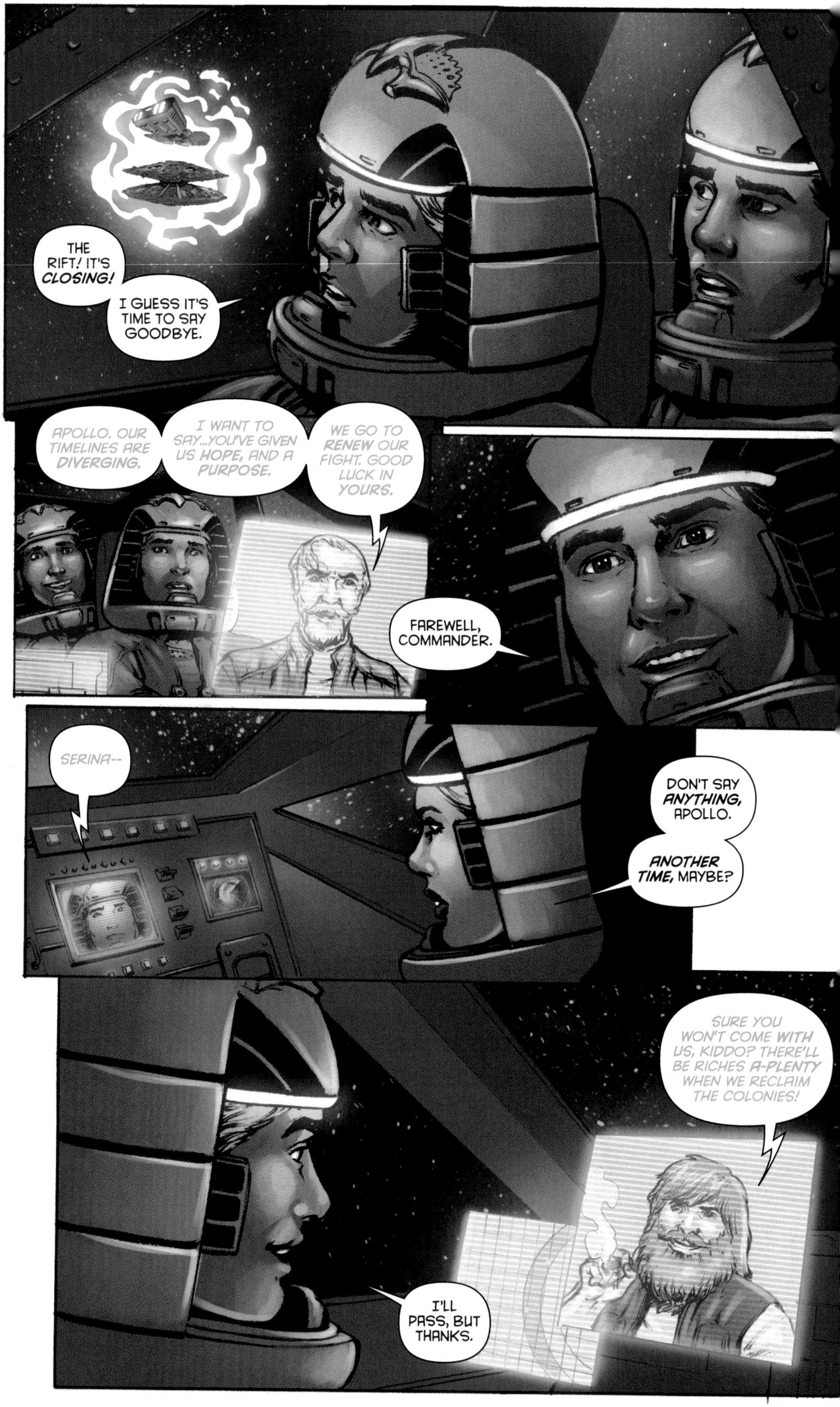
THE RIFT! IT'S CLOSING!
I GUESS IT'S TIME TO SAY GOODBYE.
APOLLO. OUR TIMELINES ARE DIVERGING.
I WANT TO SAY...YOU'VE GIVEN US HOPE, AND A PURPOSE.
WE GO TO RENEW OUR FIGHT. GOOD LUCK IN YOURS.
FAREWELL, COMMANDER.
SERINA--
DON'T SAY ANYTHING, APOLLO.
ANOTHER TIME, MAYBE?
SURE YOU WON'T COME WITH US, KIDDO? THERE'LL BE RICHES A-PLENTY WHEN WE RECLAIM THE COLONIES!
I'LL PASS, BUT THANKS.

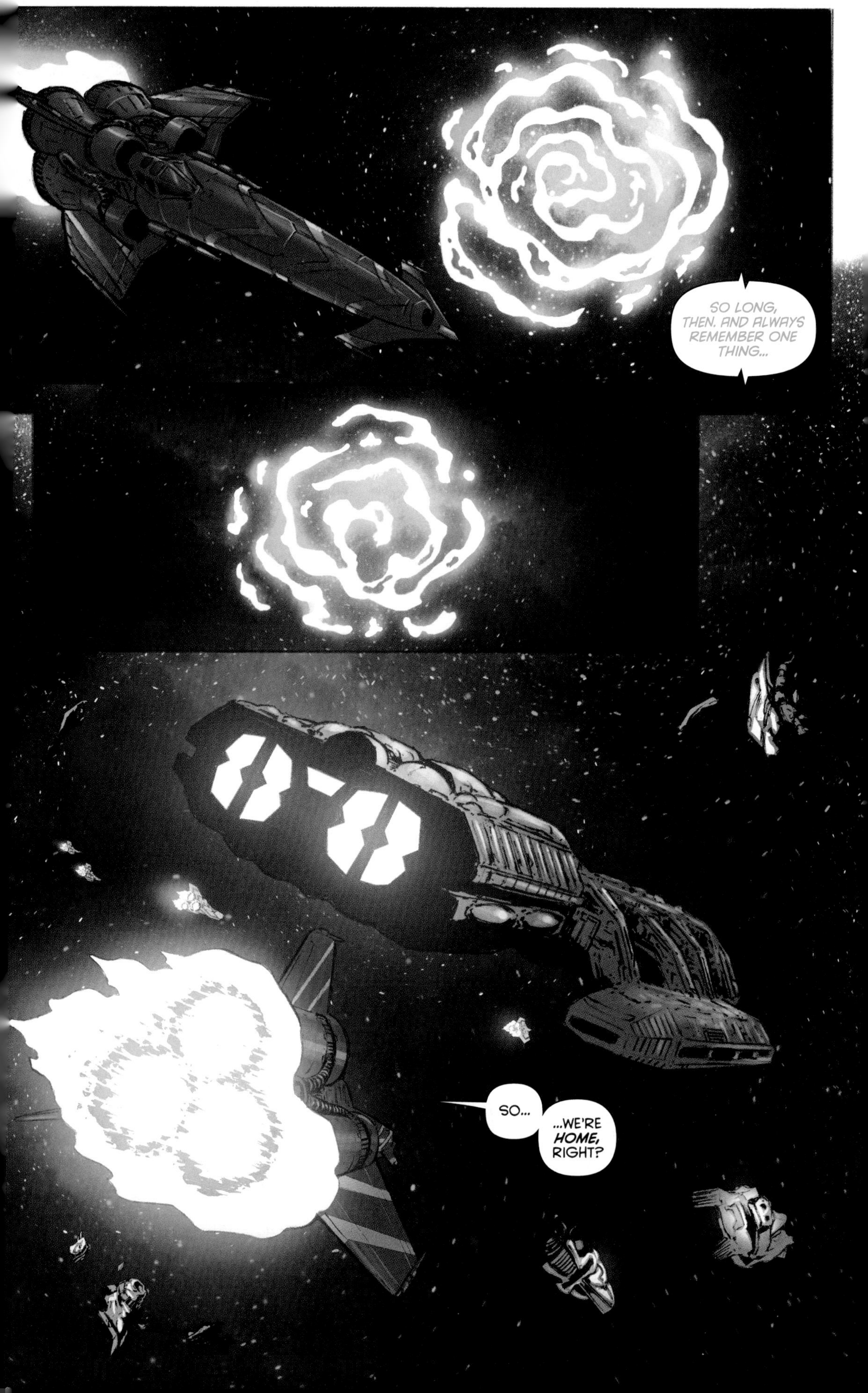

SO LONG, THEN. AND ALWAYS REMEMBER ONE THING...
SO...
...WE'RE *HOME,* RIGHT?

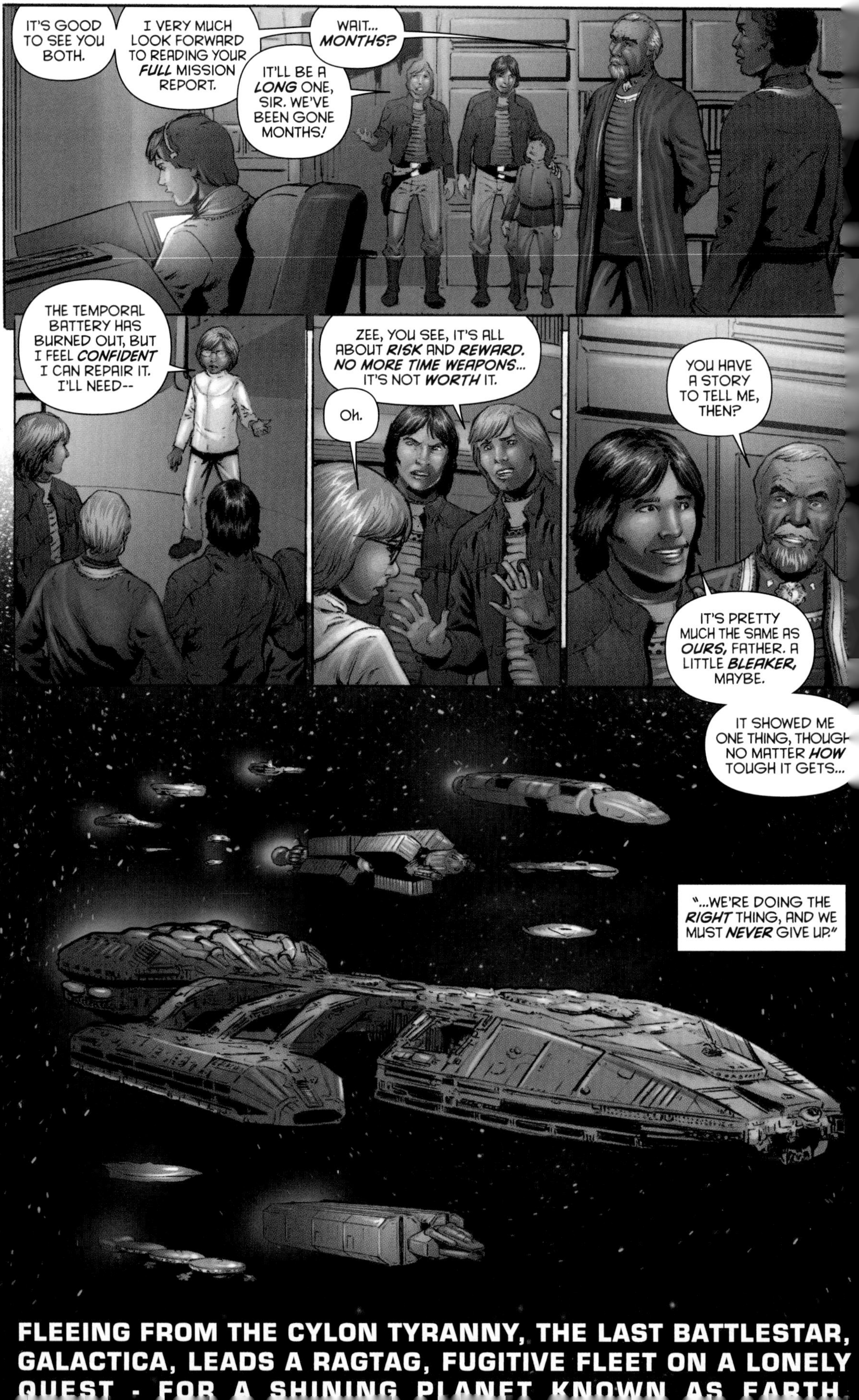
IT'S GOOD TO SEE YOU BOTH.
I VERY MUCH LOOK FORWARD TO READING YOUR FULL MISSION REPORT.
WAIT... MONTHS?
IT'LL BE A LONG ONE, SIR. WE'VE BEEN GONE MONTHS!
THE TEMPORAL BATTERY HAS BURNED OUT, BUT I FEEL CONFIDENT I CAN REPAIR IT. I'LL NEED--
ZEE, YOU SEE, IT'S ALL ABOUT RISK AND REWARD. NO MORE TIME WEAPONS... IT'S NOT WORTH IT.
Oh.
YOU HAVE A STORY TO TELL ME, THEN?
IT'S PRETTY MUCH THE SAME AS OURS, FATHER. A LITTLE BLEAKER, MAYBE.
IT SHOWED ME ONE THING, THOUGH NO MATTER HOW TOUGH IT GETS...
"...WE'RE DOING THE RIGHT THING, AND WE MUST NEVER GIVE UP."
FLEEING FROM THE CYLON TYRANNY, THE LAST BATTLESTAR, GALACTICA, LEADS A RAGTAG, FUGITIVE FLEET ON A LONELY QUEST - FOR A SHINING PLANET KNOWN AS EARTH.

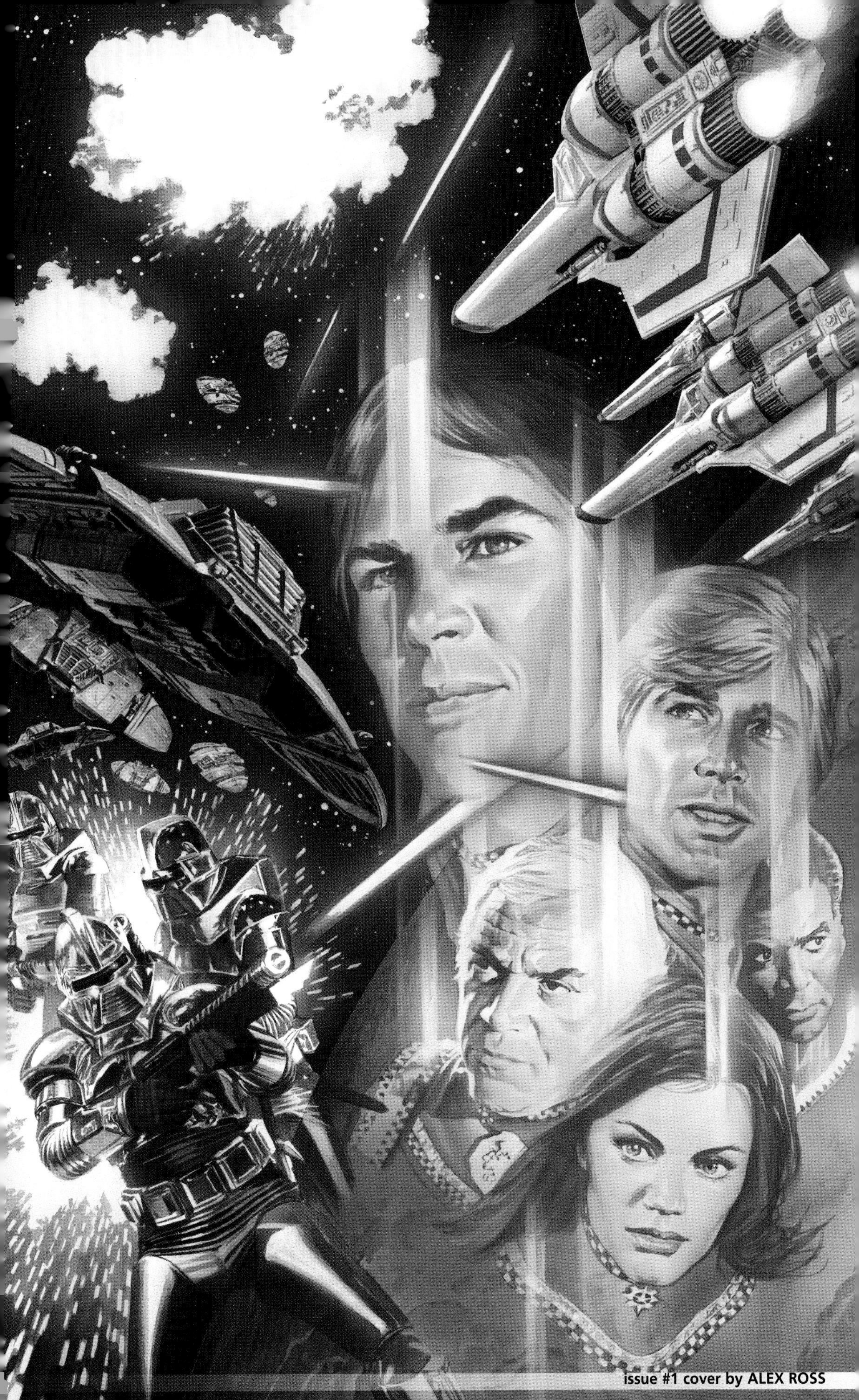

issue #1 cover by ALEX ROSS

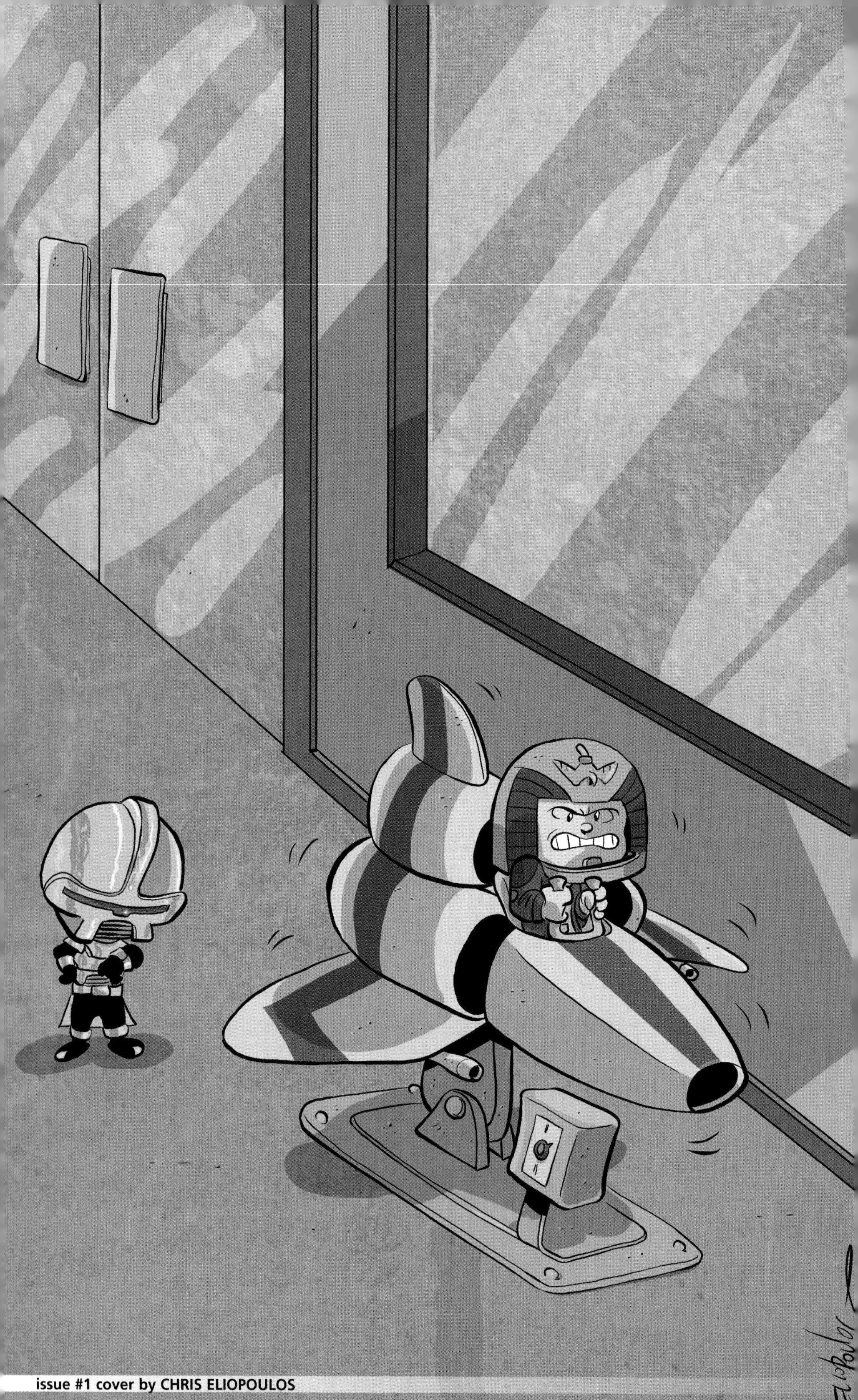

issue #1 cover by CHRIS ELIOPOULOS

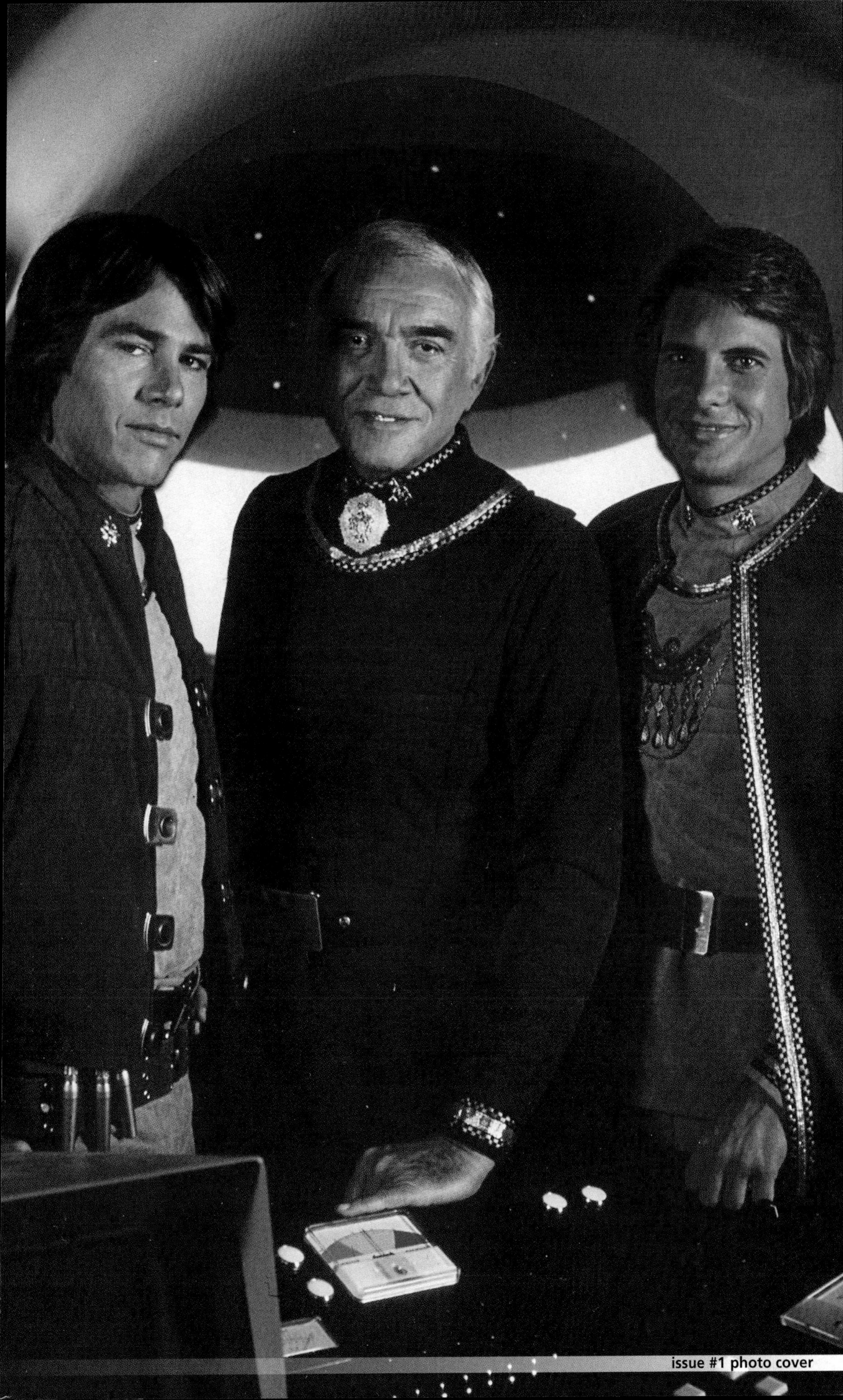

issue #1 photo cover

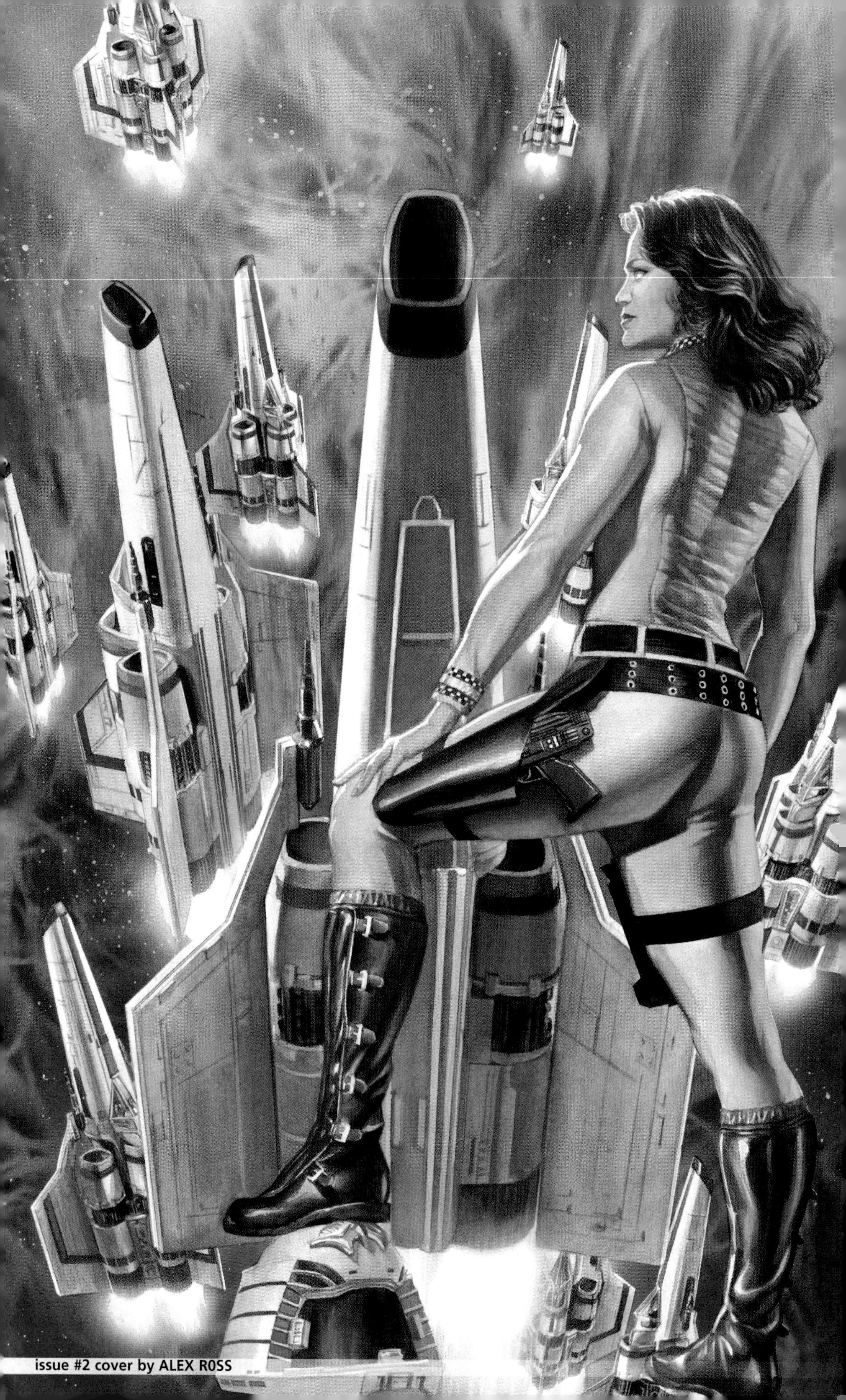

issue #2 cover by ALEX ROSS

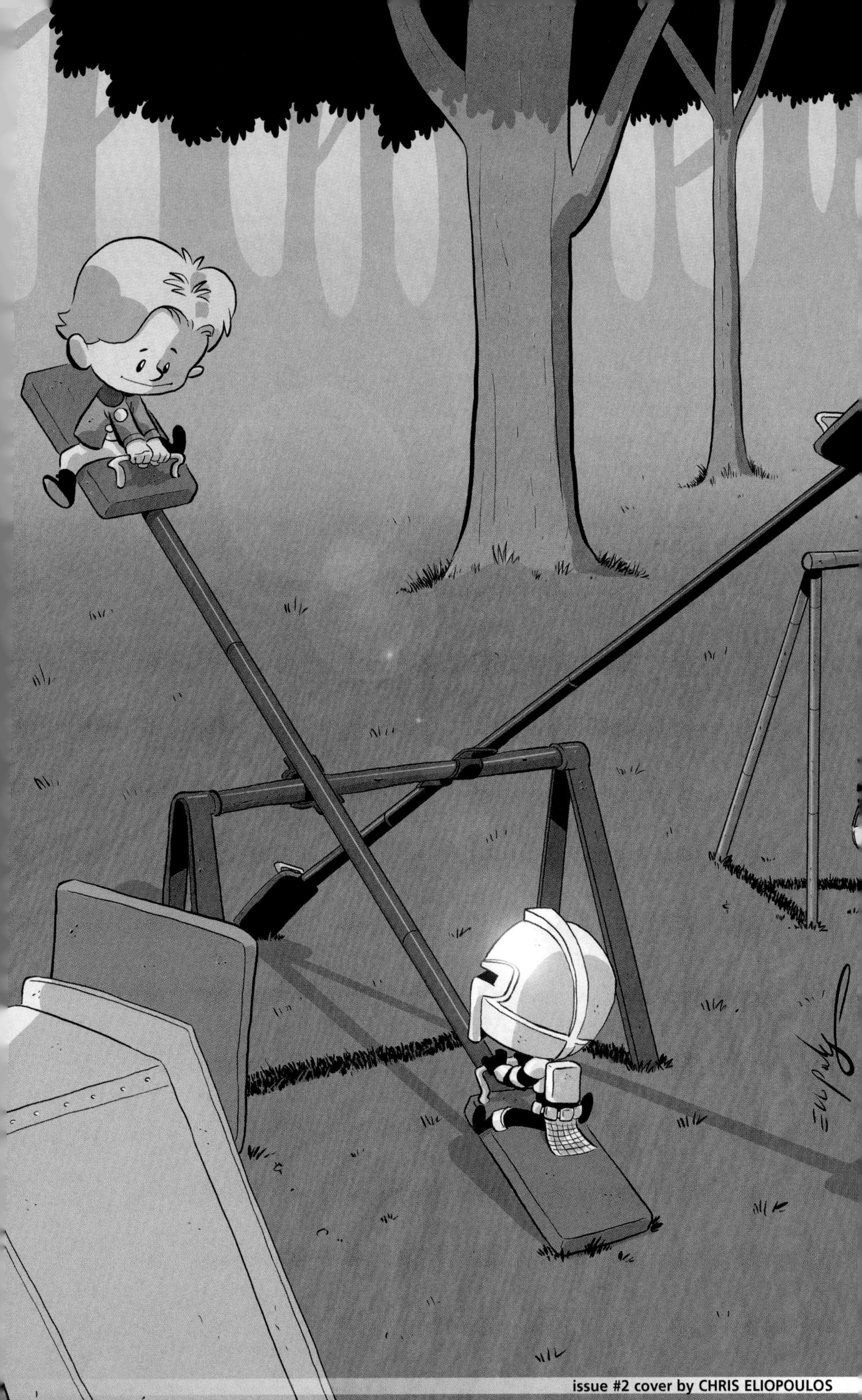

issue #2 cover by CHRIS ELIOPOULOS

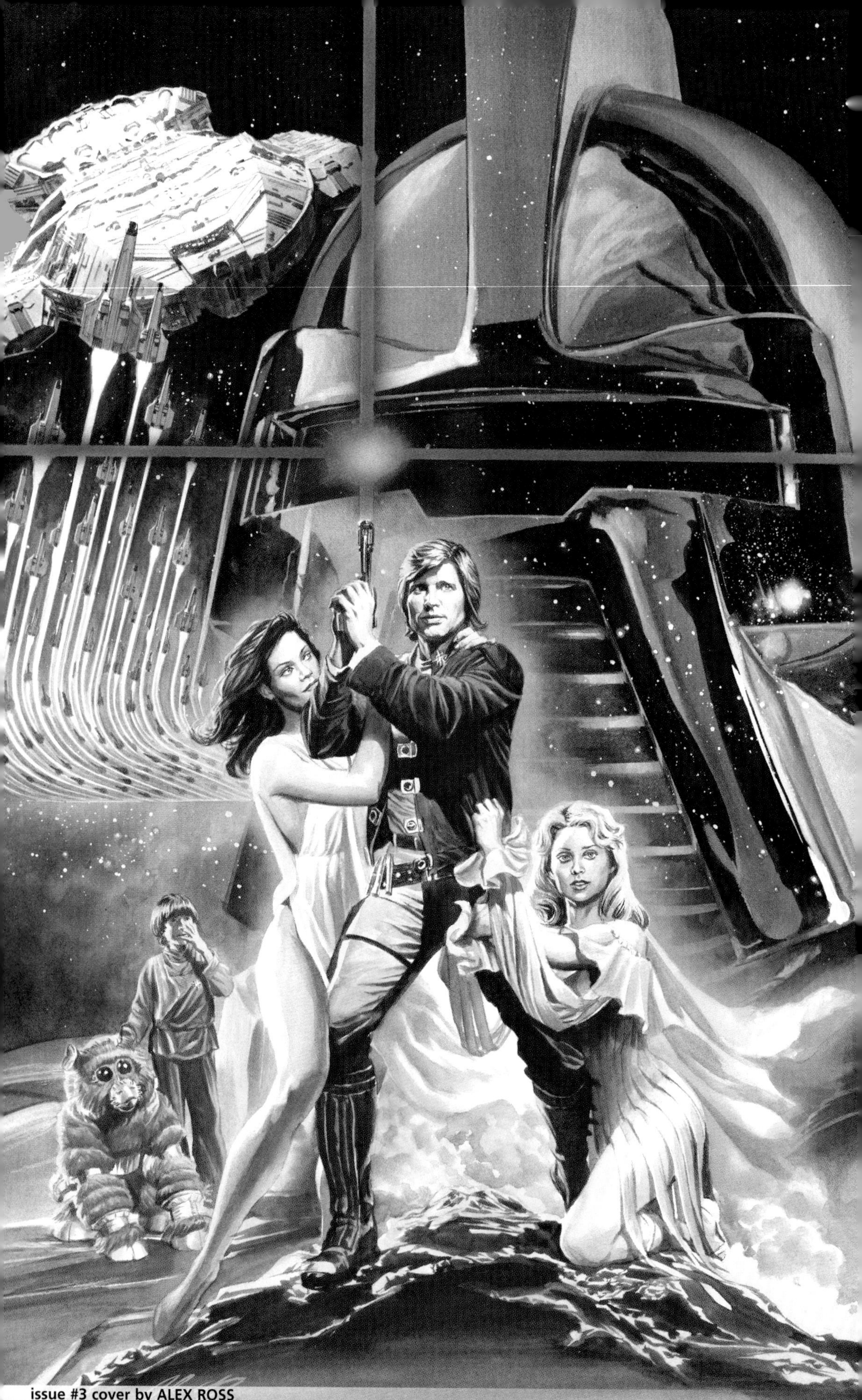

issue #3 cover by ALEX ROSS

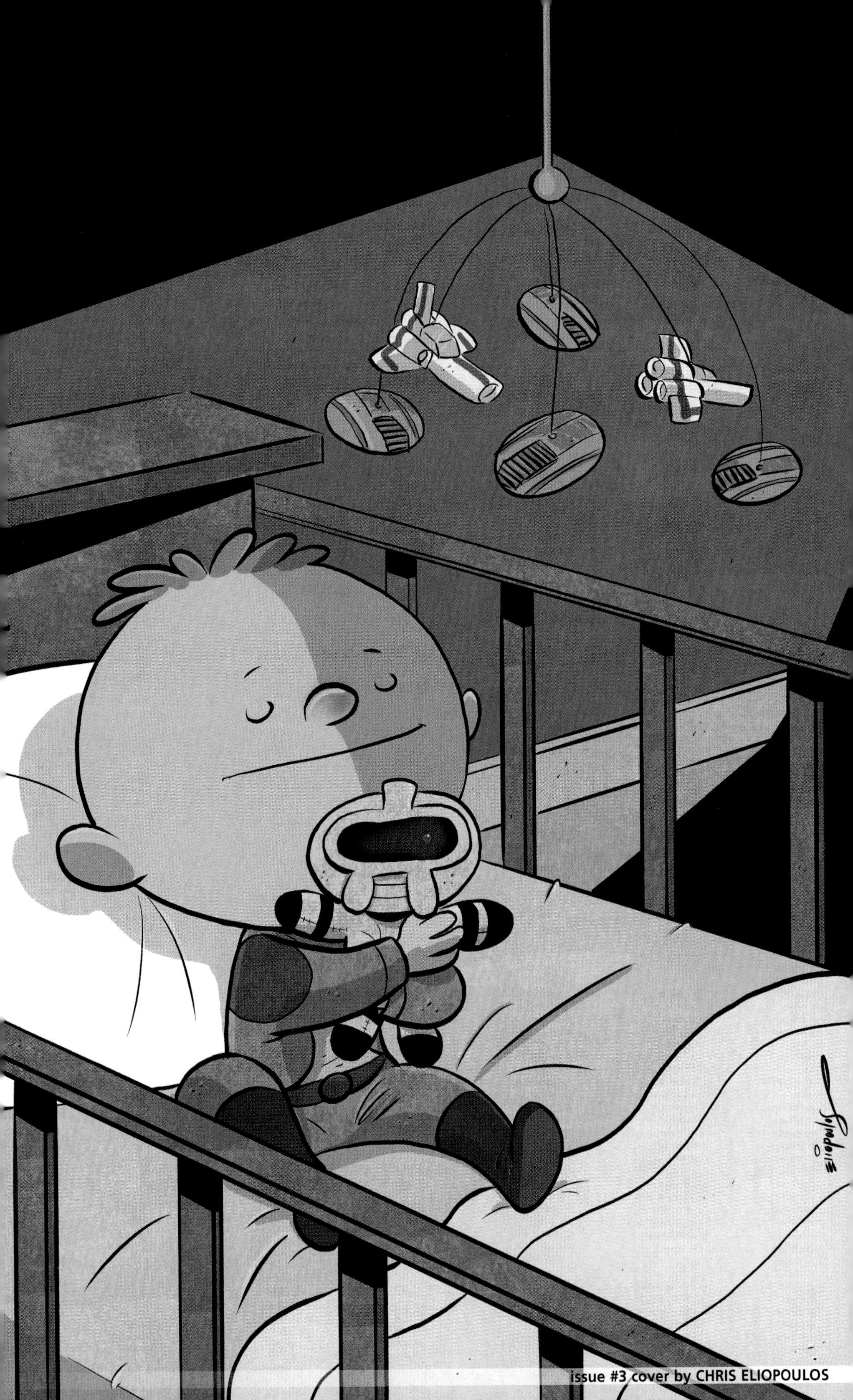

issue #3 cover by CHRIS ELIOPOULOS

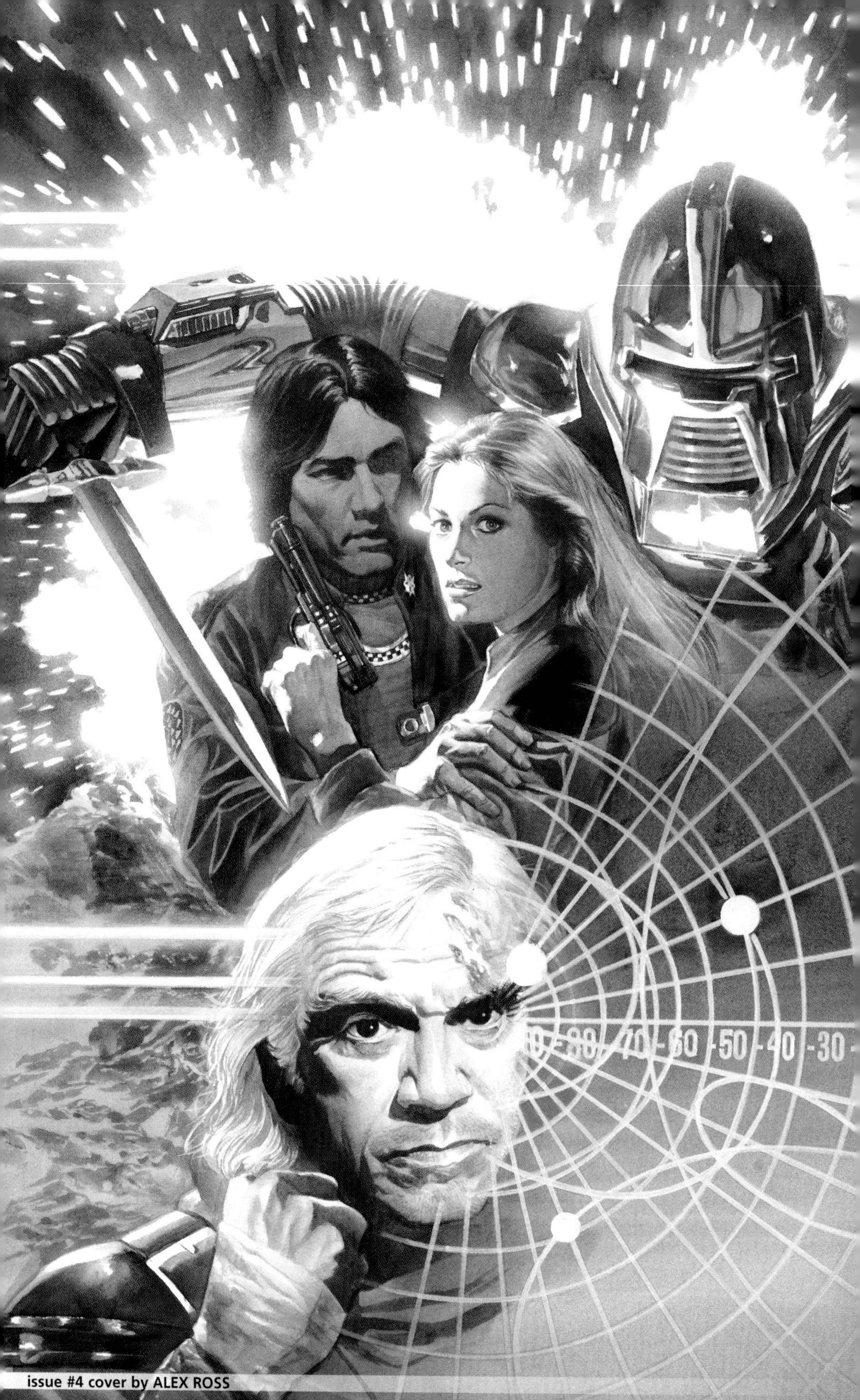
-90 -80 -70 -60 -50 -40 -30
issue #4 cover by ALEX ROSS

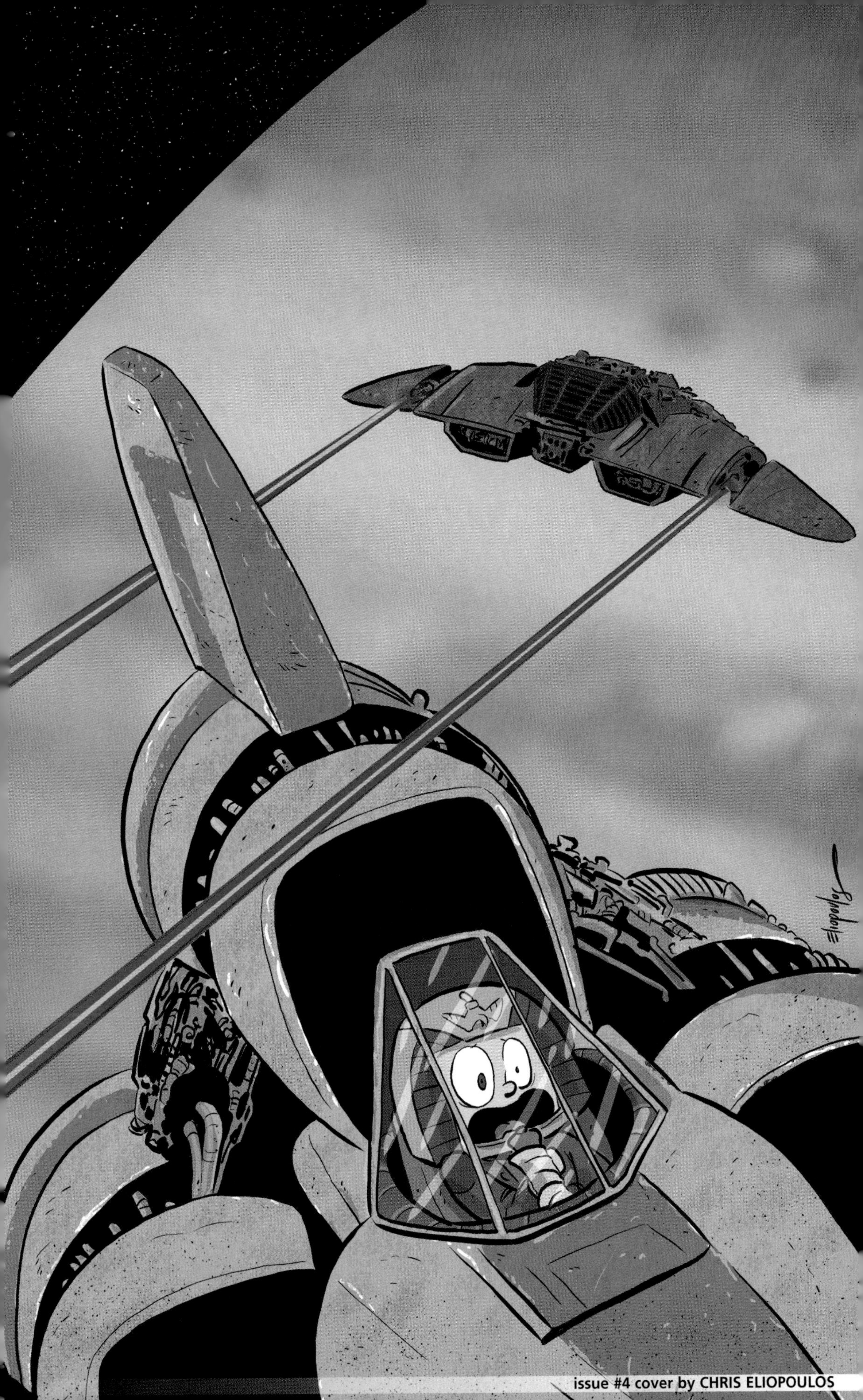

issue #4 cover by CHRIS ELIOPOULOS

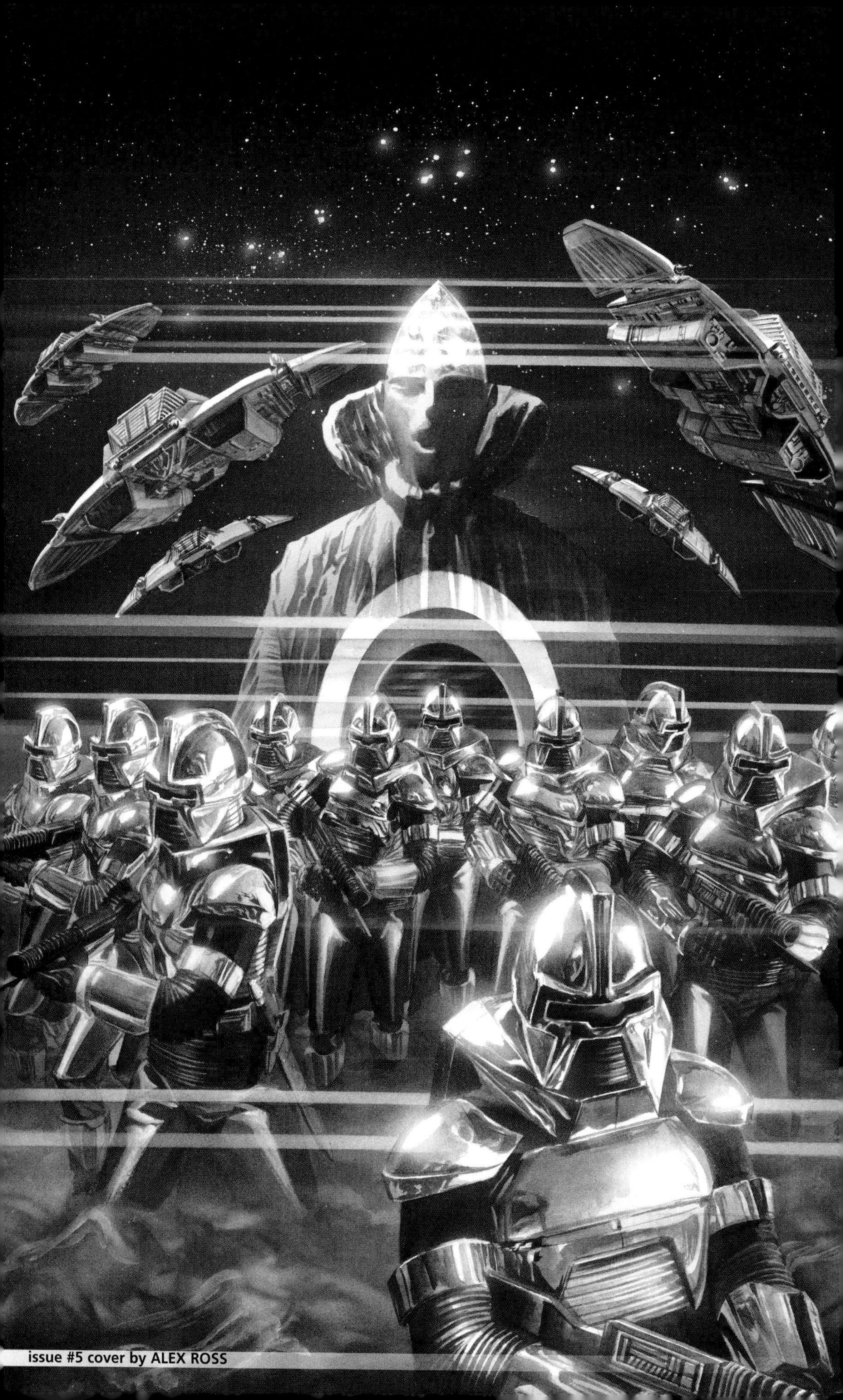

issue #5 cover by ALEX ROSS

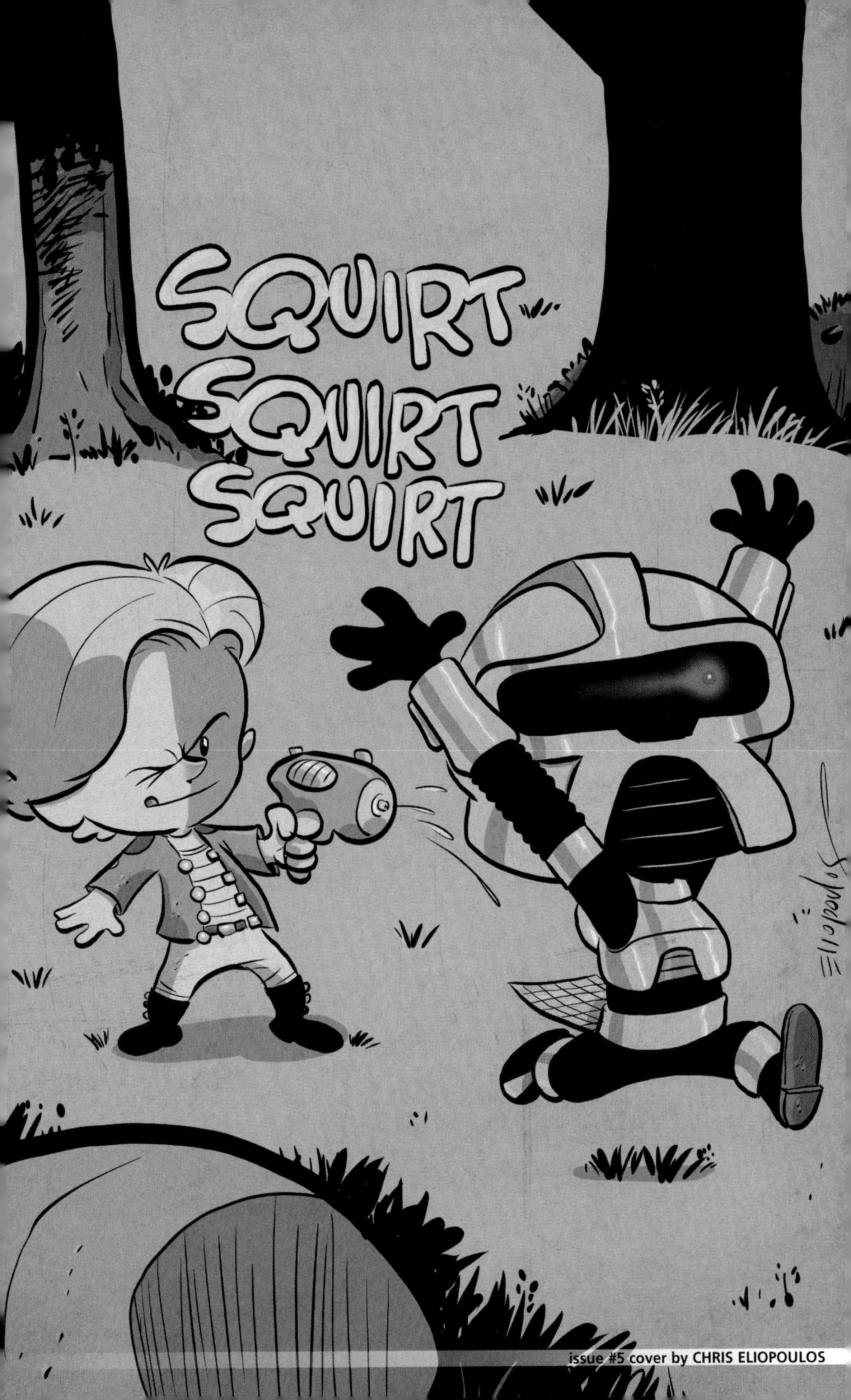
SQUIRT
SQUIRT
SQUIRT

issue #5 cover by CHRIS ELIOPOULOS

BATTLESTAR GALACTICA
MEMORIAL
Full Script for Issue One
22 pages
by DnA

"There are those who believe...that life here...began out there. Far across the universe. With tribes of humans...who may have been the forefathers of the Egyptians...or the Toltecs...or the Mayans...that they may have been the architects of the Great Pyramids...or the lost civilizations of Lemuria...or Atlantis...Some believe that there may yet be brothers of man...who even now fight to survive...somewhere beyond the heavens."

Page 1

Splash page: Impact shot of the Viper belonging to Adama's youngest son, Zac, exploding as it is strafed by Cylon Raiders (ref Episode #1 of TOS).

CAP
<u>Every</u> night.

Inset: Bottom of page: an inset page-wide panel or superimposed image of Adama and Tigh on the bridge of the Galactica watching in stunned silence, the words of President Adar come across the comms.

CAP (CONT'D)
He hears the voice of President Adar on the coms, asking "what was that, Adama? That <u>blast</u>?"

ADAMA
That was my <u>son</u>, Mr President.

CAP
Every night, the memories. His son, his wife, his people, <u>all</u> of mankind...

Page 2-3

Double page spread with inset panels running along the bottom of the page:

Dramatic spread showing the destruction of the Colonial peace fleet by the Cylon fleet. The five battlestars that made up the Colonial peace envoy, the Galactica, Atlantia, Acropolis, Pacifica and the Triton, are ambushed by the Cylons. Only the Galctica fights back, the others are peppered by Cylon weapons and explode in a conflagration. In the FG we see a battlestar (the Atlantia) ripped apart by explosions; its crew spilling into the deadly vacuum of space. In the BG the Galactica is engaged in a dog fight: it's squadrons of Vipers battling Raiders.

CAP (CONT'D)
The <u>Cylon-Colonial Peace Accord</u>. Man meeting machine. The Battlestars Atlantia,

Acropolis, Pacifica, Triton and Galactica.

CAP (CONT'D)
The inhuman treachery of the Cylons.

CAP (CONT'D)
Every night.

CAP (CONT'D)
The memories replay.

Inset panels:

1. Shot looking in the cockpit of the lead Viper on a grim faced Starbuck as he leads the Galactica's resistance. We can see the other Vipers in the BTG through the canopy of his ship.

CAP (CONT'D)
The valiant defenders.

STARBUCK
Close formation! Close fracking formation!

2. On the command deck of the battlestar: Adama is flanked by Apollo and Tigh as he issues the order for the Galactica to withdraw: they must head for Caprica and defend their home colony.

CAP
The impossible choices.

ADAMA
Withdraw Galactica.

TIGH
Commander--?

ADAMA
We must defend our home colony...

Page 4
1. Cut to a shot of the burning cities of Caprica as Adama's shuttle streaks across the smoke and flame-filled sky.

CAP
...Caprica.

CAP (CONT'D)
Hard drop in the first spare shuttle he could find.

CAP (CONT'D)
Hoping to get there in time.

2. Shot of Adama racing from his shuttle which has landed on a hill overlooking his home. He's screaming his wife's name, desperate to warn her before the inevitable can happen again.

CAP (CONT'D)
Hoping.

CAP (CONT'D)
Every night.

ADAMA
Ila! Ila!
(joined)
Get clear!

3. Shot of Ila, his wife, emerging from the house, staring up at Adam in confusion; what's all the shouting. Adama is frantic, yelling for her to get clear.

ADAMA (CONT'D)
Ila!

ILA
Husband?

CAP
Every night, memories that aren't even memories.

4. Suddenly the house explodes in a fireball.

CAP (CONT'D)
Just wishes, unfulfilled.

Page 5

Splash page: Shot of a huge Cylon heavy-weapons unit (HWU) emerging from a pall of smoke: a tank-sized centurion with tracks instead of legs, and mounted cannons and chain-guns (see ref). It is flanked by a Shock troop Squad: new designed Cylon commando troops- Cylon Special Forces foot soldiers. These units are more robotic looking than the classic Cylon design: more stripped down for speed and fighting prowess (see ref). The HWU is firing another barrage at the house, reducing it to flaming rubble.

CAP (CONT'D)
Even in his darkest wish-fulfilment dreams, he's not enough.

CAP (CONT'D)
Not fast enough. Not soon enough.

CAP (CONT'D)
Cylon heavy weapons unit. He can smell the ozone. The heat vents.

CAP (CONT'D)
It's <u>mowing</u> a path through the Caprican residences.

Page 6
1. Adama races down the slope towards the ruins of his homestead as the Cylon shock troops drag his wife, who's still alive, from the flames.

ADAMA
Ila! Come <u>on</u>!

CAP
<u>Every</u> night.

2. The centurions form an immovable wall between Adama and his wife, who has been thrown to her knees, a centurion standing over her, gun pointed at her head.

ADAMA
<u>Ila</u>!

3. On her blood and tear-streaked face as she looks up at Adama, pleading with him to help her. Adama is helpless as the Cylons restrain him.
ILA
Please--

4. Shot of the centurion firing in the FG (Ila off panel). Adama is screaming with anguish, struggling with his captors in the BG as his wife is executed.

ADAMA
<u>Nooooo</u>!

Page 7
1. On Adama surrounded by the pitiless Cylons, he's collapsed to his knees, he's devastated: his world in flames, wife and youngest son dead, his people destroyed.

[NO DIALOGUE]

2. He stares up, face streaked with tears, into the barrels of the Cylon's weapons welcoming the oblivion they offerÉ

ADAMA
Do it.
(joined)
<u>Do</u> it, then.

3. Extreme CU of the barrel of a Cylon blaster rifle as it ignites with an energy pulseÉ

ADAMA (CONT'D)
(off)
Do it, and burn in h--

Page wide black panel.

[NO DIALOGUE]

Page 8
1. Shot of Adama as he bolts awake from this reoccurring nightmare, drenched in fear-sweat and choking back a sob. NB. This version of Adama has a silver goatee: a hybrid of the clean shaven version of TOS and the full bearded one in Galactica: 1980.

ADAMA
Gnhh!

CAP
Every night.

2. Shot of him sitting up, feet over the side of his bed- looking out of his porthole at the rag-tag fleet of colonial ships that fill the space-scape. He's reaching over to a glowing holo-cube that can be seen on his bedside table.

CAP (CONT'D)
Every night the same replay. The same memories and hopeless wishes.

CAP (CONT'D)
Things that could never be.

3. Closer on him as he holds the cube, which displays a glowing holo-shot of his family from happier times: a smiling group shot of himself with Ila, Apollo, Zac and Athena.

CAP (CONT'D)
A family that will never be complete again.

4. Cut to external shot of his porthole in the side of the battlestar: Adama can be seen sitting on his bed, head in hands, sobbing.

CAP (CONT'D)
A handful of survivors searching for salvation.

5. Pull back further to show the Galactica heading up the refugee fleet set against the spectacular spacescape of the vast gas clouds of a planetary nebula which they are using to shield them from their Cylon pursuers (see ref).

CAP
Relentlessly pursued by an implacable foe.

Page 9
Splash page:
Cut to:

The next morning; Adama leading a memorial ceremony commemorating the anniversary of the attack: Adama is remembering the fallen, honouring their memories and reconfirming the mission to lead the colonial survivors to the fabled home world; Earth and calling on the blessing of God and the Lords of Kobol. This ceremony takes place in the large Worship chamber with Adama presiding over the congregation from a central raised dais which is surrounded by candles. He is wearing ceremonial robes in his role as spiritual leader. The chamber and Adama's robes are all based on Egyptian designs (in the same way the architecture of Caprica and the designs of the colonial uniforms are)- the chamber has a glowing glass pyramidal structure at its centre and is fringed with ornate columns, inscribed with hieroglyphics (see ref). The congregation are gathered in a circle around the dais.
Adama is projected on screens across the colonial fleet. Adama older; has a goatee (hallway between full beard of 1980 and clean shaven BSG).
Adama and co are in reflective mood- musing the years they've been forced to roam the galaxy, forever hunted by the relentless, merciless Cylons.

ADAMA
In the seventh millennium of time, a tribe of humanoids engaged in a terrifying conflict against a race of machines.
(joined)
The humans lost. We lost.
(joined)
Now, led by the last surviving warship, the mighty Battlestar Galactica, we few survivors move slowly through the heavens in search of our ancestral brothers.
(joined)
A tribe of humans known through ancient records to be located somewhere on a distant, shining palnet.
(joined)
A planet called Earth.

Page 10
Sequence of page wide panels showing the colonial refugees as they watch the ceremony:

1. Pan across the congregation showing Apollo, Athena with Boxey and Muffit, Starbuck with Cassiopeia. Boomer, Sheba and Greenbean in BG. Everyone solemn, reflective.
JAG
On this day, this infamous anniversary, we remember...

2. Shot of the command deck where Tigh and the crew watch the holo-screen from their battle-stations.

JAG (CONT'D)

... we remember the <u>treachery</u> of the attack that set us on this path...

3. Shot of the Galactica's engineering bays where the techs and engineers, led by Doctor Wilker and Zee, are gathered to watch the ceremony from their high-tech work stations.

JAG (CONT'D)
...we remember the fallen...

4. Shot of Adama on holo-screen on-board the cramped hold of the Gemeni (see ref) watched by refugee families.

JAG (CONT'D)
...we remember our mission...

5. Cut to a shot of a busy Medi-lab bay on the Rising Star where Doctor Salik and a group of sci-techs are watching Adama's address on holo-screens. NB. Maybe we could have a few of the known alien races seen in this sequence: Ovians, Borellian Nomen and even Borays? Plus there are a few other aliens seen in TOS which we could see in the crowds, just to add some color? (see ref).

JAG (CONT'D)
...we remember our <u>purpose</u>.

CAP
<u>Every</u> night.

Page 11
1. Raised angle shot looking down as the congregation breaks up. Focus on Apollo, Athena and Starbuck as they share a private moment with Adama and Tigh, remembering their lost family members.

CAP (CONT'D)
Like he <u>needs</u> to remember.

TIGH
A fine speech, commander.

2. Closer in on Starbuck and Apollo, who still blame themselves for Apollo's brother, Zac's death as it was their deception that put him in harm's way- wishing they could change what happened.

APOLLO
(whisper)
Zac. Zac should be here <u>with</u> us today. If we--

STARBUCK
Apollo, <u>don't</u>.

3. Adama places a hand on Apollo's shoulder and reassures them: they all have guilt about what happened that fateful day- they have to deal with it every day and must focus on doing what they can to help the survivors.

ADAMA
Starbuck's right, son. Your brother died because of our enemy's treachery.
(joined)
Not because of any mistake you made.

4. Shot of them reacting; their reflections cut short as the chamber is plunged into emergency lighting and alarms fill the air: Tigh reports from the bridge that the colonial fleet is under attack by Cylons!

STARBUCK
What the--?!

FX
BREEEEEP! BREEEEEEP! BREEEEEP!

TIGH
Commander! Bridge reports incoming Cylon attack!

Page 12
1. Cut to an external shot of the convoy beset by Cylon Raiders with several Basestars in the BG emerging from the boiling clouds of the nebula which the convoy was using to shield them from the Cylons but it shielded the Cylons from them as well.

CAP
"We have multiple basestars! They were using the local nebula as a hiding place!"

CAP (CONT'D)
"Ironic..."

2. Cut to the command bridge of the Galactica: Adama joins Tigh are taking his command position and barking orders: holo-maps hang in the air showing the danger of their situation: glowing markers signal the Cylon Basestars and Raiders in relation to the fleet. The fleet has been caught in an ambush.

ADAMA
... seeing as we were using the same nebula to cloak our position from their chase ships.
(joined)
Our ruse has shielded our enemy from us.
(joined)
Give me full situational!

3. On a grim Adama as he orders all Viper squads into the fray and the Galactica to turn and face the attack: they have to buy the fleet time to get deeper into the nebula; it's their only chance of escape.

ADAMA (CONT'D)
This is <u>bad</u>.
(joined)
Scramble <u>all</u> Viper squadrons!
(joined)
Turn the Galactica to face the attack! We have to buy the fleet enough time to get <u>deeper</u> into the Nebula and <u>evade</u> Cylon sensors!

Page wide panel split into 2 panels:
1. Shot of Apollo in the cockpit of his Viper as it speeds down the launch tube, he's responding, serious, intent.

CAP
"It's their <u>only</u> chance of escape."

APOLLO
<u>Launch</u>!

2. Shot of Starbuck in the cockpit of his Viper, grinning; cocky, self-assured. The Cylons want a fight; let's give em one they'll never forget!

STARBUCK
Let's wrap this <u>fast</u>! I've got a game of <u>pyramid</u> to finish!

Page 13
1. Awesome big shot of the Galactica banking around to face the oncoming Cylon force, opening fire with its battery of ion cannons and laser torpedoes as the space around it is filled with Vipers and Raiders in an intense dogfight. In the BG the convoy's ships are all igniting their thrusters to make their escape.

JAG FROM
Convoy! This is Adama! <u>Accelerate</u>! Best speed!
(joined)
Galactica! Turn about and <u>open fire</u>! Turbos double front!
(joined)
All weapons!

2. Shot of the Galactica as several Raiders fly straight into its hull, Kamikaze-style. Explosions ripple along it. A desperate new tactic on the Cylons are employing.

JAG
Commander! Cylon <u>suicide attacks</u>! We--

3. Cut inside as the engineering decks are rocked by explosions; the Cylons are targeting the engines. Crewmen are blown off their feet as the engine cores sustain damage.

[NO DIALOGUE]

4. On Adama, as Athena reports the damage to him from her control station.

ADAMA
Athena!

ATHENA
Damage reports coming in! Major damage to engineering... stand by...

Page 14
1. Cut to the engine section as crewmen frantically extinguish fires and pull bodies clear. An engine tech is reporting the damage to Adama- they have a choice.

TECH
We're hit _hard_! Tell the commander he has a _choice_...
(joined)
Use power to flee but _lose_ the shields, or stay put and _keep_ power to the shield and weapon systems,
(joined)
Surely we have to draw the Cylons' fire and buy the fleet time to escape...

2. On the command deck Adama responds to a holo of Doctor Wilker, who has an over-eager Doctor Zee with him. Adama is short; he has important things to deal with. Wilker is explaining how the child protégée has an urgent request.

HOLO
Commander!

ADAMA
Not _now_, Doctor Wilker!

HOLO
Commander, my protege Zee has an _urgent_ request!

3. On Adama, impatiently listening to Zee who is making his case: he begs Adama to deploy his experimental temporal weapons on the Cylons: they may give them edge they need to escape.

ADAMA
This is _hardly_ the--

ZEE HOLO
I _implore_ you to sanction the use of the _temporal weapons_ I have been developing!
(joined)
We need to _delay_ the Cylons while the fleet--

ADAMA
Those weapons are forbidden for a reason, Zee!
(joined)

Besides, I am _more_ than aware of the tactical situation. I--

4. Pull back as the Galactica is hit again and one of the control desks explodes, sending the crewman flying. Tigh and Adama are rocked by the impact.

[NO DIALOGUE]

5. CU of Adama: Because the Galactica needs time to get its engines repaired, Adama approves Zee's audacious plan.

ADAMA
We need time to get the Galactica's engines back on line.
(joined)
Gods of Kobol help me. Zee? Your weapons... are _sanctioned_.

Page 15
1. Cut to Apollo and Starbuck, removing their helmets and striding from their Vipers which are in the steam-filled docking bay of the Galactica: they are not happy at being pulled from the battle but have been ordered to report to Zee by Adama with all haste.

APOLLO
Why the _frack_ have we been pulled out of the line?

STARBUCK
The fleet needs _every_ viper it can get. There are toasters all _over_--

2. They are met by Wilker and Zee, the child genius is obnoxious and arrogant: telling them to hurry, they are delaying his experiment- which he is confident will save them all.

ZEE REAL
No! _No_! You _fail_ to comprehend, Lt Starbuck!
(joined)
You will be the _salvation_ of us _all_!
(joined
Or the _delivery mechanism_ of it, at _least_!

STARBUCK
Uh, _what_ now?

3. Starbuck and Apollo stare incredulously as Zee strides away, beckoning them to follow him through a hatchway into another bay. Wilker shrugs in a 'what you gonna do' way, as Starbuck frowns; Wilker wants to give the obnoxious little fracker a backhand too.

APOLLO
I know you think _highly_ of Zee, Doctor, but is he _really_... how can I put this..?

WILKER
Zee is a <u>strange</u> being, Apollo, an old mind in a young body, and he is <u>thoroughly</u> infuriating.
(joined)
But, in this instance, I believe he may have the <u>only</u> advantage that may save us.
(joined)
I warn you... it is <u>extreme</u> and <u>risky</u>...

4. On them as they join Zee on a balcony overlooking the chamber. We are close in,
looking at them as they stare down, stunned as Zee gestures at his handiwork a big, shit-
eating grin plastered across his face.

ZEE REAL
Behold! You <u>see</u>?
(joined)
<u>Time</u> will save us!

Page 16
Bigshot: reveal the two augmented Vipers. Zee, Apollo, Starbuck and Wilker are
descending a gantry to the deck where the Vipers are housed. Crewmen and techs are
busy prepping them for take-off- like a flight crew on an aircraft carrier. Steam rises
from pipes that snake around the decking with cables, chains and struts that hold them
in place. The Vipers have been fitted with the prototype Time Warp Synthesizers (TWS:
ref Galactica 1980). The ships redesigned like mean looking hotrods, maybe colored red
or black and yellow to distinguish them from the others, with extra shielding and huge
rear-mounted boosters that house the TWS engines- only enough materials to fit out 2
ships- it is all that Zee was allowed to play with. Behind the ships is a huge machine:
the temporal energy battery which Zee has developed to power the craft. He explains the
set up and tells Apollo and Starbuck to get on-board.

APOLLO
Modified <u>Vipers</u>?

ZEE REAL
They would only allow me <u>two</u> to refit. Resources are so <u>finite</u> in the fleet.
(joined)
Each one had been fitted with prototypes of my <u>Temporal Warper</u> weapons.

APOLLO
<u>Temporal weapons</u>? They were <u>outlawed</u> for a <u>reason</u>, Zee!

ZEE REAL
I <u>know</u>!
(joined)
They disjoint time <u>itself</u>. They are <u>formidably</u> dangerous!

3 panels running along the bottom tier, Zee's instructions/explanation running over
them:

1. On Apollo in the cockpit of his modified Viper- launch procedure.

ZEE REAL (CONT'D)
(off?)
"The Warpers are charged from the <u>main battery</u> here on the flight deck. You'll have perhaps <u>ten</u> shots maximum <u>each</u>.

2. Shot of the Viper in the launch tube.

ZEE REAL (CONT'D)
(off?)
Understand me, Apollo. Make those blasts <u>count</u>. Concentrate of the <u>basestars</u>.
(joined)
You may not have time to come back and <u>recharge</u>.

3. Reverse shot of the turbos blasting the Viper out of its launch tube into space.

CAP
"Apollo?"

APOLLO
(off?)
I <u>get</u> it, Zee. Doomsday weapons <u>and</u> a suicide mission.

Page 17
1. On the two ships as they bank in the space above the raging dogfight- Vipers and Raider locked in combat.

FROM APOLLO
Stay tight, Starbuck.
(joined)
Heat your weapon coils.
2. External shot on Apollo's cockpit in the FG, Starbuck's ship in the BG as they prepare to deploy their weapons.

FROM STARBUCK
We need to clear some of those raiders out of our visors so we can get a clean shot at the <u>basestars</u>, Apollo.

FROM APOLLO
Agreed.

3. Cut to Zee and Wilker inside the launch bay monitoring the huge temporal energy generator that powers the weapons.

WILKER
They're flooding power to the warp synthesizers.

ZEE HOLO
They <u>mustn't</u> waste the shots! They need them for the basestars!

WILKER
Apollo and Starbuck are the best pilots in the <u>fleet</u>. They <u>know</u> what they're doing.
4. Shot of the Vipers sweeping down and opening fire at the Cylon Raiders: their weapons generating a weird crackling temporal blast (color FX).

FROM APOLLO
<u>Fire</u>!

NB. It would be good to create a specific design for the temporal energy FX so that we can identify it easily. In Galactica 1980 series they used concentric blue glowing circles, so maybe a version of this but with arcs of electrical energy (see ref)?

Page 18
1. Shot of the Raiders they hit as they are enveloped in a surging net of crackling temporal energy.

[NO DIALOGUE]

2. Same shot but the Raiders have vanished all that's left in the space they occupied is a rippling flare of temporal energy.

[NO DIALOGUE] (CONT'D)

3. On Starbuck in his cockpit ye-haaawing- the Cylons won't know what hit them!

STARBUCK
Okay! <u>Total</u> temporal wipe-out!
(joined)
I might actually be <u>impressed</u>!

4. Cut to Zee, an evil little smile on his face.

ZEE REAL
<u>Yes</u>! They have been <u>temporally displaced</u>! <u>Removed</u> from our timeline as if they <u>never</u> existed!
(joined)
If Apollo and Starbuck strike the basestars <u>similarly</u>...
(joined)
...well, then, the basestars will have been <u>removed</u> from time and this attack will never have happened in the <u>first place</u>!

Page 19
1. Cut to Adama and Tigh, command deck. Adama is concerned even though the tide of the battle appears to be turning, he is worried about the use of such potentially dangerous weapons: who knows what the ramifications could be?

ADAMA
Temporal weapons.
(joined)
Tigh, have we stopped so low? To use prohibited weapons tech?

TIGH
Sir, the Cylons--

ADAMA
We forbade it for a reason, Tigh! The consequences of time-warp could--

2. Exterior shot of the Galactica as another Raider eludes the Vipers and its defences, heading straight for the hull.

JAG
Commander! Another suicide run! Shields--

3. Cut inside the Raider cockpit- the Cylon pilot.

CYLON
By your command.

4. BOOM! It impacts on the Galactica's hull blowing the shields and exploding in a fireball.

[NO DIALOGUE]

Page 20
1. Inside the labs: Zee and Wilker and their tech crew are blown of their feet as the temporal generator overloads: weird energy flares and crackles.

WILKER
UGHHN!

ZEE HOLO
The temporal battery is overloading!

2. Cut to Starbuck looking confused.

STARBUCK
Apollo? My weapons system just quit on me!

JAG
Mine too. Stand by.

3. Longshot: the modified Vipers watch as the Galactica is enveloped in a halo of temporal energy that ripples and crackles along its hull.

STARBUCK

Apollo! What the <u>frack</u> is happening to the Galactica!?

Page 21

1. Suddenly it detonates: the whole sector enveloped in a temporal vortex cantered on the Battlestar.

[NO DIALOGUE]

2. On the Vipers as they are rocked and buffeted by expanding waves of temporal distortion.

FROM APOOLO

<u>Ughnn</u>

FROM STARBUCK

<u>Felgercarb</u>!

3. Cut to Apollo, fighting his controls. Outside his cockpit is a boiling swirl of temporal energies as space and time are warped around them.

APOLLO

Starbuck? You <u>reading</u> me?

(joined)

Starbuck? <u>Galactica</u>?

4. On Starbuck he's regained control but his sensors' readings are crazy. He's getting nothing from their squad and the Galactica has gone silent. The entire region empty-filled with exotic energy.

STARBUCK

I <u>read</u> you, Apollo, but my sensor readings are <u>crazy</u>!

(joined)

It scans like there's <u>nothing</u> here at all except you, me and a <u>storm</u> of exotic energies!

Page 22

Splash page: the two Vipers are drifting alone and small against the vast desolate backdrop of the nebula.

STARBUCK (CONT'D)

Where did everyone go?

(joined)

Where did the <u>Galactica</u> go?

CAP

To be continued

ARTIST DESIGNS
BY CEZAR RAZEK

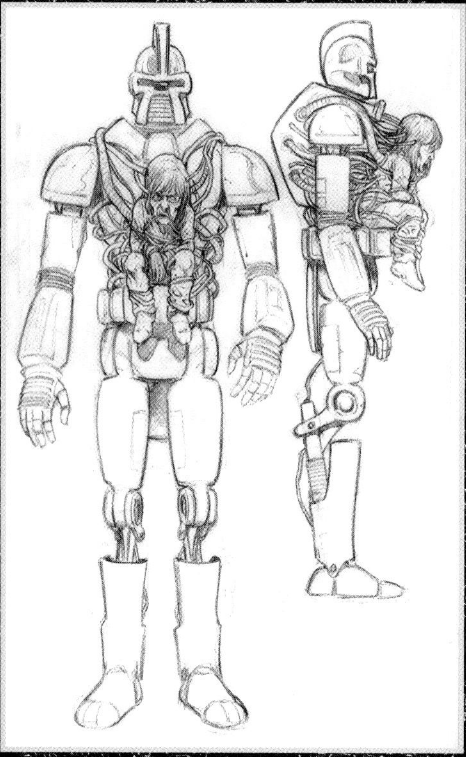

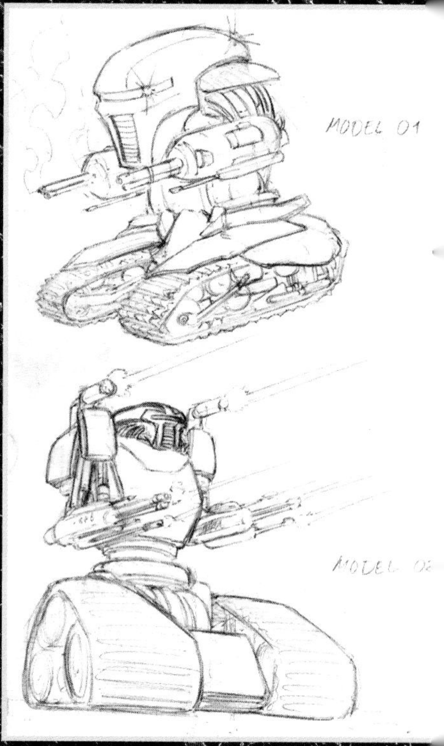
MODEL 01

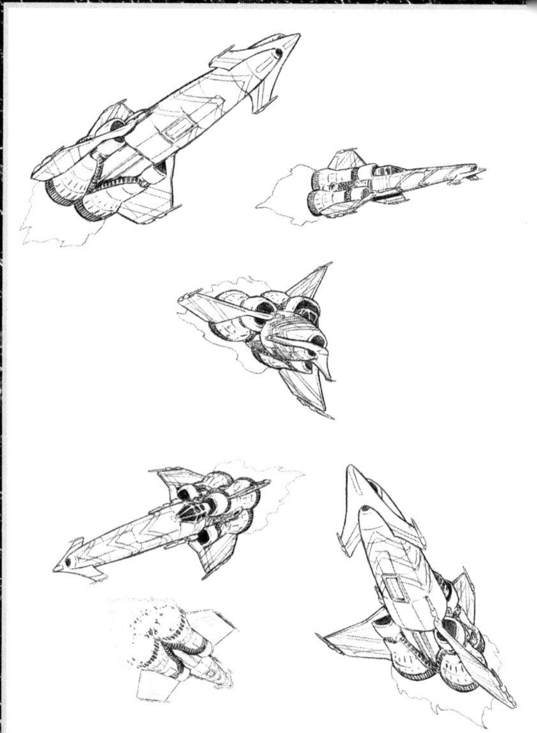

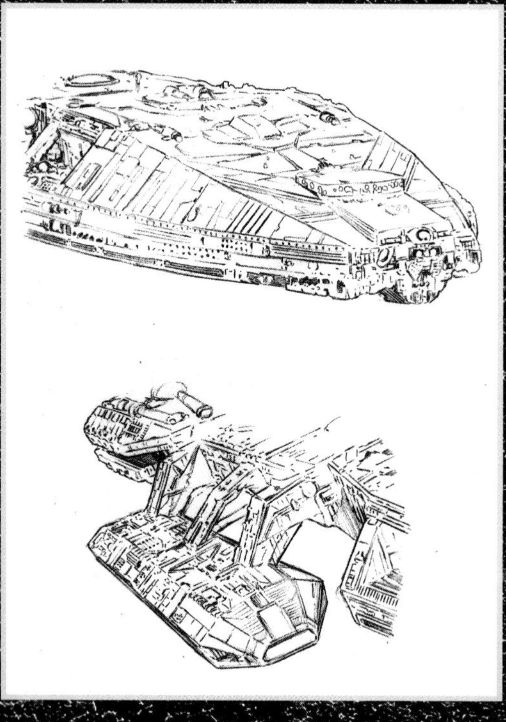

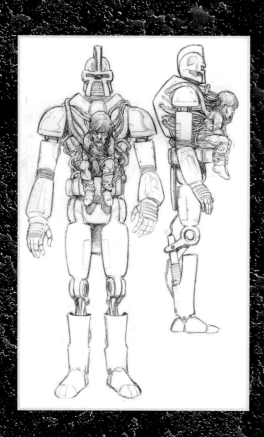